The GLOBAL SEAFARER

Living and working conditions
in a globalized industry

The GLOBAL SEAFARER

Living and working conditions in a globalized industry

International Labour Office
in collaboration with the
Seafarers International Research Centre

Contributing authors
T. Alderton, M. Bloor, E. Kahveci,
T. Lane, H. Sampson, M. Thomas,
N. Winchester, B. Wu and
M. Zhao

INTERNATIONAL LABOUR OFFICE • GENEVA

Copyright © International Labour Organization 2004
First published 2004

Publications of the International Labour Office enjoy copyright under Protocol 2 of the Universal Copyright Convention. Nevertheless, short excerpts from them may be reproduced without authorization, on condition that the source is indicated. For rights of reproduction or translation, application should be made to the Publications Bureau (Rights and Permissions), International Labour Office, CH-1211 Geneva 22, Switzerland. The International Labour Office welcomes such applications.

Libraries, institutions and other users registered in the United Kingdom with the Copyright Licensing Agency, 90 Tottenham Court Road, London W1P 4LP [Fax: (+ 44) (0) 207 631 5500; email: cla@cla.co.uk], in the United States with the Copyright Clearance Center, 222 Rosewood Drive, Danvers, MA 01923 [Fax (+1) (978) 750 4470; email: info@copyright.com], or in other countries with associated Reproduction Rights Organizations, may make photocopies in accordance with the licences issued to them for this purpose.

ILO
The global seafarer: Living and working conditions in a globalized industry
Geneva, International Labour Office, 2004

Seafarer, working conditions, conditions of employment, living conditions, globalization of the economy, developed country, developing country. 13.11.8

ISBN 92-2-112713-3

ILO Cataloguing in Publication Data

The designations employed in ILO publications, which are in conformity with United Nations practice, and the presentation of material therein do not imply the expression of any opinion whatsoever on the part of the International Labour Office concerning the legal status of any country, area or territory or of its authorities, or concerning the delimitation of its frontiers.

The responsibility for opinions expressed in signed articles, studies and other contributions rests solely with their authors, and publication does not constitute an endorsement by the International Labour Office of the opinions expressed in them.

Reference to names of firms and commercial products and processes does not imply their endorsement by the International Labour Office, and any failure to mention a particular firm, commercial product or process is not a sign of disapproval.

ILO publications can be obtained through major booksellers or ILO local offices in many countries, or direct from ILO Publications, International Labour Office, CH-1211 Geneva 22, Switzerland. Catalogues or lists of new publications are available free of charge from the above address or by email: pubvente@ilo.org

Visit our website: www.ilo.org/publns

Photo credit: SIRC Photographic Archive
Typeset by Magheross Graphics, France & Ireland *www.magheross.com*
Printed in Switzerland - PCL

CONTENTS

Abbreviations ix
Acknowledgements xiii
About the authors xv
Introduction 1

1   The political economy of world shipping 5
        Introduction 5
        Shipping and world trade 6
        Ownership, organization and finance 10
        Growth sectors: Containers and cruise 17
        The rise of the ship-management company 19
        Technological developments 22
        Politics and shipping 25

2   Flag States and regulation 27
        Introduction 27
        FOCs and second registers 28
        Regulatory regimes and practice 38
        Flag State good practice 44
        Regulatory regimes and labour issues 48

3   The labour market for seafarers 57
        Introduction 57
        The global labour market 57
        Training and certification 81
        Trade unions and collective bargaining 88

The global seafarer

4	Shipboard life and work – I	95
	Shipboard society	95
	Turnaround and voyage cycles	103
	Wages and conditions of employment	109
5	Shipboard life and work – II	121
	Food, diet and accommodation	121
	Occupational safety	131
	Occupational health	134
6	Seafarers' families	145
	Introduction	145
	Seafarers and their families	146
	Health and safety	148
	Social isolation aboard and ashore	150
	Ship–shore communication	151
	Company policies and their impact on family life	153
7	Sub-standard ships and abandoned seafarers	159
	Introduction	159
	Defining and identifying the sub-standard ship	160
	Abandoned seafarers	165
	Case notes from Sri Lanka, Tunisia and the United Kingdom	172
	Case study: The *OBO Basak*	175
	Towards global protection	182

Conclusion 189

Tables

1.1	Demolition and newbuilds, 1990–2000	8
1.2	Development of world merchant fleet, 1991–2001	8
1.3	Development of cruise shipping, 1980 and 1998	18
1.4	World's five largest cruise companies, 1999	19
2.1	Vessel numbers and gross tonnage of FOCs, 2001	31
2.2	Nationality of the five major open registry fleets, January 2001	32
2.3	Second registers, 2002	33
2.4	The 39 flag States that exceeded the average global detention rate, 1998	36
2.5	Registries with losses exceeding the world average, 1998	37
2.6	Ratifications of IMO Conventions by flag States, 2002	40

3.1	Seafarers' employment in selected countries, 1935 and 1965	59
3.2	Seafarers' employment in selected countries, 1968–92	59
3.3	Average crewing levels in selected ship types, 1993 and 1998	62
3.4	Crew nationalities aboard selected OECD fleets, 1993 and 1999	70
3.5	Selected seafarer nationalities and flags of employment, 1993 and 1999	70
3.6	Crew complaints handled by the ITF's Actions Department, 1998	92
4.1	Comparative turnaround times, 1970 and 1998	105
4.2	Average monthly wages of seafarers, 1996	111
4.3	The effect of rank on wages, 1996	112
4.4	Vessels under ITF agreements, by flag, 1998	115
5.1	Main categories of deficiencies per flag, 1997	128
5.2	Deficiencies recorded by the Paris MOU, 1996–99	129
5.3	Complaints by seafarers to port chaplains, 1994–99	130
7.1	Abandoned seafarers, 1999	168
7.2	Abandoned seafarers by ship type, 1999	171
7.3	Number of ships abandoned, by flag, 1999	172

Figures

1.1	International seaborne trade, 1970–2000	6
1.2	Annual change in OECD industrial production and world seaborne trade, 1997–2000	7
2.1	World fleet/FOC fleet, 1990–2001	30
2.2	Percentage of world fleet registered under FOCs, 1990–2001	30
3.1	Swedish wage costs under different regimes, 1988	60
3.2	At-sea seafarer population, cargo ships, 1993–2000	61
3.3	Percentage distribution of seafarers by selected ship type, 2000	62
3.4	Age of British officers, 1968 and 1998	64
3.5	Age of British ratings, 1968 and 1998	64
3.6	Age of officers from China, the Philippines, Ukraine and the United Kingdom, 1998	65
3.7	Age of ratings from China, the Philippines, Ukraine and the United Kingdom, 1998	65
3.8	Passenger/crew ratios in cruise ships, 1999	67
3.9	Seafarers' origins by world region, all ranks, 2000	74
3.10	Top ten labour supply countries for senior and junior officers, 2002	74
3.11a	Mixed nationality crewing patterns by selected ship type, 1999	76
3.11b	Mixed nationality crewing patterns across all ship types, 1999	76

4.1	Hours spent in Sandmouth by all ships, 1970	104
4.2	Hours spent in Sandmouth by all ships, 1998	105
4.3	Wage costs of ABs, selected nationalities, 1999	110

Boxes

1.1	Hyundai targets higher plain	10
1.2	Troubled Hong Kong shipping company lurches on	16
1.3	Shipping – Stay of execution?	17
3.1	Ship-management companies and their labour market tours	67
3.2	Anglo-Eastern moves into China!	69
3.3	The mixed nationality crews of the *Controro* and the *Tanker*	71
3.4	Barber pushes Polish solution to manning	77
3.5	Rizal Park, Manila: A daily "labour market"	79
3.6	Corruption in Philippine maritime training schools	82
3.7	A cautionary tale	84
4.1	"To go ashore, you had to be super-human!"	106
4.2	Ports are "far away from anything"	107
4.3	"By the end, a certain madness attacks some crew members"	108
5.1	A British college's syllabus for ships' cooks	122
5.2	The near grounding of the *Kotuku* tanker	133
5.3	"I could have quite easily jumped over the side"	139
7.1	Bid to cut disgrace of sub-standard ships	160
7.2	Europe urged to back port controls	163
7.3	Twenty-one [sic] Turkish seafarers abandoned in Dunkirk	178

ABBREVIATIONS

AB	Able seaman
BIMCO	Baltic and International Maritime Council
BMI	Body mass index
CIIPMET	China, India, Indonesia and the Philippines maritime education and training
CISD	Critical incident stress debriefing
CSR	Canary Islands Second Register
dB	Decibels
DIS	Danish International Ship Register
DTLR	Department for Transport, Local Government and the Regions
dwt	Deadweight tonnage
ECG	Electrocardiogram
EEA	European Economic Area
EU	European Union
FAS	Faeroe Islands Second Register
FIR	French International Ship Register
FOC	Flag of convenience
FPC	Fair Practices Committee
GATT	General Agreement on Tariffs and Trade
GIS	German International Ship Register
GMDSS	Global maritime distress and safety system
grt	Registered gross tonnage
gt	Gross tonnage
HIV	Human immunodeficiency virus

HKSAR	Hong Kong Special Administrative Region
IACS	International Association of Classification Societies
ICFTU	International Confederation of Free Trade Unions
ICS	International Chamber of Shipping
IER	Institute of Employment Research
ILO	International Labour Organization
IMA	International Maritime Associates
IMEC	International Maritime Employers' Committee
IMO	International Maritime Organization
INMARSAT	International Mobile Satellite Organization
ISF	International Shipping Federation
ISL	Institute of Shipping Economics and Logistics
ISMA	International Ship Managers' Association
ITF	International Transport Workers' Federation
IUA	International Underwriting Association of London
JAMRI	Japan Maritime Research Institute
LISCR	Liberian International Ship & Corporate Registry
LMIS	Lloyd's Marine Intelligence Service
LPG	Liquefied petroleum gas
MAIB	Marine Accident Investigation Branch
MAR	Madeira Second Register
MARCOM	Maritime Communications
MCA	Maritime and Coastguard Agency
MOU	Memorandum of Understanding
NCL	Norwegian Cruise Line
NIS	Norwegian International Ship Register
NUMAST	National Union of Marine Aviation and Shipping Transport Officers
OBO	ore/bulk/oil carrier
OCIMF	Oil Companies International Maritime Forum
OECD	Organisation for Economic Co-operation and Development
OS	Ordinary seaman
PAH	Polycyclic aromatic hydrocarbon
PLC	Public limited company
PSC	Port state control

Abbreviations

REB	Registro Especial Brasileiro
Ro-ro	Roll-on roll-off
SIRC	Seafarers International Research Centre
SIRE	Ship Inspection and Report Exchange
SOLAS	Safety of Life at Sea Convention
SSD	Special Seafarers' Department
STCW	Standards of Training, Certification and Watchkeeping
STD	Sexually transmitted disease
TEU	Twenty foot equivalent unit
TTC	Total Crew Cost
ULCC	Ultra large crude carrier
UNCLOS	United Nations Convention on the Law of the Sea
UNCTAD	United Nations Conference on Trade and Development
VLCC	Very large crude carrier
WMU	World Maritime University
WTO	World Trade Organization

Note: All mentions of dollars refer to the United States dollar.

ACKNOWLEDGEMENTS

We, the authors, are greatly indebted to all those in the shipping industry who, over the years, have collectively helped to shape our understanding of the circumstances of the global seafarer. There are too many people involved for each to be named and thanked individually, and in any case it is impossible to determine each person's contribution: on occasions, even a few sharp observations from a passing acquaintance has proved to be enlightening. Nevertheless, we would like to express our thanks to the several hundred seafarers of various ranks and nationalities who so willingly and openly talked to us about their lives and experiences. This book is as much *for* them as it is *about* them.

Like most of the work carried out by the Seafarers International Research Centre (SIRC), this book was produced by a team of writers/researchers, administrative staff and editors. Tony Alderton wrote the sections on trade unions and wages and conditions of service, although the passages on cruise ship wages and conditions were prepared by Minghua Zhao. Michelle Thomas is the author of Chapter 6 and, together with Mick Bloor and Helen Sampson, also wrote Chapter 5. Erol Kahveci supplied the data on turnaround times for Chapter 4 and provided the analysis of abandoned seafarers in Chapter 7. Nik Winchester wrote Chapter 2, while Bin Wu produced the statistical analysis and graphics for Chapter 3. Tony Lane wrote the Introduction, Chapter 1, those parts of Chapters 3 and 7 respectively dealing with crewing patterns, labour market organization and sub-standard ships as well as the Conclusion; he is also responsible for the final shape of the book. Louise Deeley produced the final manuscript. The SIRC team are most grateful to Margareta Simons for editing the study, and to Charlotte Beauchamp of the International Labour Organization (ILO) for coordinating the publication.

SIRC
Cardiff, United Kingdom

ABOUT THE AUTHORS

Dr Tony Alderton is a social scientist with a background in industrial relations research. He has written a number of articles on globalization and regulation in the maritime industry. He left the SIRC in 2001 to join Kent County Council as a policy researcher.

Professor Michael Bloor has been seconded to the SIRC from Cardiff University's School of Social Sciences to work on the Centre's health and safety programme. His most recent books are *Focus groups in social research* (co-authored with Jane Frankland, Michelle Thomas and Kate Robson), *Selected writings in medical sociology* and *The sociology of HIV transmission.*

Dr Erol Kahveci is a Senior Research Associate at the SIRC. His field of study is the health and safety of seafarers and their well-being aboard ship. His current research centres on car-carrier crews and the organization and provision of seafarers' welfare.

Professor Tony Lane, Director of the SIRC 1997–2003, is an ex-merchant seafarer who graduated in Social Sciences as a mature student and has been researching industrial relations, maritime history and the seafaring labour force for 30 years. He has written five books and numerous articles for academic journals and the maritime press.

Dr Helen Sampson, Deputy Director of the SIRC, is a social scientist with a background in policy-related research. Since joining the SIRC in 1999, she has worked on projects and written papers in the fields of transnationalism, gender, skills education and training, and the impact of information and communications technology on seafarers.

Dr Michelle Thomas is a social scientist who has conducted research in medical sociology, in particular on sexual risk behaviour. Her current work focuses on seafarers' families and (with Professor Bloor) the sexual risk behaviour of the crews of cruise ships. She has had articles published in journals, has edited books and is the co-author of a research methods text.

Dr Nik Winchester holds degrees from the London School of Economics and the University of Bristol in Sociology and Economics. His publications include a number of articles on globalization and regulation in the maritime industry and the SIRC book *Flag State audit 2003* (co-authored with Tony Alderton). His research interests include: flag State regulation, global governance, international political economy and social theory.

Dr Bin Wu has a Ph.D. on the subject of sustainable development in marginal agriculture in rural China. While at the SIRC, he has been responsible for the SIRC's global labour market surveys.

Dr Minghua Zhao, Deputy Director of the SIRC, joined the organization in 1998 as a Senior Research Associate. Her work focuses primarily on women seafarers in the cruise sector and on the global seafarers' labour market, especially that of China.

INTRODUCTION

A series of overarching structural changes transformed the world's shipping industry during the last quarter of the twentieth century. The containerization of the liner trades and the evolution of ship types dedicated to the carriage of specific, or narrow bands, of commodity groups were the most visible developments. On an organizational level, the industry saw the appearance of large fleets run by independent ship-management companies and the eclipse of nationally flagged fleets by flags of convenience (FOCs) and second registers. Politically, environmental issues had an influence on geo-politics generally and on the regulatory structures of world shipping in particular. Less obvious, except to those involved in the industry, national regulatory systems were progressively displaced by transnational and international ones, while the locations of the shipping industry's core cities were restructured into a global circuit of regional metropolises in the Asia-Pacific region, Europe and North America. The most momentous structural change, however, was the development of a global labour market for industrial workers.

Thirty years ago, most of the world's seafarers were citizens of the nations represented in their ships' flags and ports of registry. In the early years of the twenty-first century, not only are the crews of most internationally trading ships working under foreign flags, they are also likely to be sailing in mixed nationality crews. The causes, and especially the consequences, of these changes are the subject of this book. Merchant seafarers of the new century are unique among industrial workers. Among the higher echelons of workers in the financial services and information technology industries, it is common enough to find mixed nationality teams. However, in the shipping industry this implies a "factory type" workforce of more than a million people. Recruited in accordance with managerial preferences, crews are assembled through global networks of companies and agencies in many different permutations of nationalities. In aggregate form, the outcome of crewing policies and national preferences has been that the majority of crews are mixed: in 1999, 20 per cent of the crews of cargo ships had staff of more than four nationalities and only one-third were drawn from a single nationality. Aboard the world's cruise ships, there are rarely crews of fewer than 20 nationalities. Therefore, the title of this book, *The global seafarer*, can truly be said to represent the reality of the modern seafarer's working life.

The industry's increasingly desperate preoccupation with crew costs, which led to the formation of a global labour market, was a reflection of trading conditions. The structural problem that the industry faced was straightforward and can be summarized quite simply: a slump in world trade and a glut of ships produced a spate of intense competition and the inevitable accompanying drive to cut costs.

The 1980s were disastrous for shipping and by far the worst decade for the industry since the 1930s. The problem was essentially twofold: on the one hand there were the structural readjustments in the world economy, which led, in 1981, to a substantial fall in freight rates as world trade went into recession. Subsequent recovery was prolonged, trade did not get back to 1980 levels until 1988 and freight rates thereafter generally showed only gradual and modest improvements, despite short-lived booms in most other industries at some time or other until the mid-1990s; on the other hand, and despite high scrapping rates in the mid-1980s, there was a surplus of ships for available cargoes.

The recession of the 1980s has unquestionably left its mark on the organizational structure of the industry. The ability of the shipbuilding industry to supply cheap ships can still tempt ill-judged orders for new ships, although in all sectors there are continuing attempts to at least manage market uncertainties through vertical integration, consolidations through mergers and other organizational forms such as "alliances" and pools. These and other relevant economic issues, such as the development of ship-management companies, the organization of ship finance and technological change, which all have an effect on the labour market, are discussed in Chapter 1.

Labour was inevitably the first target when it came to making cuts, even though crew costs as a proportion of voyage costs had been falling steadily since the 1960s. By the 1980s labour productivity had already been substantially improved by a series of capital substitutions, so it followed that any further savings could only be made by finding cheaper sources of labour. These were achieved by avoiding the sophisticated labour regulatory regimes that had evolved in the embedded maritime nations[1] and instead taking advantage of the relatively cheap labour to be found in Asia, from the 1970s, and then in Eastern Europe, from the late 1980s. The route to labour regulation avoidance was already available in the shape of the FOC system, of which Liberia and Panama are the earliest examples.[2] As soon as the effects of the downturn in world trade began to bite, those who were already flagged out had an immediate competitive advantage by virtue of their unrestricted freedom to recruit cheaper crews from other world regions. In these circumstances, owners using bona fide national flags generally had little choice but to follow suit if their governments were unable or unwilling to provide subsidies through tax concessions. With an offshore registry system in place and a marked move away from the politics of social democracy towards free market policies in most of the embedded maritime nations, the process of flagging out by shipowners who had previously been strongly opposed to it was relatively uncomplicated. A number of these nations (Belgium, Denmark, Germany, France, the Netherlands, Norway and the United Kingdom) developed a variety of second register alternatives to flagging out. Although these measures delivered the same "domestic labour avoidance" solutions, they nevertheless retained some aspects of labour regulation. These and other aspects of regulation and flagging out are dealt with in some detail in Chapter 2.

Chapter 3 covers developments in the labour market and is more concerned with contemporary than recent historical questions, although the opening pages provide some relevant background. The chapter analyses the trends derived from recent SIRC global labour market surveys, which, for the first time, allow a close examination of crewing patterns and the age and rank profiles of seafarers from the newer labour supply countries. The role of crew managers in defining and organizing the labour market is also examined and critical questions of recruitment and training are explored. There is some discussion of women seafarers, who, while in a tiny minority in the cargo sector of world shipping, are a rapidly expanding presence in the cruise industry. The chapter concludes with a survey of the role of trade unions and collective bargaining in the new global era.

The four remaining chapters deal with areas that are more specific to the everyday lives and experiences of the seafaring workforce. Chapter 4 focuses on the social life of mixed nationality crews on board ship. The data are based on a uniquely large-scale research programme conducted aboard working ships, which found that, contrary to anecdotally based belief, mixed nationality crews usually work extremely well together and are widely preferred by seafarers of all ranks. This is followed by some hitherto under-reported research on turnaround times and its impact on seafarers' lives.

A survey of the limited information available on wages and conditions of employment concludes the chapter.

The second chapter on shipboard life and work (Chapter 5) summarizes the extremely limited research findings on food and diet, accommodation and occupational health and safety. Considering the industry's growing concerns about recruiting and then retaining expensively trained seafarers, none of these areas has so far attracted much attention. Chapter 6, which looks at seafarers' families, is largely informed by new research carried out in China, India, Indonesia, the Philippines and the United Kingdom, and makes clear the need for the industry to find ways of helping seafarers and their families to adjust to long periods of separation. Chapter 7 deals with sub-standard ships and abandoned crews, and examines the issues that affect the public's poor perception of the shipping industry and which frequently unsettle those industry professionals who pride themselves on operating well-found ships and looking after their crews. As in every other industry, there is a group of marginal operators whose deeds sometimes attract derogatory public attention.

As with so many other aspects of the shipping industry, far too little is known in sufficient detail to allow for effective policies to be adopted. Nevertheless, this book's conclusion is optimistic. The upheavals of the past 30 years are beginning to subside as new institutions and regulatory structures slip into place. There are many indications that the labour market is at last settling into a phase of relative stability, thanks largely to the powerful trend towards consolidation of ownership in many key sectors, the development of the machinery for global collective bargaining and the patent desire for effective regulation among all those parties concerned with extending high standards of professionalism across the industry.

Notes

[1] In this book, the term "embedded maritime nations" replaces the more familiar "traditional maritime nations" to provide a more accurate description of modern international shipping. Countries such as China, Greece, India, Malaysia and the Philippines have been involved in maritime commerce for many centuries and are, therefore, unquestionably, traditional maritime nations. However, only since the Second World War have these countries developed highly organized shipping industry infrastructures comparable to those of Europe and Japan, where developments began 50 to 100 years earlier and so can be described as having become "embedded".

[2] R. P. Carlisle: *Sovereignty for sale* (Annapolis, MD, Naval Institute Press, 1981).

1

THE POLITICAL ECONOMY OF WORLD SHIPPING

Renewing identity

Introduction

The considerable changes that have taken place in the living and working lives of seafarers in the past three decades are, unsurprisingly, related to developments in the political economy of world shipping: long-term trends, contingent events and structural flaws have all helped to produce an extremely complex state of affairs. Although changing patterns in the direction and volume of world trade are conventionally seen as the underlying determinants of the modern transformation of the shipping industry, there have been, however, other significant, contributory factors, and these are each examined in turn.

This chapter begins with a brief look at world trading patterns and the problem of overcapacity in the 1980s. This is followed by an assessment of how far the industry's patterns of ownership and financing contributed to labour market instability. The privatization of the shipping industry in Eastern Europe is looked at in this context. The organizational changes that occurred in the industry are also examined by analysing the role of ship-management companies in creating and stabilizing the global labour market. A concluding section explores two regulatory issues that have had an enormous impact on the industry: the first matter concerns the arrival of the environment as a major political issue in the developed market economy countries on world shipping; the second regulatory issue, and one that is examined at some length, is the extraordinarily rapid development of "open" and second registers; they have brought to the industry the institutional means of replacing multiple national

The global seafarer

labour markets with a single global labour market, leaving only a residual and declining rump of national labour markets.

Shipping and world trade

Considered overall, the past 30 years saw a period of steady, if patchy, growth in seaborne world trade. In the 20 years from 1972 to 1992, the total tonnage carried by the world's ships increased from 2,763 million tonnes to 4,211 million tonnes, that is, by some 52 per cent (an annual average of 2.6 per cent). In the more recent overlapping period, 1988–98, tonnage carried showed a further rise, from 3,675 to 5,064 million tonnes, that is, an increase of 2.8 per cent per annum. The overall trends for three broad commodity groups are shown in figure 1.1. Taking the industry as a whole, growth in the period was uneven, both in aggregate and among commodity groups. In fact, aggregate seaborne trade fell by 400 million tonnes in 1981 and did not return to 1980 levels until 1988, reflecting the fact that the 1980s was the worst decade experienced by the shipping industry since the 1920s and 1930s; the investment bank Warburg Dillon Read described it as a period of "valiant but mutually destructive competition". In general, the most reliable index reflecting world seaborne trade is industrial production in the Organisation for Economic Co-operation and Development (OECD) countries (figure 1.2).

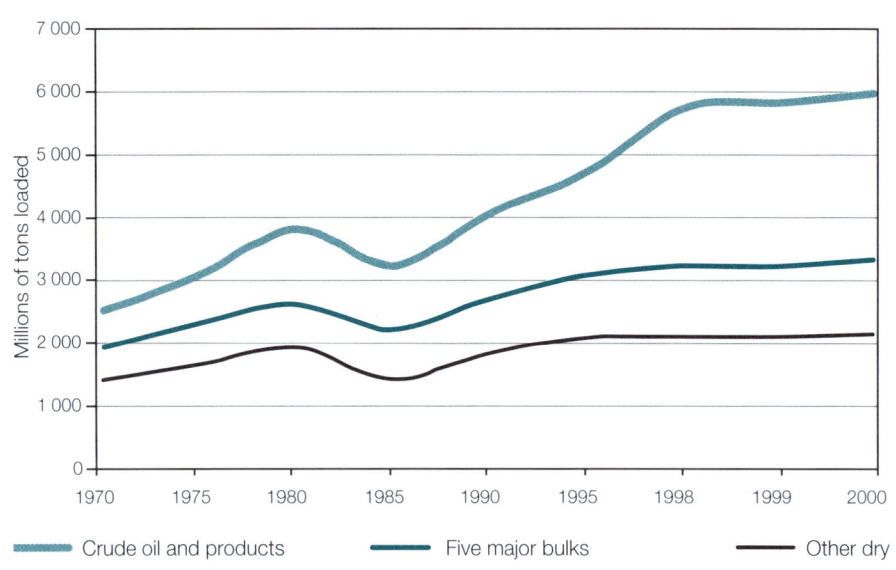

Figure 1.1 International seaborne trade, 1970–2000 (in millions of tons)

Sources: United Nations Conference on Trade and Development (UNCTAD): *Review of Maritime Transport* (New York/Geneva, various issues).

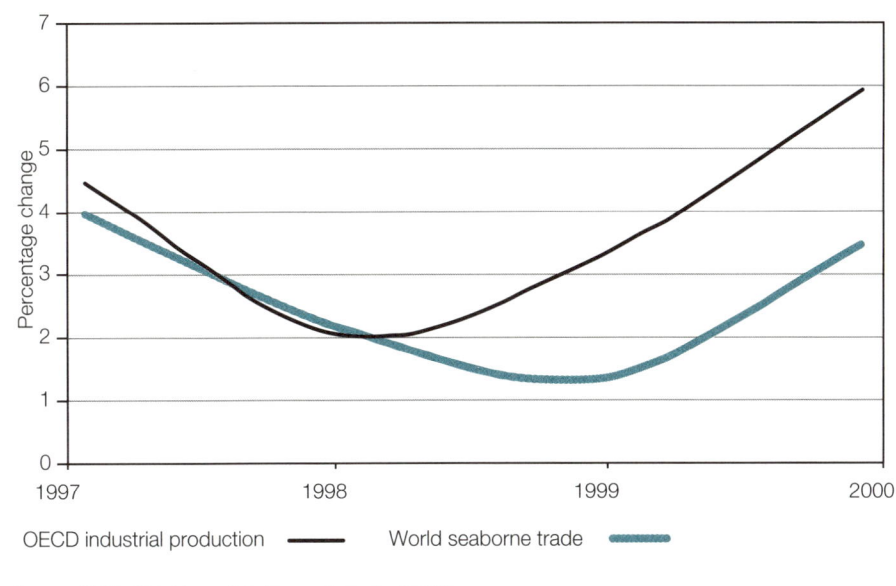

Figure 1.2 Annual change in OECD industrial production and world seaborne trade, 1997–2000 (as a percentage)

Source: OECD: *Main Economic Indicators* (Paris, April 2001).

Developments in the shipbuilding industry are not explored here in any detail, although an outline is necessary, since part of the immediate cause of the severe recession of the 1980s lay in the structure of the shipbuilding industry in the 1970s. Recollections of the causes and consequences of the 1980s crisis are sufficiently fresh in the minds of shipowners and analysts in the early years of the twenty-first century to make them alert to the likely effects of an inflated boom in shipbuilding. This sensitivity to the possibility of recent history being repeated surfaced at the 2001 autumn meeting of the Inter-Industry Round Table Group, which brings together the world's major shipowning organizations – the Baltic and International Maritime Council (BIMCO), the International Chamber of Shipping (ICS), Intercargo and Intertanko. Leading representatives of these organizations called for a more rational approach to additional shipbuilding capacity, stating that "moves towards stability and equilibrium [in the shipping industry] could be prejudiced by yards looking for short-term gains and increased market share".[1]

A flood of new and cheap ships launched from the subsidized and protected yards of the world in the late 1970s and onwards into the mid-1980s undoubtedly helped to make a bad trading period worse. Despite a high rate of scrapping in the early to mid-1980s, it was not until the 1990s that the demolition–newbuild ratio (table 1.1) began to show a consistent pattern and

The global seafarer

Table 1.1 Demolition and newbuilds, 1990–2000 (in millions of tonnes)

Year	Demolitions	Newbuilds	Demolitions as a % of newbuilds
1990	3.3	22.8	14
1991	4.7	23.7	20
1992	19.0	26.8	71
1993	16.9	31.7	53
1994	20.8	29.4	71
1995	15.3	33.7	45
1996	18.1	39.0	46
1997	14.8	36.8	40
1998	25.2	35.3	71
1999	30.7	40.5	76
2000	22.2	44.4	50

Source: UNCTAD: *Review of Maritime Transport, 1997* (New York/Geneva, 1997).

lead to a steady reduction in the volume of surplus tonnage (figure 1.2). The data in table 1.2 show reassuringly modest annual growth rates in the most volatile sectors (tankers and bulkers), negative growth in the case of cargo passengers, the displacement of general cargo 'tween deckers by container ships and the decline of ore/bulk/oil carriers (OBOs) as a viable ship type.

Table 1.2 Development of world merchant fleet, 1991–2001

Ship type	Average growth rate in gross tonnage (gt)
Bulk carriers	2.9
Cargo passenger	–5.3
Chemical tankers	4.0
Container ships	9.3
General cargo (multi-deck)	–3.1
General cargo (single-deck)	6.3
Liquid gas tankers	–0.1
OBO carriers	–7.7
Oil tankers	2.2
Passenger ships	10.1
Reefer ships	–0.1
Ro-ro cargo ships	3.1
Ro-ro passenger ships	6.3
Special ships	3.1

Source: Institute of Shipping Economics and Logistics (ISL): *Shipping Statistics Yearbook, 1994* (Bremen, 1994).

Although at the beginning of the twenty-first century the potential for future disruption from the shipbuilding industry has diminished, it has by no means disappeared. Attempts in the late 1990s by the General Agreement on Tariffs and Trade (GATT) and its successor, the World Trade Organization (WTO), to manage capacity rationalization met with very limited success, while disputes between the Republic of Korea and the European Union (EU) over government subsidies were still unresolved at the time of writing.

There is little doubt that excess capacity is a continuing problem as countries with established shipbuilding industries attempt to retain market share against new entrants. It seems that as long as there are developing countries with industrializing ambitions and an active international market enabling the transfer of technical shipbuilding knowledge and ships' ancillary equipment, the shipbuilding industry will be in a position to destabilize shipping. By the mid-1990s, world shipbuilding capacity for the production of all but the most specialized ships was centred in south-east Asia. One analyst observed that:

> [T]here is now more than adequate capacity in the Far East to build every ship the world needs and more. The sheer productivity increases of a reduced number of Japanese yards, where improvement is recognized as the only route to survival, and the capacity increases of the South Koreans and the Chinese cannot be brushed aside as inconsequential.[2]

Some 18 months later, the issues involved were neatly synthesized in a series of questions in a *Lloyd's List* leading article:

> Will, for instance, we see a trade war between Korean and Japanese shipbuilders? Will, in the short term, there be any diminution in the wish of the major Japanese corporations to maintain a shipbuilding presence, if this sector cannot provide their parent corporations with a sufficient return on investment? Will the continued overcapacity in world shipbuilding (and not many people seriously believe that this situation is going to change) simply wear down the Japanese will to remain in such an unrewarding sector? And what will be the effect on world shipbuilding of the improved productivity in China and Eastern Europe, or the political nuances of the EU towards its shipbuilding sector?[3]

The commentator left the questions unanswered but, in a world increasingly sceptical of economic protection policies (significantly underlined by China's accession to the WTO in 2001), shipbuilding seems certain to remain a mobile industry, with China as its next core destination. The essential reasoning for this "restlessness of location" can be seen in the unusually frank remarks quoted in box 1.1.

> Box 1.1 Hyundai targets higher plain
>
> The head of ship sales at Hyundai Heavy, D. Y. Han, hopes [the Republic of] Korea will outgrow shipbuilding as quickly as possible. He makes this point as a spirited defence of his country's shipbuilding prowess against European attack. "Eventually, Korea's position in the shipbuilding world will be replaced by other countries, and I hope that day will come sooner rather than later," he said. "This will be a sign that the level of the South Korean economy has advanced to a higher level of development." He pointed out that, in general, the advanced economies of the United States, Europe and Japan had many other more lucrative and technologically sophisticated industries in which to invest their capital and manpower. South Korea was, meanwhile, filling a substantial need to replace tonnage. Productivity at Hyundai Heavy has been improving every year, but Mr. Han does not want to be over proud. He sees other nations, particularly China, gathering strength. "Some day, we will have to hand over the market."
>
> Source: *Lloyd's List*, 15 June 2001.

Ownership, organization and finance

Ownership structures vary considerably between the different sectors of the shipping industry. While the privately owned and public limited company (PLC) forms of ownership can be found in all sectors, the largest firms as well as those operating the more sophisticated ship types are more likely to be equity-funded, listed companies, and these are found in those subsectors where ownership is highly concentrated. Nevertheless, it remains true that, of all the world's modern and large-scale industries, shipping seems to be the only industry in which private ownership in one form or another still predominates.

Throughout the twentieth century, the liner trades of all the embedded maritime nations showed high levels of concentration. At the beginning of the twenty-first century, the world's liner trades are, for the most part, owned by a shrinking number of global firms. Similarly, a series of mergers, takeovers and acquisitions during the 1990s progressively enlarged the major container companies, leading to a situation in the early twenty-first century in which the sector looks as if it will be dominated by perhaps as few as six carriers, each with global route patterns. The largest existing carriers, which are certain to become even larger, are not just owners of large fleets of ships running "mainline" services; through their organizational alliances with other companies and their vertical and lateral ownerships of ports and terminals, warehousing, road transport, rail rolling-stock, freight forwarding agencies and feederships, the liner companies of today are adopting exactly the same sorts of strategies developed by the first consolidations in the liner trades of the late nineteenth century.[4] It is notable, however, that some of the world's largest liner/container companies also own large fleets of other ship types – Mitsui-OSK and A. P. Moller, for example, own diverse fleets that include car carriers, tankers and bulkers. Economically, there is some logic in this approach to shipowning, if only to spread risks, since the business cycles of the different trades are incongruent. The year 2001 may have been bad for the container trades but it was a reasonable one for tankers and it is interesting to note that although Mitsui and Moller both turned in heavy losses from their liner trades, they made useful profits from their tankers that year. Other liner companies, such as the P&O Group, pursued in the late 1990s the then fashionable "back to core business" strategy. In this industry, as in others, there are always competing perspectives on strategy and development, but all the large firms in the container trades, regardless of whether they also operate in other shipping sectors, engaged in mergers in an attempt to protect their market position by enlarging their market share. Exactly the same motives resulted in parallel merger movements in other specialized sectors of the shipping industry.

Since the late 1990s, there have been a number of significant mergers at the larger end of the tanker trades, with ownership rapidly becoming concentrated in a smaller group of companies. In this particular case, concentration has been driven by an increasingly tight regulatory environment and the associated demand for more expensive double-hulled ships. The pressure to meet ever-higher structural and operating standards means that the companies that survive can only be those able to realize economies of scale. By 2001, just three companies – Worldwide, MOL and Frontline – controlled more than 100 very large crude carriers (VLCCs) between them, almost one-quarter of the world's VLCC fleet. The substantially over-tonnaged reefer trades, a contracting sector that some suggest will need to halve its current capacity, is threatened by the increasing capacity of the container lines to carry frozen and chilled cargoes. Only the larger reefer companies with the more modern fleets are likely to survive.[5]

There are only two highly specialized shipping sectors where concentration ratios approach those of the chemical and automobile industries: interestingly, these are the chemical tanker and car-carrier sectors, two expanding markets in which recent mergers have led to exceptionally high levels of concentration. In the deep-sea chemical tanker trades, two companies – Odfjell and Stolt-Nielsen – have some 50 per cent of the market, and 70 per cent of the market is controlled by four firms.[6] The picture in the car-carrier sector is a little more complicated, since different owners are dominant in different trades. Grimaldi, for example, dominates the Mediterranean to

Europe and Latin America routes, while MOL, Wallenius Wilhelmsen, NYK and Hyundai dominate the Far East routes. Nevertheless, the overall situation shows high levels of concentration and, at the time of writing, negotiations between Wallenius Wilhelmsen and Hyundai, where the latter seemed set to sell its 70 plus ships to the former, suggest that Wallenius Wilhelmsen could end up having some 50 per cent of the market (in a single fleet). In cruise shipping, bankruptcies and mergers in the period 2000–03 contributed to extremely high concentration ratios; as the entry costs into this sector are so steep, the already small number of firms seems likely to diminish even further.

The shipping industry's two largest sectors – bulk and general cargo – have low concentration ratios. In practice, and not unlike the products tanker trades, these sectors are broken down into size categories. In the case of large ships, such as cape-size bulkers, there are a number of reasonably stable pools, whereby several owners hire out their ships at collectively agreed rates, without mergers having actually taken place. This is a merger-like activity except that individual owners remain responsible for operating their own ships, do not normally pool all their ships and are free to leave the pool after agreed periods of notice.[7] Pools represent a tacit recognition of the advantages of scale but do not normally lead to mergers, even if they inevitably bring competitors closer to each other. Outside the larger ship categories, there are a number of owners with large fleets, but with the exception of those operating in certain specialist sectors such as forest products, they are unlikely to dominate their markets. The most competitive category of bulkers and general cargo carriers are those running in the short-sea trades. Here again, there are individual owners with large fleets as well as pools, but, in general, ownership is fragmented and competition intense.

The most dramatic instance of change in the ownership structure of the shipping industry came with the privatization of the Eastern European shipping enterprises. Regrettably, there is no detailed or in-depth information on developments in the major fleets of the former Soviet Union. There are the bleak and almost farcical cases of the Romanian and Georgian fleets: bankruptcy, malfeasance, abandoned and cheated crews, ships in appalling conditions detained by port state control (PSC) agencies. The relatively well-managed Yugoslav and Polish fleets went through a lengthy period of decline, in the course of which large numbers of well-trained seafarers, officers especially, quickly found employment in the flagged-out ships of the embedded maritime nations (see the section on the global labour market in Chapter 3). The East German fleet was quickly disposed of and officers wishing to continue working at sea found employment on German-owned ships. Developments in the Baltic States, Ukraine and the Russian Federation were far more complex. In a number of cases, privatized companies were refinanced through offshore registration and subsequent bareboat chartering back to the privatized company for manning by indigenous crews. In 2002, there were large numbers of ships crewed and operated by Russians, Ukrainians, Lithuanians, Estonians and Latvians that were mortgaged to Western banks and mainly flagged in the Bahamas, Cyprus, Malta and Saint Vincent and the Grenadines.

Privatization effectively left the former Soviet Union (including the Baltic States) and its closer satellites, such as Bulgaria, with two fleets. The newer and better ships were mortgaged in the West and flagged out to raise capital and establish offshore companies beyond the reach of the governments that had once owned them, while the older and presumably unmortgageable ships remained with the national flag. The flagged-out ships, having the benefit of Western commercial management experience, have generally fared better. The high PSC, detention and abandonment rates experienced by Russian- and Ukrainian-flagged ships and crews accurately reflect the relative fortunes of the two fleets, although there are now indications that at least some of the national flag fleets, especially those of the Baltic States, are rebuilding and recovering. Overall, the main beneficiaries of privatization in the former Soviet Union have been Western shipowners. Well-trained Soviet seafarers found relatively well-paid and secure employment in the West, their arrival coinciding with the area's growing shortage of well-trained officers.

Taking the industry as a global whole, bank loans are the prime source of capital for funding the purchasing of ships and providing short-term working capital on an ad hoc basis. Banks do not usually provide equity except when restructuring misjudged historical loans. There are still some companies that largely finance newbuilds or second-hand ships through retained earnings (which was common practice until the 1960s), although this is no longer widespread. The number of banks involved in ship finance varies constantly and it is not unusual for one bank to sell its ship loans portfolio, either in whole or in part, to another bank. Late 1990 estimates suggest that worldwide there are about 40 banks continuously involved in ship finance on a large scale, of which around 70 per cent are European, 18 per cent American and 10 per cent Asian.

Bank finance only began to assume any importance in the financing of the shipping industry in the boom years of tanker building in the 1960s. Such was the rate of growth in crude oil shipments in this period that the traditional method of financing newbuilds through retained earnings was no longer adequate to expand fleets quickly enough. Furthermore, the then emerging trend of building specialist ships for specialized trades also indicated the need for new sources of capital. Even the conservatively managed and equity-based liner groups aiming to establish new niche sectors found themselves turning to banks for loans. In the independent tanker and bulk trades, which are dominated by private firms, bank lending was the only possible source of new capital unless some control was relinquished by floating share issues. In the mid-1960s, at least, there was little incentive to do this: so lucrative were time charters from the major oil companies in this period that a bank loan of up to 90 per cent of the cost of a new ship could be paid off in five years.[8] Commenting on this period, H. Sohmen, whose family firm is now the world's second largest VLCC owner, said:

> Many financial institutions entered shipping for the first time, confident that high freights and expanding bulk trades suggested few risks in shipping. Syndicated loans became a common way of financing the new generation of very large tankers and bulkers. In the buoyant market conditions, a 220,000 dwt [deadweight tonnage] tanker built for US$12–14 million in 1968 might be valued at $30 million in 1971 and $47 million in 1973.[9]

Banks specializing in ship finance do not necessarily carry all or even most of the debt. They may, for example, sell some or all of the debt on to other organizations, which might be other banks or institutional lenders, such as pension funds or insurance firms, although the extent to which this is possible at any given moment necessarily depends on trading conditions in the capital markets. In a buyer's market, it is not uncommon for implausible debt to be bought by inexperienced and ill-informed lenders. The responsibility for the financial collapse of Adriatic Tankers, with its 90-ship fleet, in the mid-1990s can be evenly divided between a commercially incompetent owner and five banks and institutional lenders, which between them contributed $244 million to the (private) firm's expansion.

The relative absence of PLC structures in shipping can make it difficult for a bank to make a conventional assessment of a prospective loan. Apart from the lack of any kind of historical data series to enable comparisons to be made with the performance of other operators, a shipowner based offshore might or might not have a balance sheet and is unlikely to have either audited accounts or an impressive suite of offices providing apparently tangible evidence of a well-run firm. In these cases, bank debt can still be available on the basis of what is known as "relational banking"; that is to say, where there is a continuing relation between an individual bank and an individual owner, trust relationships often form the basis of long-term sequences of lending.

When mortgages failed, as they often did in the 1980s, banks and other lenders could either repossess ships, appointing a ship manager to operate them until a buyer could be found, or the debt could be turned into equity, thus making the bank an institutional shareholder. This latter option was never popular and was only resorted to in cases where the debt was large and shared by a number of other banks. For example, in 1986, the family-controlled firm, Wah Kwong Shipping and Investment, the third largest shipping group of former Hong Kong, owed more than $850 million to 46 creditors, who eventually agreed to reschedule the debt as equity (boxes 1.2 and 1.3).

It may not be known precisely how private and public capital is divided in world fleet ownership, but there is little doubt that equity funding is becoming increasingly important in those sectors with high concentration ratios. The cruise sector, in which ownership is most highly concentrated, is dominated by public companies. In 1995, Drewry's estimated that there were more than 300 shipping companies quoted on the world's stock exchanges, with a total market capitalization of more than $30 billion. The pace of change to PLC status, however, is unlikely to be rapid or uninterrupted, except possibly in the liner and "liner-like" trades (for example, gas and chemical tankers) and the larger end of the tanker trades, now that higher concentration ratios suggest that freight rate movements will become less erratic and profits more consistent.

For the medium term, relational banking is likely to remain predominant in the least specialized bulk trades. The inherent risk in lending of this sort is acknowledged by banks in that the exposure to any one owner is kept at relatively low levels, even if the total exposure to shipowners is high among those specializing in the shipping industry. Lending of this kind, other things being equal, will help to sustain fragmentation of ownership, speculation in the ship sale and purchase market, and consequent freight market volatility. Continued volatility will reinforce the sceptical attitudes towards the shipping industry generally held by institutional lenders and thus ensure slow progress towards concentration of ownership in all but the most specialized of the bulk trades.

There has been some debate over how far bank lending has encouraged shipowners to buy speculatively, thus exaggerating freight market volatility with all the attendant consequences for seafarers in respect of conditions of employment. At the time of the Wah Kwong restructuring in 1986, P. Slater, a prominent shipowner/financier, said publicly:

> To order a new ship, other than in the liner trades, without contractual employment [that is, without a time charter] is a total speculation. To finance that speculation with borrowed funds is an irresponsible gamble, and those banks who provide funds for such gambles and describe them as loans are guilty of gross deception.[10]

This is a persuasive argument for it was undoubtedly the banks' funding of the speculative ship purchases, in the 1970s and 1980s at least, that led to over-tonnaging, depressed freight rates and the consequent pressure on labour

Box 1.2   Troubled Hong Kong shipping company lurches on

By Michael Westlake in Hong Kong, China

With a promise of fresh but so far unquantified funding from China, a visit by the founder and chairman to Japan and the arrest of two more ships apparently acting as a spur for more creditors to sign a debt-rescheduling plan, Hong Kong's ailing third-largest shipping group, Wah Kwong Shipping and Investment Co. (Hong Kong), seems to have bought itself a little more time. The troubled company owes more than US$850 million to 46 creditors.

Wah Kwong founder and chairman T. Y. Chao, whose family owns 45 per cent of the shares, set up a meeting in Tokyo with the company's 21 Japanese creditors, which collectively account for 40 per cent of the total debt.

The low point came on 24 September with news of two further ships being arrested – the *Venture Star* in Rotterdam by the Hong Kong and Shanghai Bank's US subsidiary Marine Midland Bank and the *Brazil Venture* in Houston by the Bank of Montreal. But in Tokyo on 25 September, Chao managed to persuade at least six more creditors to sign up for the plan. The plan would give creditors control of Wah Kwong's board "whenever they wanted it". Other creditors include the Bank of Tokyo, Sumitomo Corp., Standard Chartered, Chemical Bank, Bank of Boston, Dresdner Bank and the Royal Bank of Scotland.

Wah Kwong's troubles surfaced last year, when its confident expectations of riding out the long-running shipping recession and its placing of orders for new ships while prices were low were wrecked by a series of bankruptcies in other shipping companies to which it had chartered ships.

Since then, Amex Asia, Wah Kwong's advisor, has succeeded in cajoling creditors into agreeing to two successive interim plans to keep the company afloat while it assessed Wah Kwong's long-term prospects. At that stage Chase [Manhattan Bank] went along with the proposed rescue, in the face of attempts by Lloyds Bank and Citibank to go their own way – both were eventually persuaded to join in the interim plans.

Now, Chase is owed about US$30 million secured by mortgages on three ships – the *Eastern Ranger*, the bulk-carrier *Sabodine Venture* (arrested in New Orleans on 8 September) and the multi-purpose carrier *Nigeria Venture*. However, the market value of all three now totals only about US$16 million, and Chase is not the only creditor with regard to the *Eastern Ranger*.

A Chase spokesman told the REVIEW that in view of the depressed market values, the bank might not try to sell the two arrested ships, but might try to find other work for them. The bank had already agreed with Wah Kwong to sell the *Nigeria Venture*, and the spokesman said that, contrary to earlier expectations, Chase would take the proceeds of the sale instead of leaving them in the company as part of the rescheduling agreement.

Source: *Far Eastern Economic Review* (Hong Kong), 9 Oct. 1986.

> Box 1.3 Shipping – Stay of execution?
>
> By Michael Westlake in Hong Kong
>
> Now, with Wah Kwong effectively owned by their creditors through conversion of much of their debt – US$2.6 billion and US$855 million respectively – into equity, they can operate as restructured companies with slimmed-down fleets without crippling finance costs, and can thus compete in the marketplace.
>
> But this type of rescue merely postpones what some see as a desirable – even inevitable – further shake-out among shipping companies, and shifts the debt from banks' loan portfolios to their equity portfolios. Depending on individual banking nations' rules, these "investments" might be absorbed into banks' reserves or perhaps treated as genuine long-term investments – with up to 15 years before they recoup their cost, according to one banker.
>
> Source: *Far Eastern Economic Review*, 4 Dec. 1986.

costs. Indeed, it could only have been the banks who were at fault, since retained earnings and equity were no longer important sources of capital in the 1980s, least of all in the tanker and bulk trades where over-tonnaging was especially severe.

The industry's structural problem of having too many ships to allow a reasonable return on ships run to high professional standards could not be resolved by the rescue operations the banks were obliged to mount if they were not themselves to be driven into crisis. It was simply commercially impossible for them to write off their assets by selling them for scrap, least of all at a time when scrap prices were low. Therefore, the banks were obliged to keep their assets at sea, trading and selling them at the first best opportunity. As P. Slater pointed out, the logic of the situation was ironic: "If anything, the problems are compounded as ships sold or auctioned at a fraction of their recent original costs then return to the market at rates reflecting their new low value and thus continue to depress freight rates and cause further collapses."[11] And yet, given the predominantly privately owned structure of the shipping industry, bank lending will inevitably be a major source of funding for capital projects, whether they are for private individuals or public companies.

Growth sectors: Containers and cruise

Apart from roll-on roll-off (ro-ro) passenger ships mainly operating in near-sea ferry trades, the powerful growth rates of the period were in the liner trades and in cruise shipping (table 1.2). Whereas the container trades saw steady growth for more than 30 years as they ate into more and more of the trades formerly served by geared 'tween decked cargo ships, the recent and rapid growth in cruise shipping can perhaps be best compared with the development of the packaged holiday industry in the 1960s and 1970s. Growth in the liner trades was mainly centred on the development of two main types of ship: mega-carriers dedicated to the mainline hub routes and feeder ships of various sizes flexible enough in draft and carrying capacity to be switched between spoke routes. The mainline ships offer probably the best employment conditions for crews. By contrast, the crews of feeder ships often work long hours in trades with rotations involving rapid turnarounds and sequences of short-sea passages. Overall growth in the container trades is expected to continue: in 1990, 12 per cent of general cargo was carried in containers and 27 per cent in 1999. The forecast for 2005 is a conservative 40 per cent.[12]

From the perspective of seafarers, by far the most important growth was in cruise shipping, not least because for the first time it involved a high level of demand for women seafarers. The number of cruise ships of 1,000 gt and over in the world cruise fleet rose from 147 in 1980 to 225 in 1998, with gross tonnage having increased from 2,045,000 in 1980 to 6,307,000 in 1998. The number of passengers carried rose from 1.5 million in 1980 to 7.5 million in 1998 (table 1.3). The search for economies of scale in the cruise sector led to the introduction of the "mega" ship of 100,000 gt or more, with a berth capacity of 3,000 plus passengers; one of the newer ships, *Voyager of the Seas*, owned by Royal Caribbean Cruises, weighs 142,000 tonnes and has a capacity of 3,000 passengers and 900 crew. The larger cruise companies are based in Norway, the United Kingdom and the United States. Following the 2003 merger between Carnival and P&O Cruises, the Carnival Group now owns some 30 per cent of the world's cruise ships of more than 4,500 gt. In 2002, Carnival and P&O Cruises combined carried 39 per cent of the world's total cruise passengers. The world's five largest owners and operators in 1999 are listed in table 1.4.

Table 1.3 Development of cruise shipping, 1980 and 1998 (with ships of 1,000 gt)

Sector	1980	1998	Net growth as a %
Number of ships	147	225	53
Total gt of fleet	2 045 000	6 307 000	208
Passengers carried	1 500 000	7 500 000	400

Sources: ISL: *Shipping Statistics Year Book, 1998* (Bremen, 1998); S. Thomas: "Mountains of orders steadily climbing", in Seaways (London), Mar. 1995, quoted in A. D. Couper: *Cruise ship design and seafarers* (Athens, Department of Maritime Studies, University of Piraeus, 1998); G. B. Wild: "Human resources in the cruise industry", in *Cruise + Ferry '99*, Paper Collection (London, 1999).

Table 1.4 World's five largest cruise companies, 1999

Company	Total number of lower berths in all company vessels
Carnival/Airtours	56 748
Royal Caribbean	30 996
P&O Cruises	22 996
Norwegian Cruise Line (NCL)	15 354
Star Cruise	8 214

Source: G. B. Wild: "Human resources in the cruise industry", in *Cruise + Ferry '99*, Paper Collection (London, 1999).

There are considerable economies of scale to be had from operating large cruise ships with 2,000 to 3,000 lower berths. Both capital costs and operating costs per passenger decrease rapidly with the increase in ship size. Indeed, operating cruise lines has become so profitable that, in 1999, Carnival reported a net income of $157.8 million for its first quarter, a 44 per cent rise on the previous year, making it the 31st consecutive quarter that the company has reported improvements. Royal Caribbean also reported an income growth of 16.3 per cent for the first quarter, from $77.5 million in 1998 to $90.2 million in 1999. The current economic "prizes" to be found in this sector are considerable. However, the entry costs are high and this has ensured the existence of only a small number of firms and a high merger rate. This sector of world shipping is also especially susceptible to political disturbances: cruise shipping was seriously affected by the events of 11 September 2001. And although it is possible to move ships between the main markets in North America and Europe, the economic benefits of doing so are marginal.

The rise of the ship-management company

The long crisis of the 1980s found the shipowners of the embedded maritime nations looking for radical solutions. Some left the industry to focus on other parts of their business. For example, the large British firm Ocean Transport (better known as Blue Funnel) progressively sold its shipping interests and became a logistics company. Others flagged out their ships to "open registers" of one kind or another, which allowed them to make large and immediate but unrepeatable one-off labour cost reductions. In 1983, during one of the several peaks of this exodus, H. Sohmen sharply commented that "relative advantages based on only lower manning costs are impermanent and will not finally save even the most cost-effective operator".[13]

Some companies turned to managing ships for other owners as a means of utilizing spare management capacity. For example, in 1983, P&O won a contract to manage four tankers owned by one of the Gulf States, and managed another 15 ships for various other companies. Some companies have continued this practice, albeit on a small scale: BP-AMOCO runs several liquefied petroleum gas (LPG) tankers for a Saudi Arabian company.

Third-party ship management, although not unusual among established shipowners in the embedded maritime nations, used to be on a small and almost incidental scale. In the United States, however, it became a specialist business in the 1950s, when American owners built up substantial Liberian-flagged tanker fleets. Probably the first major step towards the setting-up of similar businesses in Europe came in the 1960s, when the family-owned Scottish tramp company, Denholm's, quickly became a specialist when it took over the management of a substantial part of what had been the Naess fleet. Ship management as a recognizably specialist sector in world shipping then grew rapidly, initially in Hong Kong in the 1970s, where professionals were needed to operate the ships bought mainly by financial speculators and then to continue operating them on behalf of banks when these speculations failed. By contrast, the growth of specialist ship-management companies in Europe followed, on the whole, the "Denholm pattern", growing as extensions of, or spun off from, existing shipping enterprises, mainly in Germany, Monaco, the Netherlands, Scandinavia, Switzerland and the United Kingdom.

In-house management buyouts or the creation of self-sufficient but wholly owned subsidiaries of technical and personnel management services started to become extremely common among many of the larger shipowning companies; many of these offshoots evolved via mergers or takeovers into the now-familiar ship-management companies of the 1990s. Some became very successful and grew rapidly in the 1980s. Success was due, in no small part, to the fact that many shipowners were looking for ways to cut their overheads and saw in these new organizations the possibility of getting some of the benefits of economies of scale that were hard to achieve in-house. Economies were especially likely to be found in the area of crew management because of the difficulties involved in hiring crews either wholly or in part from cheaper but unfamiliar world regions. In these circumstances, subcontracting to specialist firms became attractive.

As ship-management firms continued to develop and expand, they eventually developed into the world's largest employers of seafarers. Such is the scale of their labour requirements and their consequent need for efficient organization that they have collectively become a powerful source of labour market stability. Unlike shipowners with small fleets who may be recurrently driven by circumstance to look for new and cheaper sources of labour, ship managers (with perhaps 5,000 seafarers spread over 200 ships) need orderly and predictable supply lines. By the mid-1990s, a number of ship-management companies had become seriously involved in the training of officers, with at least two of them running cadetships in the manner of some of the now-defunct British liner companies. Others had set up their own training establishments for ratings.

By the late 1990s, ship managers could be found in both the old and the new metropoles of world shipping: in Europe, in Hamburg, Glasgow, the Isle of Man, Piraeus and Cyprus; in the United States, in and around New York; and in Asia, in Hong Kong (China), Singapore and Kuala Lumpur. The managed fleets typically embrace a wide range of ship types, flying various but mainly open register flags and with owners and crews drawn from a number of different countries. For example, the mid-range firm, Univan, founded in Hong Kong in 1973 by a Belgian shipmaster, has a fleet of 70 plus ships flagged to the Bahamas, Cyprus, Hong Kong (China), Liberia, the Norwegian International Ship Register (NIS) and Panama, of which the major owners are located in, in order of magnitude, Norway, the United States, India, Japan, and the United Kingdom. The crews are mostly made up of Indians (90 per cent), then with nationals from Myanmar and the Philippines.[14] Other companies have a similar range of clients but usually draw upon a wider range of crewing sources: V-Ships, for example, employs large numbers of Russians, while Barber International's main sources of personnel are India, the Philippines and Poland.

The ship-management market is as stratified as any market. According to 2000 estimates, eight companies with fleets of 100 plus ships have about 36 per cent of the ship-management market and ships under management have increased from about 3,500 in 1900 to 5,000 in 2000 – a compound growth rate of 3.5 per cent per annum. In total, these estimates reveal that some 25 per cent of the world fleet are under third-party management.[15] Among these third-party managers are a large number of small firms managing less than 15 ships. Firms in this range do not have the resources to have vertically integrated organizations with tied agencies in the labour supply countries and are, therefore, more likely to be "footloose" in sourcing crews.

In at least the medium term, the organizational imperatives of the larger ship managers ensure that at any given moment they have a strong interest in sustaining the status quo in the labour market. They have established dense and personalized networks in the labour supply countries, often reaching into training and educational institutions, and social capital of this kind is not easily accumulated. On the other hand, the interest and investment in stability provide no guarantee of its continuation. It would take only one large ship-management company to seek short-term competitive advantage by opting on a large scale for a significantly cheaper source of labour to send competitors off in pursuit. The effects would be similar to those produced by the flight to offshore registries in the 1970s and 1980s.

The ship-management sector, though still growing, has now entered its mature phase and companies no longer grow mainly through mergers with small firms but through large firms taking over other large firms. In 2001, V-Ships became the largest ship manager with its takeover of Acomarit, thus assembling a fleet of 500 plus ships. Later in the same year, Anglo-Eastern took over Denholm's ship-management business, with a combined fleet of 200 plus ships.

The main centres of ship management are in northern Europe (including the Nordic countries), Greece, south-east Asia (principally Hong Kong, China and Singapore), Japan and the United States, and its main customers are from the same countries and regions. Some estimates now suggest that perhaps 10,000 ships have at least one of their functional areas run by third-party managers. Ship-management functions are conventionally designated as commercial (involving charters, mortgages, insurances and so on), technical (ship maintenance, dry-docking, periodic surveys and so on) and pertaining to crew management (the finding, organizing, payment and training of crews). By the mid-1990s, the ship-management sector was sufficiently well-established to launch the International Ship Managers' Association (ISMA). In 1994, ISMA members alone managed 1,800 ships totalling 60 million dwt; a further 1,053 were fully managed (that is, commercially, technically and in the management of crew), 717 were solely under crew-management contracts and another 70 were under other forms of service contracts. More than 80 per cent of managed ships flew second register or FOCs, with the remaining 20 per cent flying national flags. The total seagoing labour force of ISMA members was approximately 50,000, mostly from Eastern Europe, India and the Philippines. At the beginning of the twenty-first century, the clients of the ship-management companies are, for the most part, small- to medium-sized shipowners, but by virtue of the central management provided by the managers for all their clients, it might be said that ship-management companies provide at least some of the benefits of scale otherwise only found in large and powerful shipping companies.

Technological developments

The main innovative development of the past 30 years was the introduction of satellite communications, which had two main consequences for ships' personnel. Firstly, direct and immediate contact between ship and shore management became possible, which allowed and often led to the implementation of continuous, as distinct from hitherto interrupted, "line management". Secondly, the radio officer's role was displaced by the introduction of electronic distress and safety communications. Otherwise, and aside from the separate development of high-speed craft, technological change took the form of new developments in existing innovations, the most significant of which was the introduction of the automated engine room with a day-working complement; there is now only a rapidly dwindling number of ships with manned engine rooms.

The shipping industry had been steadily adopting automation and integration technology since the 1960s, and they are now applied to most shipboard systems; today, integrated bridge systems are a standard feature on new ships. The bridge has become an information and control centre for all shipboard functions, including navigation, propulsion and communications, and the layout of this system has more in common with an aircraft's cockpit than with the traditional wheel-house arrangements centred on navigation. The most radical changes were in ships' engine rooms: during the 1970s, the introduction of computers to monitor and control propulsion systems meant that machinery spaces could be left unattended; in the early twenty-first century, most seagoing vessels operate with automated machinery spaces and engineers no longer keep watches. The main effects of deck and engine-room automation and integration have been a reduction in manning levels and changes in work organization and shipboard environment.

The introduction of satellite communications began in 1976, when the International Maritime Organization (IMO) established the International Maritime Satellite Organization, which later became the International Mobile Satellite Organization (INMARSAT), to provide emergency maritime communications. Since then, communication satellites have greatly improved not only safety and distress communications but also public correspondence and fleet communications between shore and ship. On 1 February 1999, the implementation of the integrated system of satellite and terrestrial communications – the global maritime distress and safety system (GMDSS) – heralded a new era in ship distress and safety communications, improving the accuracy and response time to distress calls originating from ships. All passenger and cargo ships over 300 gt engaged on international voyages are now required to participate in GMDSS by having the appropriate equipment on board and trained personnel (almost invariably navigating officers) to operate it. The role of radio officer consequently disappeared. The use of satellites for better fleet communications, data transfer and operational control is revolutionizing the way ships are managed. The primary applications of integrated ship-management systems between ship and shore are:

- reporting systems, including automatically recorded data, such as noon position report, engine performance, cargo condition and manual input from deck, engine and port logs;
- weather routing;
- cargo/load calculations and procedures;
- management system maintenance;
- interactive electronic manuals for shipboard procedures;
- computer-based training modules;
- condition monitoring of the main engine.

These developments in shipbuilding technology led to a rapid increase in ship size, matched by advances in cargo-handling equipment and port infrastructure. The bulker and tanker sectors have now reached a stage where a further increase in ship size, although technically possible, is not commercially viable. Other shipping sectors also saw a marked increase in ship size over the past decade, the outstanding example being container vessels. In less than two decades, ship sizes doubled, from Panamax (3,000-4,000 TEUs[16]) to the latest generation of post-Panamax vessels (6,000-8,000 TEUs). It is highly probable that new generations of ships may reach the 12,000 TEU level, although, as with ultra-large crude carrier (ULCC) tankers, port-handling constraints will surely limit the number of ships with very high capacities.

In the past two decades, the use of high-speed craft (typically, catamarans and hydrofoils) has been rising rapidly in coastal areas around the world, mainly for passenger services, although larger craft are able to carry heavy goods vehicles. As supply chains in different industrial sectors move towards integration and ever higher efficiencies, the demand for high-speed craft for transporting commodities is likely to grow, although the publicly announced transatlantic high-speed service has been experiencing difficulties in raising the necessary capital. In the short term at least, these sorts of crafts will have to prove themselves in shorter-haul trades: as yet, shipowners in these trades are showing little inclination to move away from conventional higher speed ships.

Containerization, first introduced in the 1960s, remains the most important development in cargo unitization. Although container systems require a high initial investment, their benefits include extremely fast rates of handling and seamless links with other modes of transport. Container ships are equipped with special features specifically designed to optimize efficiency of handling operations. Cellular guides partly do away with the need for lashing cargo prior to a sea passage. Easy access to holds dramatically reduces the turnaround time in port. In some cases, handling rates are so fast that even shipboard ballast pumps cannot keep up with the trim and draft requirements of loading/unloading operations. The speed with which cargo operations are conducted also means that cargo calculations and stowage on board need to be carefully made in order to minimize errors, which quickly become "buried" under stacks of containers, making it extremely expensive and time consuming to rectify. Turnaround times measured in single digit hours are now close to the norm for container services.

Politics and shipping

Towards the end of the twentieth century two unrelated sets of events and developments brought the shipping industry to the attention of governments, particularly to those of the established embedded maritime nations. The first was a sequence of highly publicized strandings and other incidents involving oil tankers,[17] which came at a time when environmental issues were entering the political mainstream in the developed economies. This led directly to the formation of the first PSC regime, which came about as a result of the Paris Memorandum of Understanding (MOU), an agreement initially reached by a group of Atlantic and North Sea coast countries in 1982. The signatories agreed to a programme of ship inspections aimed at ensuring compliance with IMO Conventions.[18]

The second developments were the introduction of second registers (from the mid-1980s) and pro-shipping taxation policies (from the mid-1990s) in Europe. The aim of these two measures was to retain the institutional infrastructures (of shipowning, banking, insurance, classification, brokerage, ship management and so on) of the industry. Although politically necessary gestures towards increasing the training of national citizens as seafarers were made in some countries, policies were primarily focused on retaining these infrastructures: extensive shipping infrastructures, such as those of Denmark, Germany, the Netherlands, Norway and the United Kingdom, are substantial earners of foreign currencies and, therefore, make important contributions to their respective countries' balance of payments. Inevitably, there will be some movements of companies between the industry's metropolises, but at least for the foreseeable future there are few strategic reasons for any infrastructural sectors to move sites. In a "wired world", the economic benefits of changing location are too marginal to be worthy of serious consideration.

Politically, the industry sees the world as a "quasi-single state" in the sense that its political arenas are either agencies of the United Nations, such as the International Maritime Organization (IMO) and the International Labour Organization (ILO), or the string of international associations whose leading figures are widely known throughout shipping's infrastructure. It is commonly said that global shipping is a village in which, even if everyone is not known to everyone else, it is not hard to find an intermediary who can make an introduction. In these situations, it is easy to see how global this industry is and, at the same time, hard to see why it should change direction.

Notes

[1] *Lloyd's List* (London), 6 Sep. 2001.

[2] *Lloyd's List*, 6 Mar. 1996.

[3] *Lloyd's List,* 5 Aug. 1997.

[4] M. Falkus: *The Blue Funnel legend* (London, Macmillan, 1990); E. Green and M. Moss: *A business of national importance* (London, Methuen, 1982); S. G. Sturmey: *British shipping and world competition* (London, Athlone Press, 1962).

[5] *Lloyd's List*, 9 Aug. 2001.

[6] *Lloyd's List*, 21 Feb. 2000.

[7] W. V. Packard: *Shipping pools* (London, Lloyd's of London Press, 1995).

[8] Z. S. Zannetos: *The theory of oil tankship rates* (Cambridge, MA, MIT Press, 1966).

[9] H. Sohmen: *Profitability in shipping* (Tübingen, J. C. B. Mohr, 1983).

[10] Quoted in *Far Eastern Economic Review*, 4 Dec. 1986.

[11] ibid.

[12] UNCTAD: *Review of Maritime Transport* (New York/Geneva, various issues).

[13] Sohmen, op. cit.

[14] *Lloyd's List Ship Management Supplement*, Jan. 1994.

[15] *Lloyd's List*, 27 Oct. 2000.

[16] TEU = twenty foot equivalent unit. Container ships are measured in TEUs, that is, by the number of containers they can carry.

[17] *Amoco Cadiz,* coastal France, 1978; *Exxon Valdez*, Alaska, 1989; *Braer*, Shetland Islands, United Kingdom, 1993; *Sea Empress*, Milford Haven, United Kingdom, 1996.

[18] The various provisions of these Conventions offer a wide range of opportunities to "capture" defective ships: structural deficiencies, inadequate life-saving and fire-fighting appliances, poorly stocked medicine chests, deficient food and accommodation, and insufficiently or improperly certificated officers are all grounds for delaying a ship's departure.

2

FLAG STATES AND REGULATION

Maintenance work

Introduction

One of the primary responsibilities of a flag involves regulating the activities of the ships flying its flag. Indeed, it is the duty in law of the flag to maintain a regulatory environment that encompasses the following: the operation of the ship; the physical status of the ship; the activities of the shipowners; and the working conditions of the seafarers. The flag, in the first instance, underwrites the safe operation of those ships under its flag.

The principal legislation affecting ship registration is the United Nations Convention on the Law of the Sea (UNCLOS) of 10 December 1982. Article 91 of the Convention states that:

> Every State shall fix the conditions for the grant of its nationality to ships, for the registration of ships in its territory, and for the right to fly its flag. Ships have the nationality of the State whose flag they are entitled to fly. There must exist a genuine link between the State and the ship.[1]

Under current practice, this Article has been interpreted as enabling the flag to set the conditions for registering a ship as it sees fit.[2] In so doing, the flag can define its regulatory environment autonomously. Article 94 of the Convention, entitled "Duties of the flag State", states that "every State shall effectively exercise its jurisdiction and control in administrative, technical and social matters over ships flying its flag".[3] Article 217 of the Convention, entitled "Enforcement by flag States", describes these functions in more detail.

However, as M. Stopford states: "As far as the flag of registration is concerned, the 1982 Convention endorses the right of any to register ships, provided there is a 'genuine link' between the ship and the states. Since the flag can define the nature of this link, in practice it can register any ship it chooses."[4]

When shipowners elect to register vessels under a specific flag, they become subject to a particular regulatory environment that entails a number of rights and obligations. Because of the current enactment and interpretation of international law concerning ship registration, flag States enforce and define these rights and duties in any manner they see fit. In short, shipowners can choose which environment they feel is most amenable to their approach to vessel operation.

The aim of this chapter is to look at the development, trends and implications of the varying practices of regulation in the maritime industry. The discussion has a number of objectives, namely to:

- identify the key trends in vessel registration;
- look at the impact of these trends on vessel operation;
- consider the range and kinds of regulatory practices occurring in flag States;
- locate the overall picture of the regulatory qualities of forms of flag States;
- discuss the reasons why this situation has occurred and consider the prospects for the future.

FOCs and second registers

Flagging out vessels to States other than the shipowner's own country of origin has a long history. In the earliest examples of this phenomenon, shipowners usually did this for political or military reasons, while the grounds for the more recent examples are much more likely to be economic. It is only in the period between the two World Wars, however, that certain nations (Honduras, Liberia and Panama) were specifically developed as "open" or FOC registers,[5] that is, States that will accept the registration of vessels from any other nation with only minor restrictions.[6]

The latter half of the twentieth century saw a significant shift in ship registration from embedded maritime nations to open registers. Whereas in 1950, Liberia and Panama, the two major open registers, accounted for 6 per cent of tonnage registered, by 1975 this figure had risen to 27 per cent.[7] In more recent years, the trend towards open registers has continued. In the period 1990–2001, the number of vessels in the world fleet increased by 16 per cent, while during the same period the number of vessels registered with all

FOCs increased by 70 per cent. The gross tonnage figures are even more revealing. During this period, total world tonnage increased by 106 per cent, while FOC tonnage increased by 90 per cent (figures 2.1 and 2.2). The average size of open registered vessels in 2001 stood at 15,647 gt, roughly two-and-a-half times larger than that of the world fleet in general at 6,533 gt.[8]

Equally clear is the extreme concentration of the open register fleet. The five largest open register fleets – the Bahamas, Cyprus, Liberia, Malta and Panama – account for 60 per cent of the total in terms of the number of vessels and for 84 per cent of the total FOC gross tonnage (table 2.1). These five also account for 14 per cent of the total world fleet in terms of numbers and 45 per cent in terms of gross tonnage. Some States are expanding their fleets more rapidly than others. The four fastest growing fleets between 31 December 2000 and 31 December 2001 – Cambodia, the Canary Islands, Gibraltar and Luxembourg – were all open registers, and all had gross tonnage growth rates in excess of 30 per cent. Conversely, however, two of the ten fastest shrinking fleets in this period were also FOCs, with Belize showing a decline in gross tonnage of 18.8 per cent.[9]

The lack of a substantial economic link between shipowners and the flag for most of the vessels registered to FOCs is most graphically depicted in an analysis of the beneficial ownership of such fleets. Seven out of ten of the major flag States, ranked by total deadweight tonnage, do not feature within the top 35 embedded maritime nations in terms of beneficial ownership.[10] Of the five largest FOCs, most of the deadweight tonnage on the Maltese and Cyprus registers is owned by Greek interests and 40 per cent of the Panamanian fleet is controlled by Japanese owners (table 2.2), while there is no significant tonnage owned by nationals of any of the seven flag States concerned.[11]

It would once have been conceivable to speak of a British-flagged ship, owned by a British company and crewed by British seafarers, but this kind of single nationality ship operation has now become the exception to the norm. Because of the growth of FOCs (both in terms of tonnage and the number of States offering such facilities), the sourcing of labour from many nationalities and the appearance of single-ship style offshore company incorporation (indeed almost without exception open registers offer tax-free offshore company incorporation at minimal cost and transparency), the structure of ship ownership has become a complex and, at times, opaque affair.

As a response to intensified competition in the market for ship registration, from the late 1980s onwards a number of States have created second registers to provide some or all of the advantages of open registers while simultaneously maintaining a primary register. The aim is to minimize the loss of tonnage from a flag by effectively encouraging a shipowner to remain under

The global seafarer

Figure 2.1 World fleet/FOC fleet, 1990–2001 (in gross tonnage)

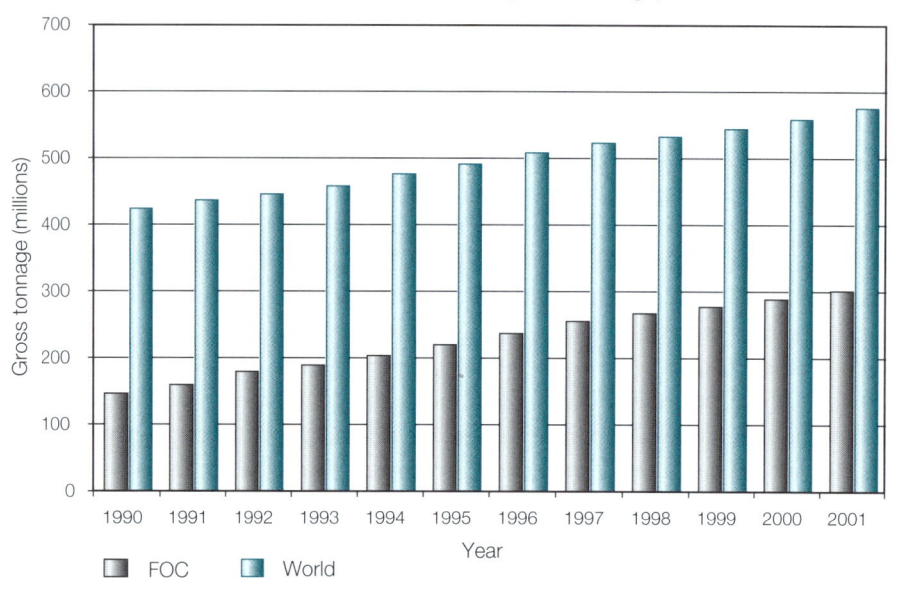

Sources: Lloyd's Register–Fairplay: *World Fleet Statistics* (London, various years).

Figure 2.2 Percentage of world fleet registered under FOCs, 1990–2001 (in gross tonnage)

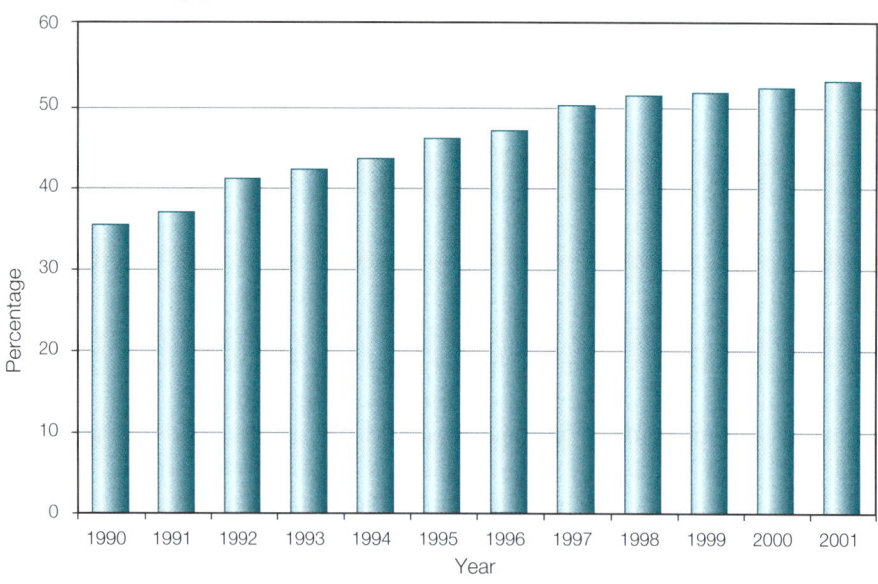

Sources: Lloyd's Register–Fairplay: *World Fleet Statistics* (London, various years).

Table 2.1 Vessel numbers and gross tonnage of FOCs, 2001

Registry	Number of vessels	Gross tonnage
Antigua and Barbuda	840	4 688 330
Aruba	3	592
Bahamas	1 312	33 385 713
Barbados	68	687 331
Belize	1 516	1 828 190
Bermuda	121	5 312 780
Bolivia	78	174 042
Cambodia	564	1 996 738
Canary Islands	200	1 630 353
Cayman Islands	144	2 053 934
Cook Islands	10	5 202
Cyprus	1 407	22 761 778
Equatorial Guinea	60	37 225
German International Ship Register (GIS)[1]	635	4 410 124
Gibraltar	79	816 323
Honduras	1 183	966 511
Lebanon	99	301 653
Liberia	1 566	51 784 010
Luxembourg	68	1 469 208
Malta	1 421	27 052 579
Marshall Islands	360	11 718 971
Mauritius	42	96 945
Myanmar	124	379 819
Netherlands Antilles	176	1 249 762
Panama	6 245	122 352 071
Saint Vincent and the Grenadines	1 318	7 072 895
São Tomé and Príncipe[2]	64	190 428
Sri Lanka	69	153 708
Tuvalu	8	35 516
Vanuatu	316	1 496 422
Totals	20 096	306 109 153

Notes: [1] Estimated by the International Transport Workers' Federation (ITF) at 70 per cent of tonnage and numbers of German register. Germany's Federal Office of Maritime Shipping and Hydrography (Bundesamt für Seeschiffahrt und Hydrographie) stated that, in 2001, the GIS possessed 353 ships totalling 5,435,964 gt. [2] São Tomé and Príncipe was added as an FOC in 2001.

Sources: Lloyd's Register–Fairplay: *World Fleet Statistics, 2001* (London, 2001). Details for Aruba from the Lloyd's Marine Intelligence Service (LMIS).

The global seafarer

Table 2.2 Nationality of the five major open registry fleets, January 2001 (by percentage)

Country of effective ownership	Flag States				
	Bahamas	Cyprus	Liberia	Malta	Panama
Greece	19.10	71.30	14.50	62.50	11.70
Japan	1.50	0.90	7.00	1.00	42.50
United States	24.40	0.10	8.80	1.30	1.80
Hong Kong, China	1.80	0.10	3.10	1.50	10.10
Norway	21.90	0.90	8.20	9.00	2.80
United Kingdom	3.80	0.10	1.20	0.20	0.40
China	0.00	0.60	4.00	0.80	5.50
Republic of Korea	0.00	0.30	1.70	0.10	9.90
Sweden	2.30	0.00	1.80	0.00	0.40
Germany	0.20	11.00	15.70	1.50	0.40
Saudi Arabia	4.90	0.00	8.80	0.00	0.10
Taiwan, China	0.00	0.00	1.30	0.00	5.10
Singapore	1.40	0.10	3.90	0.00	1.30
Denmark	0.90	0.00	0.30	0.10	0.20
Russian Federation	0.00	4.60	6.00	2.10	0.00
Switzerland	0.90	0.20	1.00	3.50	1.60
Italy	1.40	0.00	0.90	3.30	0.20
Belgium	1.50	0.20	1.40	0.10	0.30
France	0.90	0.00	0.00	0.00	0.20
Spain	1.80	0.40	0.10	0.00	0.20
Monaco	1.50	0.00	0.80	0.90	0.30
Australia	0.00	0.00	0.70	0.00	0.30
Others	9.80	9.20	8.80	12.10	4.70
Totals	100	100	100	100	100

Source: UNCTAD: *Review of Maritime Transport, 2001* (New York/Geneva, 2001).

the auspices of that State while benefiting from a number of enticements such as lower taxation and less regulated crewing requirements. This action is the pragmatic recognition of the force of international competition from open registries – and of their competitive advantages because of their flexibility. With few exceptions, such as the German second register, these flags also attempt to attract international shipping as well as maintain the national fleet.

In terms of numbers, there are 26 registers that can be classified as second registers, a list of which is given in table 2.3. The creation of these registers began in the late 1980s with the French Kerguelen Islands in 1987, the NIS in 1987, the Danish International Ship Register (DIS) in 1988,

Table 2.3 Second registers, 2002

Country	Second register
Brazil	Registro Especial Brasileiro (REB)
China	Hong Kong;[1] Macao
Denmark	DIS; Faeroe Islands; Faeroe Islands (FAS)
Finland	Åland Islands
France	Kerguelen Islands (French Southern and Antarctic Territories); Wallis and Futuna Islands
Germany	GIS
Italy	Second Register
Netherlands	Netherlands Antilles
New Zealand	Cook Islands
Norway	NIS
Portugal	Madeira (MAR)
Spain	Canary Islands (CSR)
Turkey	International Shipping Register
United Kingdom	Anguilla; Bermuda; British Virgin Islands; Cayman Islands; Channel Islands; Falkland Islands; Gibraltar; Isle of Man; Turks and Caicos Islands

Note: [1] The Hong Kong Special Administrative Region (HKSAR) is authorized by the Chinese Government to maintain a separate shipping register and issue certificates using the name "Hong Kong, China". However, its status as an administrative region means that it is, technically, a second register. As discussed above, this does not imply the form of the relationship between Hong Kong and China.

Portugal's Madeira in 1988, and the German International Ship Register (GIS) in 1988. After this initial period of activity, there was a significant lull in the further creation of second registers, with the sole exception of Spain's Canary Islands (1992). However, since 1997 there has been renewed activity in this area, with the creation of a Turkish second register in 1997, a Brazilian register and an Italian second register in 1998.

The blanket term "second register" does not necessarily indicate the form of the relationship between the primary and second register or the rationale and operation of their respective registers. A number of these second registers are extremely small and show little, if any, growth. Furthermore, they cover only small ships. Their status as a second register is due to the fact that they are based in a non-metropolitan territory of another State, although in terms of shipping registration there may be no formal links with the State's primary register. These registers can be classified as non-active, in terms of both their operations and international significance. The following seven registers can be included in this category: Anguilla; British Virgin Islands; Channel Islands; Cook Islands; Falkland Islands; Turks and Caicos Islands, and Wallis and Futuna Islands.

Other second registers are active in the flag market as well as significantly autonomous in their operations, but they do not exist solely with a view to attracting shipping from the metropolitan State. The relationship between the territory and its State tends to be visible through the content of laws. For example, in Bermuda and the Cayman Islands, the principal shipping legislation in force is the United Kingdom Merchant Shipping Acts; the Isle of Man's legislation is also principally based on these Acts.

Although a number of second registers are in fact "open", they are at once similar to and different from most open registers. The Red Ensign Group, the Canary Islands and Madeira may be run as commercial enterprises, but because all these various territories have a formal and legal and political relationship with embedded maritime nations that have well-established regulatory frameworks, they are susceptible to "home State" intervention. In the case of the Red Ensign Group, for example, there may not be any formal control, but there is no doubt that the British Government has begun to take an active and almost monitoring interest in its operations. The same is no less true of the Spanish and Portuguese Governments in respect of their territories' registers. Where Denmark, Germany, France and Norway are concerned, their international/second registers are all formally administered by bona fide agencies, which, in their practices and their personnel, are hard to tell apart from what might be called their "first" registries. These registers are not run as commercial enterprises. They have been set up by the home State and their purpose is the preservation of the home State's maritime industry infrastructure. In original intention and in fact, they are typical examples of the sort of defensive economic development strategy to be found everywhere in Europe and variously applied to cities, regions and industries.

Activity in the early years of the twenty-first century suggests that the option of utilizing a non-metropolitan territory has become less attractive, and new second registers are exclusively concentrated in the nominal constitution of second registers within the primary countries themselves. Both the recent second registers and those countries engaged in debate over this issue favour this option. The disadvantages attached to the use of a non-metropolitan territory led the French Government to agree, in 2003, to set up a second national register within France, the French International Ship Register (FIR), to replace the Kerguelen Islands. Concerning the attempt to retain tonnage, the GIS has been the most successful. When Germany introduced its second register in 1988, 52 per cent of German tonnage was registered abroad; the figure subsequently fell to 38 per cent but was up to 65 per cent in 1997.[12] According to Germany's Federal Office of Maritime Shipping and Hydrography, 96 per cent of German-registered tonnage appears on this register. The GIS is also unusual in terms of second registers in that only ships acceptable to the primary register may be entered on it.

FOCs and second registers are steadily becoming more important within the global maritime industry, although the reasons for this may be diverse. As suggested by Bergantino and Marlow, "flagging out is primarily caused by the desire to minimize costs".[13] The same authors also suggest, however, that other factors such as the quality of available labour, management costs, fiscal considerations and questions of effective control are important elements in such decisions. The ITF is even more explicit on this point:

> FOCs enable shipowners to minimize their operational costs by, inter alia, tax avoidance, transfer pricing, trade union avoidance, recruitment of non-domiciled seafarers and passport holders on very low wage rates, non-payment of welfare and social security contributions for their crews and avoidance of strictly applied safety and environmental standards.[14]

This definition does, however, overlook one vital point: although it is probably easier for open registers to minimize their costs in such ways, some national registers are as equally deficient in these respects as the worst FOCs. The data on detention and casualty rates, for example, also reveal that many national flags have extremely poor records. The average global detention rate in 1998 was 6 per cent,[15] and of the 39 countries who exceeded this rate (table 2.4), ten were FOCs whose combined total gross tonnage represented just 20 per cent of the entire FOC fleet. A similar pattern emerges when considering the list of targeted flag States defined by the various PSC regimes. The *2000 Port State Control (PSC) Report* of the American Coastguard lists 13 countries on its targeted list; of these nine, or 69 per cent, are FOCs.[16] Of those flag States that exceeded the three-year detention rate of 7.1 per cent (1998–2000) in the Asia-Pacific region (Tokyo MOU), six, or 35 per cent, of these were open registers.[17] Nine of the 26 States appearing on the "black list" in the 2000 Paris MOU report are open registers, with FOCs accounting for 35 per cent of those States identified as "very high risk" in the black list.[18] Making similar comparisons on the basis of second registers is problematic in that second registers, which are centrally run and operated, are normally included within the statistics for the first register of that particular State. However, none of the second registers for which figures are available appears on any of the targeted lists produced by PSC regions.

As for the number of casualties (that is, ships lost), the picture is similar. Of the 21 States whose losses as a percentage of its fleet exceeded the world average losses of 0.1 in 1998, eight were FOCs (table 2.5) and their combined total gross tonnage accounted for only 25 per cent of the FOC total. Once again, comparisons with second registers are difficult, as in most cases the data elide the difference between primary and second registers. Where data are available, only one second register (the Isle of Man) reported a loss rate above the world average in 1998.

The global seafarer

Table 2.4 The 39 flag States that exceeded the average global detention rate, 1998

Registry	Number of inspections	Number of detentions	Percentage detention/inspection
Albania	10	7	70
Democratic People's Republic of Korea	22	10	45
Equatorial Guinea	16	7	44
Bolivia	8	3	38
Mauritius	12	4	33
Lebanon	72	22	31
Sudan	11	3	27
Cape Verde	17	4	24
Georgia	14	3	21
Syria	152	32	21
Croatia	60	12	20
Guinea	10	2	20
Indonesia	89	18	20
Belize	611	114	19
Nigeria	11	2	18
Tonga	11	2	18
Bangladesh	18	3	17
Turkey	889	151	17
Cambodia	202	32	16
Libyan Arab Jamahiriya	31	5	16
Honduras	570	84	15
Bulgaria	122	17	14
Saint Vincent and the Grenadines	1 274	172	14
Azerbaijan	31	4	13
Pakistan	45	6	13
Egypt	60	7	12
Morocco	65	8	12
Romania	233	28	12
Islamic Republic of Iran	85	9	11
Malta	2 131	207	10
Turkmenistan	10	1	10
Malaysia	248	22	9
Samoa	11	1	9
Algeria	90	7	8
Cyprus	3 107	236	8
Russian Federation	1 997	132	7
Sri Lanka	29	2	7
Thailand	247	18	7
Ukraine	520	38	7

Note: Registries in italics are FOCs.
Source: IMO.

Table 2.5 Registries with losses exceeding the world average, 1998

Registry	Number of ships lost	Percentage of flag fleet lost
Congo	1	29.13[1]
Austria	1	2.84
Equatorial Guinea	1	1.62
Democratic People's Republic of Korea	1	1.48
Belize	10	1.12
Cambodia	2	0.78
Argentina	1	0.73
Honduras	3	0.72
Syria	1	0.68
Saint Vincent and the Grenadines	6	0.64
Philippines	2	0.64
Antigua and Barbuda	3	0.42
Isle of Man	1	0.41
Turkey	3	0.36
Chile	1	0.32
Indonesia	3	0.31
Spain	1	0.30
Cyprus	6	0.26
South Africa	1	0.22
Bahamas	6	0.19
China	3	0.16

Notes: Registries in italics are FOCs. [1] According to Lloyd's *World Fleet Statistics*, in 1998 there were 21 ships on the Congo register. The loss of one vessel would, therefore, represent a 4.76 loss rate.

Sources: International Underwriting Association of London (IUA): *IUA Marine Report and Statistics, 1998* (London, 1998).

The growth of open registers shows no sign of abating, in terms of both the percentage of tonnage registered to them and the number of States opting to enter this market. Second registers have become an increasingly popular choice for embedded maritime nations as a way of maintaining a national fleet. However, the extent to which this strategy is effective remains to be seen over the medium to long term. Evidence concerning the consequences of the dominance of open registers is somewhat inconclusive. However, it is clear that the claim that all FOCs result in poor vessel maintenance and operation is simply not true. Although some FOCs report high rates of detention and losses, these are matched, and sometimes overtaken, by a number of national flags, although none of these could be termed embedded maritime nations. Regarding second registers, the evidence is somewhat sparse, owing to the fact that many of the data do not make a distinction between primary and second registers within a flag State.

Although PSC rates and vessel losses may give an indication of the standards of vessel operation in flag States, these data say little of the actual regulatory practice of different types of registers in the flag market. Additionally, because PSC inspectors concentrate on matters of vessel standards, the data do not provide much insight into how these flags regulate and interact with seafarers. In the following section, these aspects of regulatory practice are discussed in greater detail in order to examine the forms of regulatory environment on offer in the vessel registration market.

Regulatory regimes and practice

The development of open registers has led to the appearance of flag States with highly divergent histories in the regulation of vessel operations. Additionally, the competitive nature of the flag market has meant that the type of regulatory regime offered affects the economic viability of the flag itself. When a shipowner is deciding which flag to choose, the regulatory regime offered by the flag is an element that will influence this choice. Maintaining stringent standards is a cost element to the shipowner with an obvious effect on the profitability of ship operation. It is because of these developments that different regulatory regimes in the marketplace for ship registration have emerged.

The nature of these differences is examined in the rest of this chapter by way of a number of illustrated examples, followed by a brief analysis of the development of these differences.

PSC statistics continually point out the differences in the physical standards of ships on different registers; reports from trade unions and welfare organizations describe similar variations in both the working conditions and treatment of seafarers. Many of them can be considered with reference to the varying levels of regulatory control exercised by flag States and styles of regulatory environment enacted by them. There are a number of dimensions that characterize the kind of regulatory regime put in force by a flag State, namely:

- the extent to which the shipowner comes under the regulatory authority of the flag States;

- the extent of the existing rule of law;

- the extent to which the context of the flag provides resources to counter the effects of the breakdown of power.

These aspects are analysed by examining: the extent of ratification of international Conventions; the requirements for registering a vessel; health-screening procedures; welfare provision; seafarer training; and general labour issues. This list is not designed to be exhaustive but is a selection of the range and types of activities that flag States are involved in regulating.

Prior to discussing specific examples of regulatory practice, it is worth taking a brief look at international law. International Conventions represent a sustained attempt to harmonize regulations pertaining to ships and seafarers in the globalized maritime sector. Indeed, the effective regulation of the maritime sector depends, in the first instance, upon the ratification of these Conventions by flag States. The international Conventions applicable to seafarers derive from two main sources, and these are discussed in turn.

IMO Conventions concern the various aspects of the operation of ships. These define the required standards for ship operation in terms of the physical standards of the vessel; the minimum standards of competence of the seafarer; and certification requirements. Those that relate to the "human factor" in ship operation are not concerned with general labour conditions, such as contracts and welfare provision, but focus on issues of crew competency and certification. There are 53 IMO Conventions; table 2.6 below shows the extent of ratification for a selection of flag States.

The highest level of ratification of IMO instruments occurs in those flag States that are often termed embedded maritime nations, with new entrants to the flag market, such as Bolivia and Equatorial Guinea, showing the lowest level. Although a number of open registers do have fairly high rates of ratification, for example, the Marshall Islands and Liberia, in general they tend to have noticeably lower rates of ratification than the embedded maritime nations.

There are a large number of ILO Conventions that apply exclusively to the work of seafarers, the most important of which is the Merchant Shipping (Minimum Standards) Convention, 1976 (No. 147). This Convention extends previous instruments and reiterates the commitment to those Conventions already in force. It is aimed at ensuring that there are laws or regulations by countries for ships registered in their territory that adequately provide for: safety and health on board ships; appropriate working and living conditions aboard ships; the training and qualifications of seafarers; and appropriate social security measures for those working on ships. In 1997, the ILO noted that:

> Convention No. 147 has become the basic point of reference in the maritime industry for minimal acceptable standards on living and working conditions of seafarers. Although more than 50 per cent of the world fleet is now covered by this instrument, six of the top 15 shipping countries have still not ratified it: Panama, Bahamas, Malta, China, Singapore and the Philippines.[19]

In comparison with embedded maritime nations, open registers have significantly lower rates of ratification of this instrument. Additionally, the

The global seafarer

Table 2.6 Ratifications of IMO Conventions by flag States, 2002

Flag	Number of IMO ratifications	Percentage of all Conventions ratified
Norway	44	83.0
United Kingdom	43	81.1
Denmark	42	79.2
Spain	41	77.4
Germany	39	73.6
Marshall Islands	37	69.8
Liberia	35	66.0
Vanuatu	35	66.0
Bahamas	32	60.4
Barbados	32	60.4
Cyprus	30	56.6
Malta	26	49.1
Panama	24	45.3
Saint Vincent and the Grenadines	24	45.3
Antigua and Barbuda	22	41.5
Turkey	18	34.0
Cambodia	17	32.1
Equatorial Guinea	17	32.1
Belize	16	30.2
Bolivia	14	26.4

Source: IMO.

time delay in ratification is often substantial. For example, Convention No. 147 is dated 1976, yet the Bahamas did not ratify it until 2001, Cyprus in 1995 and Barbados in 1994 (a notable exception is Liberia, which ratified this instrument in 1981). By contrast, embedded maritime States have tended to ratify the Convention with greater speed, for example France ratified it in 1978, Norway in 1979 and Greece in 1979. This also applies to international labour Conventions in general: open registers ratify fewer Conventions and do so more slowly than embedded maritime nations. In fact, both Vanuatu and the Marshall Islands are not even ILO member States.

Although the content of the laws gives an insight into differences in regulatory regimes, the question of enforcement must be borne in mind. As the IMO has noted: "The enforcement of IMO Conventions depends upon the Governments of Member Parties. Contracting Governments enforce the provisions of IMO Conventions as far as their own ships are concerned and also set the penalties for infringements, where these are applicable."[20] Similarly, the ILO document, *Characteristics of international labour standards*, declares that "transforming these universally accepted goals and rules into a binding legal obligation is each State's sovereign privilege".[21] International regulation in the maritime industry is enacted on a State-by-State basis and the flag itself is entrusted with the responsibility of enforcing these standards. Such enforcement is not uniform across flag States. As an example, the Panamanian administration has an annual budget of about $20 million and 6,245 vessels, whereas the British administration has an annual budget of $78 million to monitor and control a fleet that is less than a quarter of the size of the Panamanian fleet. It is clear that such budgetary differences will result in differing enforcement capabilities, and shows that States attach different levels of priority to the enforcement of these Conventions.

Control over the quality of the vessels flying the flag of the State is, in the first instance, determined by the requirements that need to be fulfilled before a ship is registered. If a flag is only interested in increasing the number of ships on its register, irrespective of their condition, then the registration requirements will be, at best, minimal, and, at worst, of no consequence at all. Clearly, if a State establishes lax procedures, then it has displayed limited interest in maintaining the quality of ships appearing on its register and is often placing the shipowner outside the regulatory network of the State.

In the United Kingdom, the eligibility requirements are as follows:

- British citizens;
- Citizens of an EU member exercising their rights under Articles 48 or 52 of the EU Treaty in the United Kingdom;
- British Dependent Territories citizens;
- British Overseas citizens;
- Companies incorporated in one of the European Economic Area (EEA) countries;
- Companies incorporated in any British overseas possession that have their principal place of business in the United Kingdom or those possessions;
- European Economic Interest Groupings.[22]

By contrast, the requirements of the Maltese flag are less stringent:

All types of vessels, from pleasure yachts to oil rigs, may be registered, provided that, inter alia, they are wholly owned by Maltese citizens or Maltese bodies corporate. The formation of a Maltese company is a straightforward operation; there are no nationality requirements as to both the shareholders and directors.[23]

Panama has even weaker minimal restrictions. Its registry does not require the owners of a vessel to be nationals and it accepts vessels for registration as long as they have a legal representative in the country. There are also no age limitations for vessels. This absence of restrictions as to age, type and size of vessels makes almost any vessel eligible for registration. Cambodia's regulations are even more lax. There are no restrictions on the ownership of any vessel registered in the Cambodian Ship Registry. Any legal entity capable of owning vessels under the law of the country in which it is established or domiciled may be registered as owner. Any vessel used in navigation, including non-propelled vessels, fishing vessels and pleasure yachts, can be registered. Additionally, the Cambodian Registry operates a 24-hour service and is able to process applications within an hour on the strength of faxed documentation alone. Provisional registration is available on the payment of fees and a temporary safe manning certificate can be issued without even a cursory inspection.

It is clear that there is a sliding scale of stringency in terms of registration requirements. Although the United Kingdom and other embedded maritime nations seek to restrict eligibility, FOCs attempt to open up these restrictions as far as possible – to the furthest extent in Cambodia, where there are no restrictions at all. Although a number of registers may require company incorporation, this is undermined as a means of placing the shipowner within the regulatory network of that State by the nature of the rules governing offshore company incorporation.

The link between open registers and offshore company incorporation is clear. Most FOCs offer offshore company incorporation at low cost and demanding minimal participation within that State; indeed, it represents a further enhancement of the income-generating property of the register.[24] For example, offshore company incorporation in Panama can be effected in 24 hours at a cost of $2,600: there are no requirements for local meetings, directors or company secretaries; there is no government register of shareholders; and there are no requirements for the company to submit either annual returns or accounts. The growth of open registers and single-ship companies is synonymous.

The status of company law as it pertains to non-resident companies is an important consideration in determining how far shipowners can place themselves at arm's length from their investment. Significant benefits can be gained from registering an offshore company in a particular jurisdiction. Whereas the registration of a ship under a flag will confer taxation advantages, the incorporation of a company under that flag (whose assets are limited to that ship alone) attracts the additional advantage of limiting liability by restricting company assets to a minimal level; and the prevention of the arrest of sister ships in lieu of a maritime lien.

In general, corporations act within States and, therefore, have an impact on that State. In terms of the maritime sector, the effect upon that State is often at a distance; therefore, the responsibility of corporations to a flag State is substantially more complex. On 5 October 1999, Norway unveiled a proposal to link shipowners' tax liability directly to their environmental performance. The Government of Norway's draft budget recommended increasing tonnage tax by 50 per cent universally, and then offering rebates on it to shipowners whose fleets score highly on the so-called "environment factor" index, scaled from zero to ten. This system came into force in January 2000. Shipowners may, on a voluntary basis, submit an environmental declaration, which, according to the score on the index, can give them a maximum discount of 25 per cent on the tonnage tax. This form of legislation is a simple and novel method of introducing the concept of public responsibility into the shipowning corporation through the auspices of the flag State.

Carrying out surveys of ships enables the flag to monitor the quality of vessels that are accepted on that register. Although most registers offer some form of provisional registration, all require a ship survey, or a certificate of survey, before permanent registration is granted. However, the regulations pertaining to surveys differ across flag States.

United Kingdom regulations are carried out under the auspices of the MCA. On the issue of surveys, the MCA states that:

> Every ship must be surveyed before it can be registered. MCA's general policy is for this survey to be carried out by an MCA surveyor; however, under certain circumstances, arrangements can be made for this survey to be carried out by a class surveyor on behalf of the MCA.[25]

Additionally, the process of ship surveying is ongoing and not simply routine:

> We [the MCA] will carry out unscheduled inspections on United Kingdom ships, including small passenger ships, fishing vessels and foreign registered cargo and passenger ships using United Kingdom ports. These inspections will check for compliance with national and international safety, pollution prevention and crew welfare standards. Some inspections will target one particular feature or item of the ship and its operation in depth, for example, packaged dangerous goods.[26]

By contrast, open registers require only a survey certificate issued by a classification society. Attempts to control standards of inspection have included restricting the number of classification societies authorized to carry out such surveys. For example, the Bahamas has authorized only seven classification societies and Liberia only authorizes surveyors if they are a member of the International Association of Classification Societies (IACS).

The global seafarer

However, a number of registers, such as Cambodia and Tonga, accept survey certificates from virtually all such societies and show a distinct preference for their own network of surveyors. Although this may look like a return to regulatory control, it is in fact another source of income generation. These inspections are conducted by independent surveyors operating on behalf of these flag States, with little centralized control over their operation.

It is clear that some ships are operated in a non-compliant manner, and it is the responsibility of the flag to take action where such deficiencies occur. The British administration noted that:

> Vessels which fall short of the required standards will be subject to sanctions depending on the seriousness of the deficiencies found. These include the detention of the vessel in port, the suspension of its certificate, or the issue of improvement and prohibition notices which prevent the use of a specific practice/equipment until defects are rectified.[27]

The suspension of registration means that a ship may not carry on trading under that flag, nor can it be legally reflagged elsewhere.[28] The problems with the vessel must be rectified or else it will no longer be allowed to trade legally.

By contrast, Cypriot regulations accept international PSC action as prima facie grounds for deleting ships from its registry. Although this may appear to be a commitment to improve standards, it is a withdrawal from the responsibility of the flag State. The deletion of a ship from a register leaves the ship free to flag itself elsewhere, without being forced to make any changes to that vessel. The *suspension* of registration represents a tool for exercising control over the shipowner, while the *deletion* of registration represents the flag renouncing control.

Flag State good practice

It could be expected that an administration committed to maintaining the welfare of seafarers would involve itself in health-screening procedures for seafarers serving on board vessels flagged to their State. Indeed, it could be argued that it is within the remit of any effective flag to be involved in health screening as a matter of course. An absence of such procedures suggests that the flag shows limited interest in the status of seafarers.

Norway's regulations, which apply to ships flagged to both the primary and the second (NIS) registers, are as follows:

> The Seamen's Act of 1975 (as amended by regulations in 1986, 1989, 1992 and 27 January 2000) specifies that any person accepted for service on Norwegian vessels

over 25 grt [registered gross tonnage] (or over 100 grt in the case of fishing vessels), shall, after a medical examination, produce a health certificate issued by a doctor indicating that the person is medically fit for duty. Certificates must be based upon thorough examinations carried out pursuant to instructions issued by the Directorate of Health, and must be renewed annually. Those doctors issuing certificates must not only be registered medical practitioners, but must also provide the Maritime Directorate with proof of their knowledge of the health conditions of seafarers, and show probability of providing medical examinations of seafarers on a scale large enough to maintain and further develop their competence in maritime medicine. There is an appeal mechanism for those seafarers declared unfit for duty. A health certificate issued to an EEA national can be accepted, provided the doctor issuing the certificate is approved by the authorities of the country concerned.[29]

In contrast to this active approach to health screening, the Panamanian administration takes a somewhat more passive role. Although there is an acknowledgement of the need for some kind of health screening, the administration itself is not involved in the process to any significant degree. A seafarer on board a Panamanian-flagged vessel has the right to receive an identity card issued by the Panamanian Government. In order to receive this card, the seafarer must make an application at the Panamanian Consulate armed with a medical certificate, three photographs and documentation listing the applicant's experience and/or training. Although this approach is passive, it at least acknowledges the need for health screening of some kind. However, in administrations such as those of Cambodia, Equatorial Guinea and Honduras there is no involvement in the health screening of seafarers in any way.

One of the factors that reveals the commitment to maintaining the well-being of seafarers serving on board ships flagged to their State is the provision by that flag State of welfare services. These provisions show that the flag State is taking an active role in promoting the welfare of seafarers. Once again, there are significant differences across registers.

Of all flag States, Norway has the most extensive welfare provision. The Norwegian Government Seamen's Service provides cultural and recreational activities for seafarers on board Norwegian/NIS-flagged vessels, including: language courses; a library service; a newspaper service; leisure parcels; a magazine service; photography competitions; a sports service; shopping and sightseeing; social services; and video films. These services are provided directly to the seafarers at home, through their shipping companies, local stations or contacts in Norway and in ports around the world. The providers of these services work closely with other welfare bodies, such as the

International Seafarers' Clubs. The newspaper service includes English, Filipino, Indian, Norwegian and Polish newspapers and magazines. The library service includes boxes with English or Norwegian books that circulate among the ships, or a personal service sent directly to the seafarer. Seafarers can choose from a wide range of languages and other types of educational material and courses are also available.

Similarly, the United Kingdom has a well-established role in the provision of welfare services. The principal establishment concerned with the welfare of seafarers in the United Kingdom is the Merchant Navy Welfare Board, a registered charity that has more than 44 constituent members engaged in all aspects of seafarers' welfare. It is governed by a council of management, consisting of equal numbers of representatives of shipowners, seafarers' trade unions and national charities. The principal objectives of the board are to assess the welfare needs of merchant seafarers and their dependants, and to coordinate the work of the societies and charitable organizations concerned with providing these services.

In contrast to this pro-active and extensive understanding of welfare provision, open registers tend to restrict welfare to either repatriation or disability payments. Panama's regulations are that if a seafarer is temporarily disabled, the seafarer is entitled to full wages for up to two months and then 60 per cent for up to ten months while disabled. In the case of partial or total permanent disability, the seafarer has the right to a pension for two years based on 60 per cent of his or her salary. An officer who has served 12 months of uninterrupted service is entitled to paid annual leave of 18 days per years of service and ratings to 12 working days per years of service. Cyprus has no specific contributions for the welfare of seafarers other than a provision in the annual budget for the rehabilitation and repatriation of distressed seafarers. Rather than understanding welfare as an ongoing issue, these administrations treat it in its most restricted form: welfare is relegated to the regulation of activities when things go wrong, rather than being seen as a way of improving the quality of life at sea.

A flag involved in the training and education of seafarers is one exhibiting a more extensive involvement in the maritime sector than merely providing a service for the registration of ships. This involvement allows a State to control and maintain the standards of seafarers plying their trade around the world. Where there is a close relationship between the flag State, the shipowner, the training of seafarers and the sourcing of labour from that flag State, the flag is in a strong position to maintain and enforce standards of the seafarers serving on board its vessels. However, the widespread resort to FOCs and second registers has severed the links of common citizenship between shipowners and seafarers and between training/certification and the flag State. It has also signalled the diminution of comparable levels of competence and remit across all flag administrative agencies. The ITF has noted that:

> There are very few significant manpower suppliers among the FOC flags. FOCs do not engage in the expense of training crew. They leave it instead to the developing countries which supply the crews and to individual shipowners and managers.[30]

An illustration of the extent to which the link between training and ship registration has been severed can be found in the BIMCO/International Shipping Federation (ISF) *2000 Manpower Update*. In reference to this report, the ITF noted that:

> In 1995, demand for crew on Panamanian ships was 54,559 officers and 49,862 ratings – a total of 104,421 seafarers. The fleet has grown in size since then, and yet the contribution of Panama to the manning of the world fleet as at year 2000 was just 325 officers and 2,611 ratings. The Marshall Islands, the 14th largest fleet in the world, supplied only 40 seafarers.[31]

In terms of training provision, there are certain general characteristics of open register:

- The register is either privately operated, hence the training of seafarers is not within the remit of the register operator, or the register is run but its sole purpose is to generate income from the registration of vessels, hence it is not involved in seafarer training.
- Registering a ship under the flag does not require sourcing labour from that State.
- There is hardly any training of seafarers in that State.

There are two main consequences of this situation: the involvement within the maritime sector by FOCs is restricted to the process of registration itself; and the shipowner's responsibility is restricted to fulfilling limited registration conditions.

Where States do train seafarers, such provision is not directly related to the vessel register itself. The Philippines is by far the largest supplier of seafarers to the world fleet (providing some 230,000 seafarers) and there are over 50 maritime training establishments within the State. The regulations governing the shipping register of the Philippines indicate that all crew members on board Filipino-flagged ships should be Philippine nationals (except in the case of specialized vessels). However, this is the full extent of the responsibility of the shipowner when opting for this flag. The shipowner is not required to contribute in any way to training.

Almost without exception, there is no connection between the registration of a ship and the wider participation of the shipowner in the training of seafarers. However, the United Kingdom has recently developed a regime in which this link is, to some degree, re-established. In exchange for a preferential tonnage tax regime on the British flag, the shipowner needs to make a training commitment:

> A company participating in the tonnage tax regime will have to meet a minimum obligation to train one cadet per year for each 15 officer posts in existence on the vessels operated by that company, or where this is not possible, to make a cash payment to the Maritime Training Trust in respect of each training place which it is unable to offer. The Maritime Training Trust and the Department for Transport, Local Government and the Regions (DTLR) will supervise the training requirement.[32]

The maritime administration of the United Kingdom is, therefore, putting a wider remit of responsibility onto the shipowner. In exchange for a reduced tax burden, the shipowner accrues additional responsibilities and becomes a true participant in the maritime sector of that State.

In sum, open registers restrict themselves to the vending of flags. The constitution and understanding of the role of these registers mean that seafarer training occurs neither in that State, nor is it the responsibility of shipowners. Even where States are significant providers of training, this is not related to shipowners flagged to that State; training and ship registration are entirely separate. Only the British tonnage tax system attempts to place the shipowner in the wider maritime field of training provision, thus establishing a wider understanding of the implications of ship registration and the regulatory remit of a flag State.

Regulatory regimes and labour issues

During the last few decades of the twentieth century, many industrialized countries deregulated their labour markets. In the shipping industry, the elaborate networks of institutions experienced a process of attrition as national labour markets gave way to a global labour market. Both with respect to safety standards and labour market regulation, the world's shipping industry is in a transitional stage between weakening national regulation and strengthening newly emerging global regulation as the industry rediscovers that an orderly labour market is an asset to the industry as a whole. Despite the fact that the role of international regulation is fully recognized as far as technical issues relating to the ship and its operation are concerned, the need for global regulation of conditions of work and life through the relevant ILO standards is not so fully appreciated.

By the 1970s, after more than a century of development, the structures, institutions and organizations concerned with seafarers looked remarkably similar in all the embedded maritime nations. Naturally, political systems and practices varied from country to country, but whether it was Japan, France or the Nordic countries, the State, shipowners, seafarers and various ancillary organizations (typically with charitable status in Europe) had developed ways of working together to produce orderly systems of "regulation". The market was regulated through a legal framework that specified standards of technical competence, shipboard safety, work discipline, accommodation and victualling, crew engagement and discharge – including the keeping of registers of seafarers. Training and education were provided by the State or by State-supported institutions, with governing bodies based on "constituency of interest" principles. The terms and conditions of employment and crew recruitment were settled and supervised by corps of permanent officials working to agreed rules and precedents agreed by representatives of shipowners and seafarers. National and local committees considered matters of health and welfare.

Shipowners and seafarers' representatives, examiners and surveyors, senior civil servants, nautical college principals, Missions' chaplains and officers of various charitable organizations in their specific roles – but also as members of various industry-based committees – all took part in a "regulatory system" that was so similar in its effects and applied to such a large proportion of the world's internationally trading ships that it effectively set or applied international standards. In this context, ILO standards were applied, sometimes without ratification. This regulatory system, where the actors were familiar with ILO standards, served as a vehicle for the application of the relevant instruments. The weakening of the system lay not so much in its standards but in its rootedness in national institutions that, by themselves, were unable to resist the impact of globalization. As soon as it became possible for shipowners to make substantial short-term reductions in labour costs by flagging out, it was inevitable that the regulatory labour systems that had been introduced and nurtured by the traditional and nationally based players of the international shipping industry would be dismantled. Whether British, German, Japanese or Norwegian, these players nevertheless had a shared understanding of the basic conditions of good practice.

In the opening years of the twenty-first century and in those countries with increasingly large registers, few representative organizations of the social partners, especially of seafarers, still exist. Consequently, there is no national tripartite machinery for the consideration of labour issues. The national consultations required in the application of ILO standards do not function

The global seafarer

properly. There are no national lobbies to give priority to maritime labour issues and, as a result, progress on these issues is slow.

As the examples given above illustrate, there are a number of differences in the type and extent of the regulatory environment displayed by flags. In summary form, these flags can be placed into three general categories.

1. Regulatory efficient States in which the State seeks to regulate the full extent of maritime operations. These flag States are run centrally from within governmental structures. From the initial survey of the ship before its registration to the welfare provision of seafarers, these States seek to provide an efficient and effective regulatory environment backed up by both the full range of international law and effective political will. Examples of such flag States are Norway and the United Kingdom.

2. Regulatory inefficient States. Within such States there is generally a somewhat opaque route between the shipowner and the flag States. Vessel registry tends to be nominally owned and privately operated. The registration requirements are not negligible but nor are they stringent. The ratification of IMO Conventions tends to be moderate and responsibility for compliance is passed onto classification societies. The main distinction between this category and regulatory efficient States lies in the treatment of labour issues: welfare provision in its widest definition is, at best, moderate, and, at worst, perfunctory, and is reflected in low ratification levels of international labour Conventions relating to seafarers. Examples of such flag States are Liberia, Malta and Panama (in general, the established open registers).

3. Unregulated States. The regulatory environment within these registers is almost non-existent. The register is privately operated. The link between the shipowner and the flag State is extremely minimal. The ratification rate of ILO and IMO Conventions is low and there exist few, if any, structures or personnel in both the flag State and register operator that could enforce these effectively; additionally, there is little political will to enforce these Conventions. These registers provide a regulatory-free environment for ship operators to act in a manner of their choosing with little regard for the consequences. Examples of such registers are Cambodia, Equatorial Guinea and Tonga.

The first and second categories present two very different prospects in terms of regulation. The regulatory environment of the first group is positive and extensive and covers all aspects of ship operation. This environment is weakened in the second category in which ships and seafarers are treated quite differently. In the former category, the regulations are limited to certain minimum acceptable standards of ship condition, which are monitored by classification societies. As for the latter, restrictions, regulations and the enforcement of labour standards are minimal, with little political will involved. The third category is an intensification of the tendencies of the second: shipowners can carry out all aspects of ship operation in an almost totally unregulated environment. Of course, within these three categories the flag States also exhibit differences: some have slightly more stringent survey requirements than others; some provide minimal welfare procedures, where others provide none; and flag States have ratified differing numbers of international Conventions. However, these general categories still offer an insight into the styles of regulatory environments that exist in the flag market. Hence, it is necessary to ask why such a situation occurred.

Those flag States that belong to the regulatory efficient group can be termed embedded maritime nations. For some considerable time, they have built ships, owned ships, trained and provided seafarers, financed and insured ships, and registered ships. Indeed, the registration of ships is but one element in an extensive range of maritime operations carried out within the State. Such States have been involved in the regulation of all aspects of the maritime industry for some time. Regulatory structures have had the time to create a coherent and effective regulatory environment. Additionally, specific maritime expertise has developed and become entrenched within the State and, importantly, within the State's bureaucratic apparatus.

Additionally, these States conform to a broadly defined, liberal democratic model. This has meant that routes have been developed in which interest groups, in both the spheres of capital and labour, can present their case and effect a certain degree of influence in the operation of the flag State. These groups are consulted, as a matter of routine, in major changes to the flag State. These States have also been centrally involved in the creation of international regulatory structures and thus the harmonization of the rule of law as it applies to both ships and seafarers. With the recent development of second registers within these States, the onus turned to enticing shipowners by offering enhancements to make ship operation as profitable as possible. These changes relate, generally, to: removing national crewing requirements; reducing taxation rates (or introducing preferential tonnage tax schemes); and reducing registration charges. However, these changes have not had a detrimental effect on the regulatory environment. So, for example, although nationality requirements have been modified, health-screening and certification procedures remain unchanged.

Although such a history and understanding of the nature of the flag within these nations might go some way to explaining their regulatory efficient nature, they cannot be identified as the sole causes of regulatory efficacy. The specific historical trajectory of these embedded maritime nations led to this efficiency, but this type of historical evolution of regimes is not the only way in which to achieve effective regulatory environments. Open registers could conceivably seek to reproduce the regulatory structures, comprehensive legislation and enforcement capabilities of the embedded maritime nations in order to produce a regulatory efficient environment. However, it would take a substantial change in the constitution and operation of the flag State, and such a situation has singularly failed to occur; the reasons behind this relate to the nature and development of the open register market.

Without exception, open registers are run on a business model. Their aim is to maximize profit by increasing revenue streams and keeping costs low. The competition is further intensified owing to the unique nature of the maritime industry. Usually when an organization wishes to locate a production site, the decision results in a certain investment implication. If, after that decision has occurred and been carried out, another State offers a more attractive business environment, the time and cost consequences to relocate could be both considerable and prohibitive (for example, new premises may have to be built and staff recruited and trained). Making the choice of flag, the shipowner does not have to take these kinds of issues into account. The thoroughly globalized nature of the maritime industry and the subsequent separation of ownership, control and crewing from the remit of the flag mean that the shipowner can make a choice of flag that can subsequently be easily altered. Following the regulatory requirements prescribed by flag States is within the cost/benefit analysis of the shipowner. Hence, the regulatory environment maintained by the flag becomes a matter that affects the continuing profitability of that register. A unilateral increase in regulatory standards would have severe effects on the attractiveness of a ship register to both new and existing clients and therefore lessen the profit-making potential of that register.

The advent of a systematic method of vessel inspection within the PSC system has meant that the quality of ships appearing on a vessel register has become an issue in the revenue-generating properties of a shipping register. Where the vessels of a flag are shown to be of a consistently poor standard, ships flying that flag become targeted: they are more likely to be inspected; the probability that a ship is detained may rise; and insurance rates may increase on the basis of that flag.[33] This alters the cost involved in operating a ship under a particular flag. In such an environment, the flag has to maintain a balance between regulatory levels that attract the shipowner but deter the attentions of PSC inspectors. Therefore, maintaining a certain level of standards under IMO regulations becomes an issue in the successful operation of a register. The split between the formal conditions of vessels and certification requirements, contrasted with the labour conditions reproduced in the ambits of the IMO and ILO respectively, plus the fact that PSC inspectors have focused almost exclusively on IMO factors, has meant that the issue of regulatory environments has focused on the ship and not the seafarer. Thus, the seafarer remains in a highly unregulated condition in the absence of effective control by the flag State.

Regulation has developed because of economic concerns and not because of an understanding of the flag as a site for effective regulation. Free markets are notoriously bad at producing regulations for themselves; it is only when regulations affect profitability that regulatory enhancement occurs.[34] Indeed, regulation is often considered to occur at the intersection of the government and the economy. Where the political system acts as a receiver of monies and ship registration exists wholly within the economy, the potential for effective regulation is diminished. Where the ship registration is understood as solely a revenue generator, the flag State is unlikely to put an autonomous check on the ships registered to it. Indeed, were the State wishing to impose some authority, the ease at which a ship can "hop" to another flag may threaten the economic viability of that register. In fact, one of the features of the gradual increase in regulation by established FOCs has been the emergence of super-unregulated registers, such as those of Bolivia and Cambodia (a peculiarity of the flag market is that the start-up cost and time required to create a flag State is minimal). So it could be said that the steady increase in regulation in open registers may lead to a certain level of deregulation overall.

The market for vessel registration is increasingly dominated by open registers, and in the absence of an external shock to the system, this trend is likely to continue. The rise of second registers has occurred as a response to this situation, although the long-term success of this tactic is by no means assured. Not only has the tonnage registered to FOCs continued to rise, but recent history has shown a significant increase in the number of open registers. There is no simple correlation between the type of flag and general indicators of vessel condition and operation. However, there are clear differences in the kind of regulatory environments offered by flag regimes. The specific conjunction of the characteristics of the modern maritime industry has led to a tiered nature of regulatory regimes, the factors of which can be summarized as follows:

- the freedom of flag States to determine the conditions for the registration of ships;
- the likelihood of ship registration being run on a profit-making model, as the operations of flag States may be privately owned;
- the highly competitive market for ship registration;
- the separation of ownership, control and crewing of the vessel from the flag;

- the ease with which vessels can change flags;
- the extreme opacity of vessel ownership;[35]
- the low barriers to entry into the flag market.

Because of these features, flag States have emerged with little expertise in regulating the maritime industry (or any international regulation per se) and with no well-developed structures in which the interests of capital and labour can influence policy, all within a situation in which increased regulation can affect income streams. It may be going too far to suggest that embedded maritime nations are wholly committed to maintaining standards in an altruistic way. However, by virtue of the register operating within and controlled by the political structure of a State in which there is sufficient expertise and funding, regulation becomes a semi-autonomous factor in the constitution of the regulatory environment, and one that is informed and influenced by interest groups. In this way, there is no need to rely on the market as the source and impetus behind the effective regulation of both ships and seafarers.

Notes

[1] United Nations: UNCLOS, Part VII, Section 1, Article 91, available at: http://www.un.org/ [22.08.2003].

[2] For an overview of this point, see M. McConnell: "Darkening confusion mounted upon darkening confusion: The search for the elusive genuine link", in *Journal of Maritime Law and Commerce*, 1985, Vol. 16. In this article, McConnell states that: "many of the international standards of the Conventions are vague. [...] The question of attribution of nationality and 'genuine link' is not clarified to any extent by the 1982 Convention. [...] Since 1958 the problem of conflict with sovereignty has meant that 'genuine link' has been left undefined as a pre-requisite for attribution of nationality." For a legal interpretation that discusses the content of the concept of the "genuine link", see R. R. Churchill and C. Hedley: *The meaning of the "genuine link" requirement in relation to the nationality of ships* (London, ITF, 2000), available at: http://www.icons.org.au/images/ITF-Oct2000.pdf [22.08.2003].

[3] United Nations, op. cit., Part XII, Section 6, Article 94.

[4] M. Stopford: *Maritime economics* (London, Routledge, 1997).

[5] In this chapter, the terms "open register" and FOC are used synonymously. Stopford's definition is as follows: "Open registers have been set up with the specific aim of offering shipowners a registration service, often as a means of earning revenue for the flag State." (Stopford, op. cit.)

[6] International Maritime Associates (IMA): *Economic impact of open registry shipping* (Washington, DC, 1979).

[7] National Union of Seamen: *Flags of convenience* (London, 1981).

[8] Lloyd's Register–Fairplay: *World Fleet Statistics* (London, various years).

[9] ITF: *Flags of Convenience Campaign Report 2001/02* (London, 2002), available at: http://www.itf.org.uk/seafarers/foc/report_2001/ [22.08.2003].

[10] These seven States are: the Bahamas, Cyprus, Liberia, Malta, the Marshall Islands, Panama and Saint Vincent and the Grenadines.

[11] UNCTAD: *Review of Maritime Transport, 2001* (New York/Geneva, 2001).

[12] *Lloyd's Ship Manager* (London), Sep. 1999.

[13] A. S. Bergantino and P. B. Marlow: *An econometric analysis of the decision to flag out* (Cardiff, SIRC, 1997).

[14] ITF: *Flags of Convenience Campaign Report 1998/99* (London, 1999).

[15] The detention rate data are supplied by the IMO and include data from the following countries: all the countries within the Paris MOU, that is: Belgium, Canada, Croatia, Denmark, Finland, France, Germany, Greece, Iceland, Ireland, Italy, Netherlands, Norway, Poland, Portugal, the Russian Federation, Spain, Sweden and the United Kingdom; ten of the 18 countries/territories within the Tokyo MOU: Australia, Canada (west coast), China, Hong Kong (China), Japan, New Zealand, Philippines, Republic of Korea, the Russian Federation and Singapore; eight *Viña del Mar* MOU countries: Argentina, Brazil, Chile, Cuba, Ecuador, Mexico, Panama, Uruguay; two of the 15 Indian Ocean MOU countries: India and South Africa; four of the nine Mediterranean MOU countries: Cyprus, Egypt, Israel and Malta; and four other countries not within any specific MOU: Paraguay, Saudi Arabia, Slovenia, Ukraine and the United States.

[16] United States Coastguard: *2000 Port State Control (PSC) Report*, available at: http://www.uscg.mil/ [22.08.2003].

[17] Tokyo MOU: *Annual Report on Port State Control in the Asia-Pacific Region 2000*, available at: http://www.tokyo-mou.org/ [22.08.2003].

[18] Paris MOU: *2000 Annual Report*, available at: www.parismou.org [22.08.2003].

[19] ILO: "Maritime conference adopts better conditions for seafarers", in *ILO Focus*, Winter/Spring 1997, Vol. 10, No. 1 (Geneva), available at http://us.ilo.org/news/focus/maritime.html [22.08.2003]. Both the Bahamas and Malta ratified Convention No. 147 in 2001.

[20] IMO: Conventions (undated), available at: http://www.imo.org/ [22.08.2003].

[21] ILO: *Characteristics of international labour standards* (Geneva, 2000), available at: http://www.ilo.org/ [22.08.2003].

[22] The Maritime and Coastguard Agency (MCA): *Eligibility* (undated), available at: http://www.mcga.gov.uk/ [22.08.03].

[23] Malta Information: *Registration of ships (including yachts) under the Malta flag* (undated), available at: http://www.malta.co.uk/ [22.08.03].

[24] Indeed, the operators of the Liberian register, Liberian International Ship & Corporate Registry (LISCR), offer company incorporation services themselves (see: http://www.liscr.com/).

[25] MCA: Inspection and Enforcement, undated, available at: http://www.mcga.gov.uk/ [22.08.2003].

[26] ibid.

[27] ibid.

[28] Of course, vessels could be reregistered elsewhere illegally, and anecdotal evidence suggests that this occasionally occurs.

[29] Norwegian Maritime Directorate: Personal correspondence (Oslo), 16 May 2000.

[30] ITF: *Flags of Convenience Campaign Report 2000* (London, 2000), available at: http://www.itf.org.uk/seafarers/foc/report_2000/pages/section-06-30.html [22.08.2003].

[31] ibid.

[32] MCA: Tonnage tax (undated), available at: http://www.mcga.gov.uk [22.08.2003].

[33] It is worth noting that insurance rates are also affected by the vessel casualty rate of a flag.

[34] The oil industry has introduced its own practices designed to squeeze out sub-standard ships. In 1993 the Oil Companies International Maritime Forum (OCIMF) established the Ship Inspection and Report Exchange (SIRE), a ship inspection database accessible to both members and non-members. The scheme was designed to ensure that ships taken on hire by the oil majors met good structural and operational standards. As the SIRE system has developed, it has become increasingly concerned with the competence and conditions of service of the crew. Within just three years of operation, the London ship-broking community was persuaded that it was no longer possible to fix a sub-standard ship with any of the oil majors. The SIRE regime, taken together with the state-based PSC system, has received support from all the industry's representative organizations and has undoubtedly gone a long way towards improving safety generally and especially for crews. It is fair to wonder, however, how much of this new regulatory regime would have developed without the arrival of the environment as a major political issue and whether this kind of strategy could be effective in a sector without the particular characteristics of the oil-tanker market.

[35] This can be explained by looking at profit maximization; offshore company incorporation can be included within the profit-generating capabilities of shipping registers.

3

THE LABOUR MARKET FOR SEAFARERS

Seafarers of Turkish, Sierra Leonean, Indonesian, Egyptian, Maldivian and Filipino origin at boat drill

Introduction

The last two decades of the twentieth century saw the emergence of a global labour market for seafarers. The associated development of a worldwide network of agencies and organizations dedicated to crew management made it possible for crews to be recruited from different regions of the world. This chapter discusses these developments and examines modern crewing patterns from the perspectives of rank, nationality and gender, and the effects of globalization on crew composition, recruitment practices and certification and training.

National labour markets have not been entirely eclipsed. But now that open register ships account for more than half the world's internationally trading fleet and many OECD countries have relaxed or virtually abolished crew nationality requirements, ships whose flags and entire crews share the same nationality are mainly owned in the world's developing countries. These same countries are also, for the most part, the suppliers of seafarers for the ships of the open register and OECD countries' fleets. It is this movement of seafarers between flags, created by the freedom of shipowners and managers to choose combinations of different nationalities when assembling crews, that allowed for a global labour market to be established.

The global labour market

At the beginning of the twentieth century, almost all ships were predominantly crewed by nationals of the ship's flag – a situation that continued into the 1970s.[1]

Although this crewing practice was typically a legal requirement that varied in strength from country to country, it was also a matter of the practicalities of organizing the recruitment of crews during a period in which the international movement of people was costly and difficult. Some notable exceptions to the employment of national crews arose as a result of the creation of the Panamanian register in 1922 and the Liberian register in 1949, since neither of these countries had internal seafarers' labour markets. However, the existence of these anomalies posed few threats to the highly organized labour markets of the embedded maritime nations in Europe and Japan until the prolonged recession that hit world trade in the 1970s and 1980s.

The former pre-eminence of national crews and their concentration in the ships of the embedded maritime nations can be seen in table 3.1. Although three countries – France, Sweden and the United Kingdom – showed a slight decline in the number of seafarers between 1935 and 1965, in all the other countries the numbers rose, and in some cases considerably. Relevant data for Japan are not readily available for the period, but the rapid rebuilding in the 1950s and 1960s of the Japanese fleet back to its pre-Second World War position as one of the world's largest fleets suggests that the Japanese labour force grew at a similar rate to those of Greece and Norway.

The employment data in table 3.2, although showing a long-term decline of the seafaring labour force in OECD countries, contain two interesting trends. The decline in the period 1968 to 1974 was largely a result of capital intensification. The displacement of conventional geared cargo liners by container ships, of 'tween decker tramps by big bulkers and of large tankers by even larger ones saw a substantial growth in ship size but a fall in the number of ships and crews. Big tankers had the same size crews as smaller ones, while gearless bulkers and container ships both saw similarly substantial gains in labour productivity as crew size declined both relatively and absolutely. Employment decline after 1974 was still due partly to productivity gains in all sectors and especially in the container and bulk tramp trades, but by the 1980s was almost entirely due to the phenomenon of flagging out by OECD shipowners and the substitution of OECD seafarers by those from developing countries and, later in the 1990s, by seafarers from Eastern Europe.

The pace and the scale of change in the 1980s in the composition of the workforce generally and, consequently, in the nationality/ethnicity of crews, was unprecedented. In 1987 alone, the employment of Filipino seafarers in European-owned ships increased from 2,900 to 17,057 people. Translated into crews, this meant that the number of European-owned ships with a substantial Filipino component went from approximately 200 to 1,130 in just 12 months. Almost all the displaced seafarers were domiciled in the embedded maritime nations of Europe. Throughout the 1980s, the shipping industry press regularly

Table 3.1 Seafarers' employment in selected countries, 1935 and 1965

Country	1935	1965	1965 as a % of 1935
Denmark	12 200	17 710	145
France	45 424	34 818	192
Germany	37 199	41 969	111
Greece	19 000	33 456	176
Italy	34 723	44 065	128
Netherlands	19 071	33 190	174
Norway	36 387	62 230	171
Spain	10 294	15 410	150
Sweden	22 353	20 401	91
United Kingdom	152 793	143 330	94

Sources: ILO: *Maritime Statistical Handbook* (Geneva, 1936); OECD: *Maritime Transport Statistics* (Paris, yearly issues 1969–92).

Table 3.2 Seafarers' employment in selected countries, 1968–92

Country	1968	1974	1982	1992	1992 as a % of 1968
Denmark	18 145	17 641	14 442	7 722	43
France	28 849	18 858	11 630	7 004	23
Germany	44 161	31 914	24 562	18 747	43
Greece	39 835	51 096	46 021	n.a.	–
Italy	35 479	n.a.	n.a.	34 170	96
Netherlands	25 570	13 719	16 117	10 530	41
Norway	57 504	39 738	35 216	40 055	70
Spain	16 990	24 458	18 406	10 229	60
Sweden	17 160	13 946	12 102	14 209	83
United Kingdom	121 750	112 721	53 772	33 037	27

Notes: n.a. = figures not available; – = figure not calculable.

Sources: OECD: *Maritime Transport Statistics* (Paris, yearly issues 1969–92).

reported news of new crewing sources and the cost savings potential to be had by drawing on them. In many cases the savings could only be made by reflagging to States entirely devoid of both indigenous labour markets and functioning systems of labour regulation. By 1986, for example, 45 per cent of German-owned ships were operating under other flags with these labour market characteristics and the same trend applied no less in Japan, the Netherlands, Norway and the United Kingdom. The savings to be made by flagging out were undoubtedly

The global seafarer

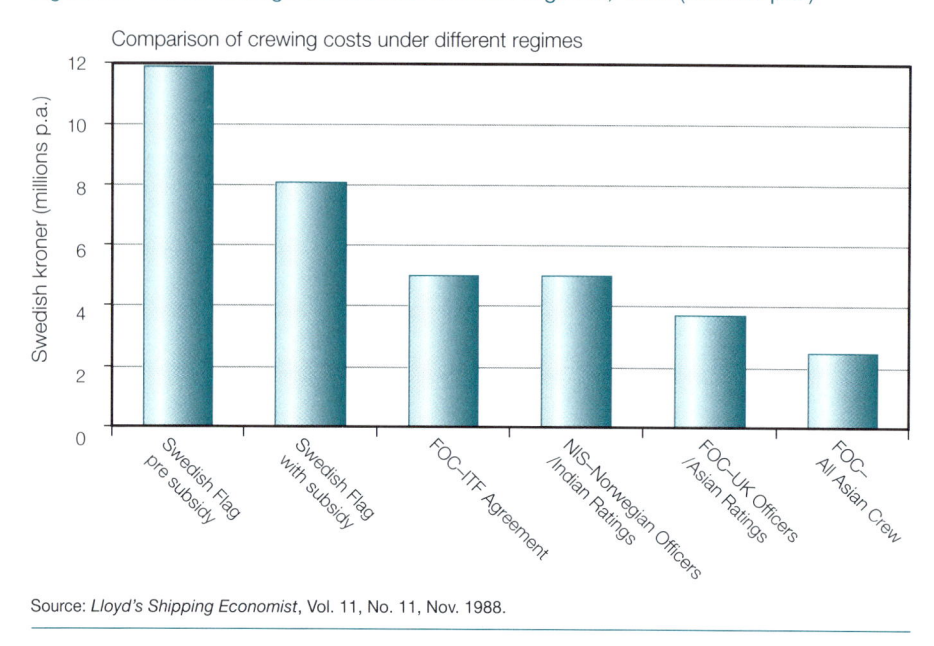

Figure 3.1 Swedish wage costs under different regimes, 1988 (millions p.a.)

Comparison of crewing costs under different regimes

Regime	Swedish kroner (millions p.a.)
Swedish Flag pre subsidy	12
Swedish Flag with subsidy	8
FOC–ITF Agreement	5
NIS–Norwegian Officers / Indian Ratings	5
FOC–UK Officers / Asian Ratings	~3.7
FOC–All Asian Crew	~2.5

Source: *Lloyd's Shipping Economist*, Vol. 11, No. 11, Nov. 1988.

considerable. The figures released by Swedish shipowners in their attempts to demonstrate to their Government their cost disadvantages can be taken as reliable, even if some allowances should be made for exaggeration (figure 3.1).

The sudden switch to employing seafarers from non-established sources, most of whom had not previously worked on ocean-going ships, entailed an unavoidable reduction in standards of competence, except in those relatively unusual cases where shipowners invested in training. Seafarers from south-east Asia, and principally from Indonesia, the Republic of Korea and above all the Philippines, were the newcomers to the world fleet. With the exception of India, which had been providing crews for European ships on a large scale since the middle of the nineteenth century, the new supply countries were very new indeed. In the ILO's report to its second Asian Maritime Conference in 1965, Korean seafarers received no mention whatsoever, although Indonesians and Filipinos were reported as working on small inter-island ships. Small numbers of the latter two nationalities had, in fact, worked on a few Dutch and American-owned ships but not on a scale sufficient to provide the basis for a rapid and large expansion into international shipping. A similar situation applied to Koreans: small numbers domiciled in Japan had been sailing on Japanese ships for many years. And yet by 1988 there were estimated to be 50,000 Korean seafarers, half of them working aboard Japanese-owned ships flagged mainly in Panama. Only six years later, in 1994, and in a neat illustration of price sensitivities in the seafarers' labour market,

The labour market for seafarers

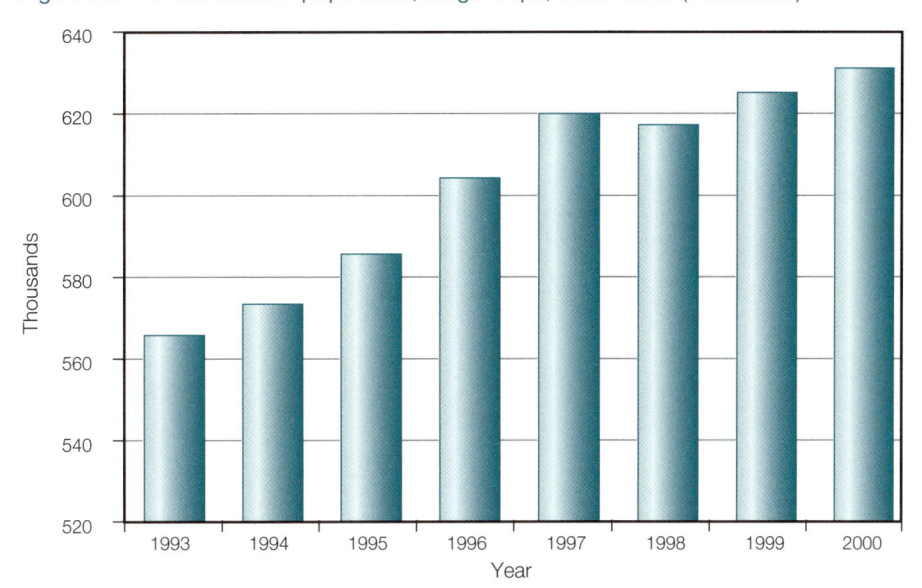

Figure 3.2 At-sea seafarer population, cargo ships, 1993–2000 (thousands)

Source: T. Lane et al.: *Crewing the international merchant fleet* (Redhill, Lloyd's Register–Fairplay, 2002).

Korean shipowners were pressing their Government to be allowed to employ Chinese seafarers, who could be paid half the Korean wage.

There are two recent estimates of the overall size of the world's labour force. The BIMCO/ISF 2000 study estimates that the global labour force stands at 1.2 million people.[2] The 1997–2000 SIRC global labour market survey, based on a sample of crew lists deposited by shipmasters with immigration control agencies in various ports, estimates the figure to be 1.03 million seafarers.[3] The data in figure 3.2 show a slight upward trend in the size of the at-sea labour force in cargo ships – from about 570,000 people in 1993 to 630,000 in 2000.[4] Figure 3.3 shows the distribution of seafarers among the principal types of cargo-carrying ship.

The upward trend in employment of approximately 8,500 people per year is likely to continue for the foreseeable future. As Chapter 1 shows the labour intensive cruise sector is growing rapidly, so the demand for crews will inevitably increase. Growth in the cargo sector is more modest but also seems set to continue in line with world trade. There is no indication that ship size is likely to rise sufficiently to produce any significant labour economies of scale. Cargo-sector crewing levels are low but they have been fairly stable for almost a decade and there is even some evidence of a slight increase (table 3.3). Further small rises may result as the enforcement of safety standards becomes more effective and more maintenance is done at sea. There are several financially successful tanker owners – Concordia is the best-known – that run older ships with relatively large

The global seafarer

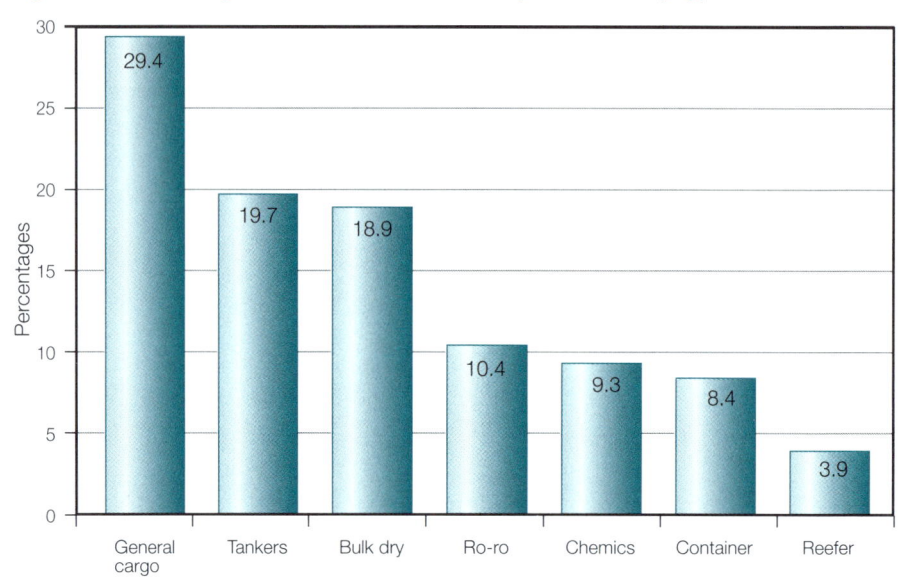

Figure 3.3 Percentage distribution of seafarers by selected ship type, 2000

Ship type	Percentage
General cargo	29.4
Tankers	19.7
Bulk dry	18.9
Ro-ro	10.4
Chemics	9.3
Container	8.4
Reefer	3.9

Source: T. Lane et al.: *Crewing the international merchant fleet* (Redhill, Lloyd's Register–Fairplay, 2002).

Table 3.3 Average crewing levels in selected ship types, 1993 and 1998

Ship type	Average 1993	Average 1998	Number as a % 1993	Number as a % 1998
20,000–50,000 dwt				
Oil	19.0	24.8	3	42
Bulk	22.4	23.3	17	326
General cargo	22.5	22.7	4	58
Container	21.3	22.1	61	124
5,000–20,000 dwt				
Oil	20.6	24.4	10	14
Bulk	22.5	19.3	6	33
General cargo	18.5	19.3	17	165
Container	18.7	18.2	30	37

Source: T. Lane et al.: *Crewing the international merchant fleet* (Redhill, Lloyd's Register–Fairplay, 2002).

crews to ensure high maintenance standards. These are exceptional cases, although there are other owners crewing their ships with four or five extra hands.

Regarding the shipboard division of labour and skill requirements, the past 30 years saw remarkably few changes in the cargo sector and among the marine crews of cruise ships. The average cargo ship crew in 2002 may be some 60 per cent smaller than it was in 1970, but the organization of the crew into deck, engine-room and catering departments has remained intact. General purpose ratings' schemes with interchangeable deck and engine-room personnel have been tried on a limited scale since the 1960s but have not been widely adopted. On some ships, the catering crew might be required to turn out to assist the deck crew on entering and leaving port, otherwise they cook and prepare food and clean accommodation as before. Crew reductions were achieved not through radical changes in the traditional division of labour but mainly by automation within departments and large reductions in trainee ratings and officers. The grades of boy deck and catering ratings have been virtually eliminated in OECD-owned ships. The recruitment of officer trainees was substantially cut in the 1980s and 1990s, although in some OECD countries there have been attempts since the late 1990s to revive officer training.

The age structure of the seafaring population has changed in parallel with the shift of recruitment away from the older embedded maritime nations and towards the newer seafarer supply nations of Asia and Eastern Europe. If it is assumed that the age data for British seafarers in 1968 and 1998 (figures 3.4 and 3.5) was and is similar to that of other European OECD countries, then interesting comparisons can be made with the age structure of seafarers from countries such as China, the Philippines and Ukraine (figures 3.6 and 3.7).

These data on the age structure of seafarers from leading labour supply countries are revealing. Firstly, the age distribution of British seafarers is highly skewed to the older age groups. Secondly, and especially with regard to officers, while the modal age group for Filipinos and Ukrainians is between 35 years and 44 years, for the Chinese the modal group is ten years younger. These differences are largely a result of the rapid growth of the Chinese fleet compared with the relative maturity of the Filipino and Ukrainian labour forces. The comparative absence of younger people under the age of 25 may be explained in part by the economic costs of labour market entry, which are often personally incurred in many of the newer seafarer supply nations. The fact that overall the labour force is older than it was in the 1960s is probably of little consequence and may even be an advantage, since wastage rates are commonly quite high among young seafarers.[5]

Crewing requirements in the cruise sector are completely different. As in the hotel and catering industry on land, cruise shipping is labour intensive, although only in respect of those crew members employed as "hotel" staff. According to the 1997–2000 SIRC labour market survey, 84 per cent of crew members are employed in passenger service roles in the cruise sector as a whole. Cruise ship marine crews, though larger than those found aboard cargo ships of similar tonnage, follow a similar organizational pattern: the

The global seafarer

Figure 3.4 Age of British officers, 1968 and 1998

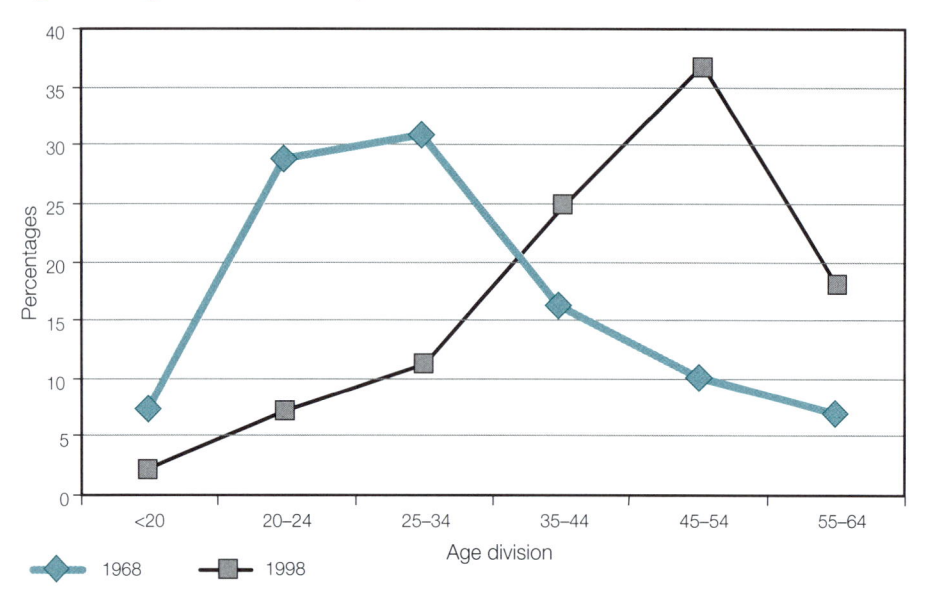

Source: T. Lane et al.: *Crewing the international merchant fleet* (Redhill, Lloyd's Register–Fairplay, 2002).

Figure 3.5 Age of British ratings, 1968 and 1998

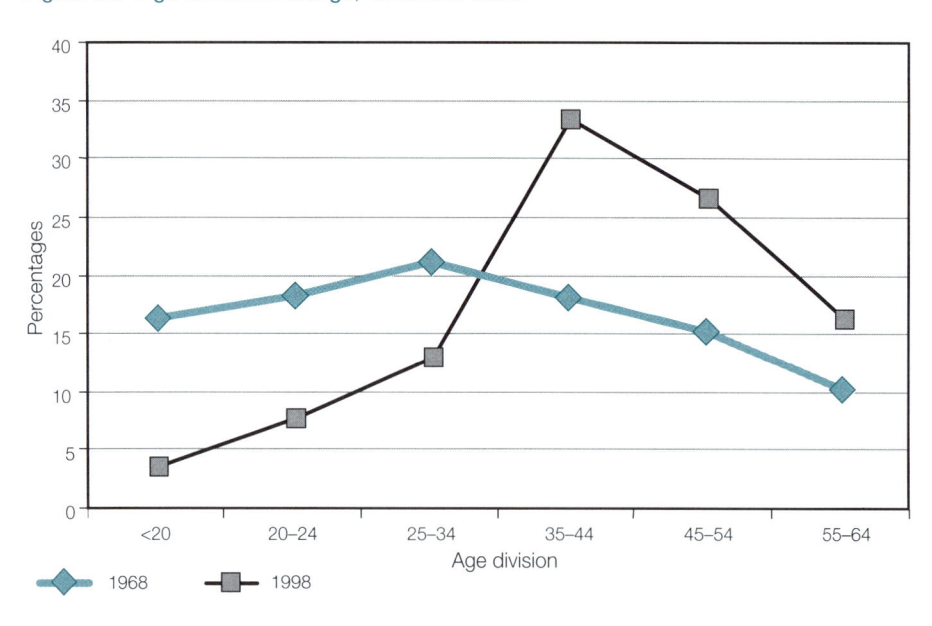

Source: T. Lane et al.: *Crewing the international merchant fleet* (Redhill, Lloyd's Register–Fairplay, 2002).

The labour market for seafarers

Figure 3.6 Age of officers from China, the Philippines, Ukraine and the United Kingdom, 1998

Source: T. Lane et al.: *Crewing the international merchant fleet* (Redhill, Lloyd's Register–Fairplay, 2002).

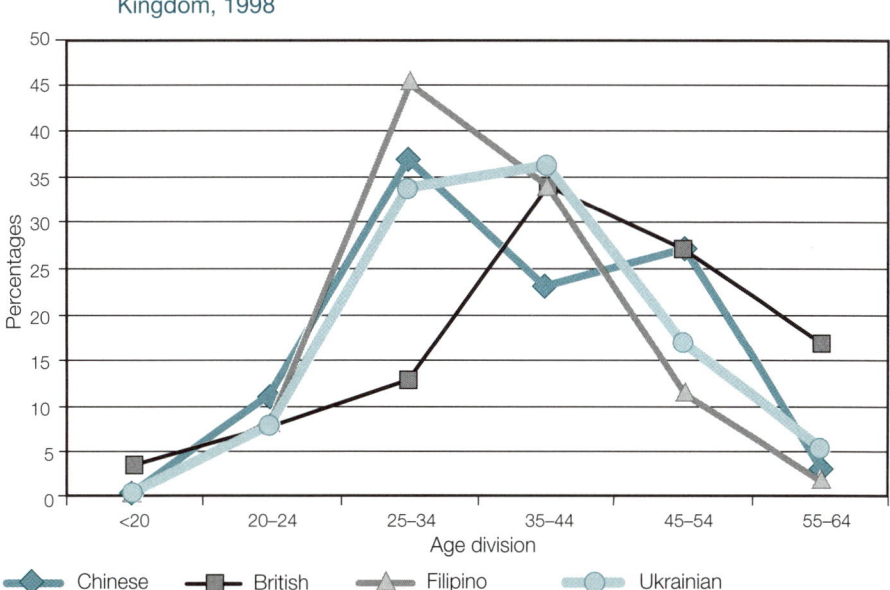

Figure 3.7 Age of ratings from China, the Philippines, Ukraine and the United Kingdom, 1998

Source: T. Lane et al.: *Crewing the international merchant fleet* (Redhill, Lloyd's Register–Fairplay, 2002).

officer/rating ratio is at 40:60 in both sectors. There is, however, one quite noticeable feature regarding cruise ship marine crews, namely that their complements do not increase significantly with the size of ship and numbers of passengers carried. Where the number of passengers to hotel crew is fairly constant across the size range of ships, the number of marine crew per passenger actually declines with the increase in ship size.

The data in figure 3.8 show that, although the number of hotel crew per passenger remains almost constant irrespective of the size of the vessel, the number of passengers per marine crew ranges from nine in the smaller ships to almost 24 in the larger vessels.

As seen in Chapter 1, the creation of the global labour market was the unintended result of the cuts in labour costs made by shipowners and ship managers in the embedded maritime nations of the OECD bloc. When, in the 1980s, these owners and managers ended their dependency on the established and regulated labour markets of the nations in which their businesses were sited, every world region able to offer cheaper seafaring labour immediately became a potential source of supply. Thereafter, nationality became irrelevant and employees were selected on the basis of a trade-off between price and the quality of their training and accumulated experience. Of these characteristics, the irrelevance of nationality is the most important. The freedom to assemble crews of any nationality on one engagement and then to make completely different choices of nationalities at subsequent engagements is the defining feature of the global labour market for seafarers.

In principal, anyone with a good general knowledge of the industry and with funds to invest in a maritime directory, a telephone, fax machine and a computer with an Internet connection can take advantage of the global labour market's opportunities open to manning agents. However, firms that have large crewing requirements and are able to afford personnel/crew management departments with a global reach are in a position to benefit most from the situation. No doubt this is why growing numbers of shipowners with relatively small fleets hire ship-management companies to organize their crewing for them. The scale of the crewing requirements of the larger ship-management companies and the range of owners' crew preferences these companies have to satisfy inevitably lead ship managers to use established networks of agencies in the labour supply countries.

Ship-management companies commonly have to guard against supplies of labour drying up or the possibility of equally well-qualified but cheaper sources of supply becoming available. It is for this reason that major employers with a diversified "portfolio" of supply countries and agents routinely search for new sources of seafaring labour and "experiment" with nationalities new to their ships. In box 3.1, two senior managers of two extremely large ship-management companies describe the labour market tours they undertook in 1994 and 2000.

The labour market for seafarers

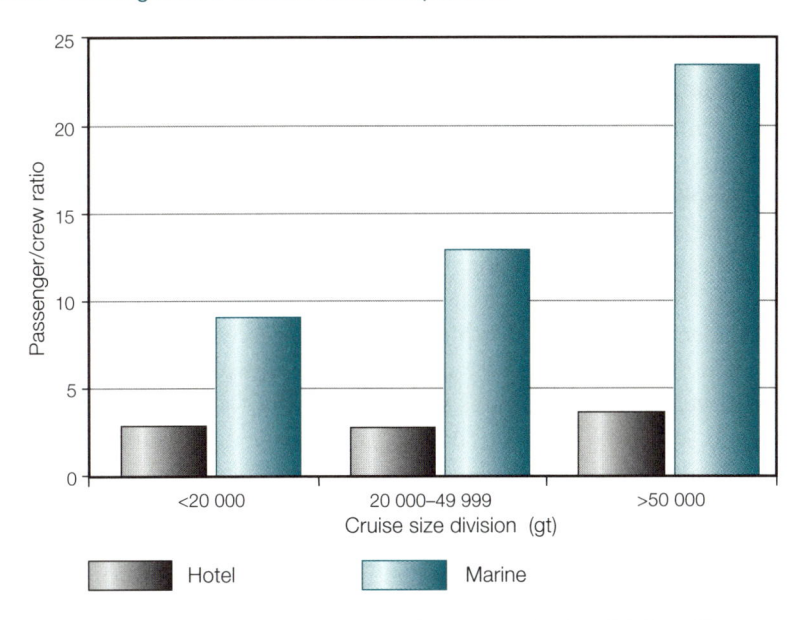

Figure 3.8 Passenger/crew ratios in cruise ships, 1999

[Bar chart showing Passenger/crew ratio by Cruise size division (gt) for Hotel and Marine categories:
- <20 000: Hotel ~3, Marine ~9
- 20 000–49 999: Hotel ~3, Marine ~13
- >50 000: Hotel ~4, Marine ~23.5]

Source: T. Lane et al.: *Crewing the international merchant fleet* (Redhill, Lloyd's Register–Fairplay, 2002).

Box 3.1   Ship-management companies and their labour market tours

Manager 1, 1994
In the last year [apart from the Philippines], I have been in about seven other countries … Myanmar and Indonesia were two. China, we know about, but I was back there. We haven't looked at Viet Nam, although we have seen plenty of reports on it. We haven't visited West Africa – I have mixed feelings about it. Latvia is all right. I think the Baltic States are somewhat further ahead. Croatia is getting expensive: you're paying a Croatian tanker master $4,600 a month; an Indian master would be about $3,500.[1]

Manager 2, 2000
We looked at Romania, where we now have a contract in place, and we also have a contract in Bulgaria. In other words, we have the ability to take people from there if we need them. We have looked at Ghana, Senegal and Côte d'Ivoire. We have had another look at Indonesia and we have recently set up a joint venture crewing agency in China. We have looked at Venezuela, Ecuador, Peru, Cuba, Jamaica. We are always looking.[2]

[1] Quoted in T. Lane: "The social order of the ship in a globalised labour market for seafarers", in R. Crompton, D. Gallie and K. Purcell (eds.): *Changing forms of employment* (London, Routledge, 1996). [2] E. Kahveci, T. Lane and H. Sampson: *Transnational seafarer communities* (Cardiff, SIRC, 2002).

67

The process of search and experimentation advertises the availability of new sources and thus helps to shape a labour market which always carries within itself the seeds of instability. While the larger crew managers have the resources to explore, sample and test new labour supply sources, and do so, at any one moment their immediate needs are such that they are inevitably drawn into at least semi-permanent organizational arrangements in a few of the labour supply nations. Crew managers with large labour requirements are, at least in the short term, a significant force for labour market stability. It is nonetheless true that ship managers also operate in competitive markets and it is normal for them to let it be known, either by press releases or advertisements, that they are able to supply attractively priced, cost-efficient labour. The following sequence of announcements and advertisements taken over a 13-year period illustrates the importance of ship managers in shaping the labour market. In 1988, Barber International announced that it had separately agreed with Portuguese and Korean Republic unions to provide crews of 22 seafarers of each nationality for ships on the NIS at 40 per cent of the price of a Norwegian crew.[6] Five years later, in 1993, the company said it was pleased with the performance of its Polish crews, who were, in price terms, "competitive with the Far East", and had set up, jointly with the Polish trade union, Solidarity, a recruiting office in Szczecin.[7] Eight years later, in 2001, another of the larger ship-management firms, the Anglo-Eastern Group, announced that it could now offer "exciting new opportunities" by supplying Chinese officers and ratings (box 3.2). As these examples show, single nationality crews are being offered, although, as explained below, crews of this kind are only found aboard approximately one-third of ships trading internationally.

Only in coastal shipping is the labour market relatively unorganized, in the sense that it is not dominated by crew managers and manning agents. Particularly in the coastal tramp and feeder container trades, it is still possible for individual seafarers to find jobs aboard ships for themselves. In ports such as Piraeus and Rotterdam there are small clusters of domiciled Cape Verdeans, East and West Africans, Egyptians, Filipinos, Indonesians, Latin Americans, Poles, Portuguese, Russians and Turks who have lodged themselves in the informal networks that find crews for small ships. Similar communities, though composed of a different range of nationalities, can also be found in the larger ports of Japan and the Asia-Pacific region. But whether in Europe or Asia, these are often precarious communities whose members may be residing illegally. Intermediaries from within these communities historically played an important role in linking shipowners with seafarers and still do so, but these local brokers or "compradors" only bear a superficial resemblance to the highly organized crew managers. As for the communities themselves,

Box 3.2

Anglo-Eastern moves into China!
Now offering Chinese Officers and ratings for world-wide deployment – selected and trained to international standards by Anglo-Eastern

According to BIMCO statistics, with a pool of 34,197 qualified officers and 47,820 ratings - China is the second largest source of officers and ratings in the world - yet only 10 percent are used on non-Chinese owned vessels.

Anglo-Eastern have recently finalized a co-operative Venture with GMG Yinghua Crew Management Company. As a result, Anglo-Eastern is now able to offer – for the first time – Chinese officers and ratings qualified to international standards, who have gone through a specialized intensive two months training programme in preparation for international deployment.

This training is carried out jointly by Anglo-Eastern's professional trainers, in conjunction with GMC and covers

- Intensive English training, using Marlins training and ISF/Marlins assessment
- Port State Control requirements
- ISM Regulations
- Commercial Reporting
- Safety Procedures
- Emergency Procedures
- Company specific training

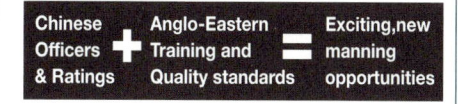

Chinese Officers & Ratings + Anglo-Eastern Training and Quality standards = Exciting, new manning opportunities

For details, please contact :
Mr Peter Cremers, Chairman
Tel: 852 – 2893 6111   E-mail: aesmhk@aesm.com

THE ANGLO-EASTERN GROUP
23/F 248 Queen's Road East, Wanchai, Hong Kong.
Tel: (852) 2863 6111/Fax (852) 2863 2861/homepage: www.aesm.com.hk
Denholm Crew Management Ltd • Anglo-Eastern Ship Management Ltd
(Anglo-Eastern Group Member Companies)

although they may be no more than residues of the once large but transient cosmopolitan waterfront districts of the world's larger ports, they do fill an essential labour market role. Apart from providing a significant proportion of crews for the smaller and hard-running ships working in coastal waters, enclosed seas such as the Mediterranean, the Black Sea and the island archipelagos of south-east Asia, they can also supply the small numbers of seafarers needed to make up the complements of deep-sea ships unexpectedly obliged to land sick or injured crew members.

The global labour market, then, is a reality for most of the world's seafarers except those working in the coastal and near-sea trades of either the less developed countries of Asia or in those industrializing or developed countries with cabotage policies, such as Brazil and the United States. There are, of course, still a large number of internationally trading, nationally flagged ships crewed by nationals, but, with the exception of China, none of these fleets is large. It is a sign of the times that China, now the only nation with a sizeable fleet of merchant ships crewed by nationals who have been trained and certificated in a well-regulated system of colleges and universities, simultaneously licenses manning agents to supply seafarers for foreign-flagged

The global seafarer

ships. Elsewhere in the world, the national flag flown by a ship rarely corresponds with the nationality of a significant proportion of the crew. The world's largest fleets are attached to either FOCs or second registers, and the nationalities of these fleets' crews do not correspond with the flags of their ships, as can be seen in tables 3.4 and 3.5.

This lack of correspondence between crew and the flag a ship flies is a growing feature of flagged fleets as remaining nationality requirements are steadily removed. Late in 2001, the prominent Taiwanese liner company, Evergreen, began a process of reflagging a number of ships to the British flag. The only British crew requirement was that specified ranks among the Taiwanese officer corps should be successfully examined for British certificates of competency. This ultimate relaxation of British nationality requirements brought the flag into line with crewing practices aboard ships attached to British dependent territories, such as the Isle of Man and Bermuda, where

Table 3.4 Crew nationalities aboard selected OECD fleets, 1993 and 1999

Flag	Nationals as a % 1993	1999	Others as a % 1993	1999
Greece	56	51	44	49
Japan	71	31	29[1]	69[1]
Netherlands	56	44	44	56
United Kingdom	75	71	25	29
United States	100	100	0	0

Note: [1] Filipino.

Source: SIRC Global Labour Market Database (Cardiff).

Table 3.5 Selected seafarer nationalities and flags of employment, 1993 and 1999

Nationality	Own flag as a % 1993	1999	Others as a % 1993	1999
British	37	29	63	71
Croatian	0	5	100	95
Filipino	2	5	98	95
German	78	43	22	57
Indian	30	3	3	97
Korean (Rep.)	43	8	57	92
Polish	23	2	77	98

Source: SIRC Global Labour Market Database (Cardiff).

Box 3.3 The mixed nationality crews of the *Controro* and the *Tanker*

Controro **(NIS-flagged ship)**

Nationality	Rank
Norwegian	master
Filipino	chief officer
Filipino	2nd officer
Filipino	3rd officer
Myanmar	radio officer
Myanmar	chief engineer
Myanmar	2nd engineer
Myanmar	3rd engineer
Myanmar	4th engineer
Myanmar	electrical engineer
Filipino	bosun
Filipino	able seaman (AB)
Filipino	AB
Filipino	AB
Filipino	ordinary seaman (OS)
Filipino	OS
Filipino	deck fitter
Filipino	deck fitter
Filipino	deck cadet
Myanmar	deck cadet
Myanmar	engine-room fitter
Myanmar	motorman
Myanmar	motorman
Myanmar	motorman
Filipino	chief cook
Myanmar	2nd cook
Filipino	mess boy

Tanker **(Isle of Man-flagged ship)**

Nationality	Rank
Italian	master
Polish	chief officer
Polish	2nd officer
Polish	2nd officer
Polish	radio officer
Italian	chief engineer
Polish	1st engineer
Polish	2nd engineer
Polish	fitter
Italian	cook
Filipino	pumpman
Filipino	AB
Filipino	AB
Filipino	AB
Filipino	deck boy
Filipino	engine-room boy
Italian	deck apprentice
Italian	engine-room apprentice

Source: SIRC Crew Lists Archive (Cardiff).

mixed nationality crews are predominant. Crewing patterns aboard the ships attached to these island dependencies are similar to those found in the other major European second registers of Norway (NIS), Denmark (DIS) and Germany (GIS) and these, in turn, are very similar to those found aboard the ships of the FOC fleets. In box 3.3 the mixed nationality crews aboard two OECD-flagged ships – the *Controro* and the *Tanker* – are listed.

Mixed nationality crews are hardly a new phenomenon, but what makes the modern mixed nationality crew distinctive is the extent to which it is consciously composed. Since seaborne international trade began on a significant level around 500 years ago, mixed nationality crews have been common and, during some periods, even commonplace. However, the apparent similarity between today and times past is, in critical respects, misleading. Except for those twentieth-century ships crewed by European owners with European officers and variously African, Chinese and Indian ratings, crews were assembled through the mechanisms of local and nationally based labour markets: ships announced their crewing requirements, and seafarers either presented themselves for engagement or were presented through intermediaries.

Preferences for particular nationalities and views about their "mixability" are often influential in deciding the composition of crews. The SIRC global labour market surveys of 1992–93 and 1997–2000 show that Russians and nationals of the Republic of Korea are normally found only in single nationality crews when engaged aboard FOC or second register ships. Where Russians do sail in the company of other nationalities, they do so usually in ones and twos rather than in homogeneous groups of officers or ratings. By contrast, the surveys show that, although Filipino, Indian and Polish seafarers frequently provide large proportions of crews, they are less likely to form whole crews in FOC or second register ships. English-language ability is probably the decisive factor in most of these cases. Where standards of English-speaking are relatively low, as they are widely held to be among Russian and Korean seafarers, then it is presumably prudent to employ them in monoglot crews. The English of Filipinos, Indians and Poles is generally thought to be of a high enough standard for them to be placed with English-speaking senior officers of other nationalities.

Nationalities also often seem to be chosen on the basis of what might be called inter- and intraregional preferences. In some of these cases, preferences seem to be a residue of historic imperial associations: it is noticeable that the only groups of Indonesians and West Africans found in the sample aboard European ships worked respectively in Dutch and British ships, and that the largest employers of nationals of the Republic of Korea were the Japanese. Then there are a number of cases of Egyptian officers and ratings sailing with Greeks in what might be called a "Mediterranean association"; a "Baltic connection" might account for Poles providing a high proportion of the crews of small German and Norwegian ships; and a "south-east Asian connection" presumably explains the predominance of Indonesians, Malaysians and Thais aboard Singaporean ships. However, these nationality choices are more likely to be made on the basis of availability and price than on sentiment or cultural familiarity.

A good illustration of the implicit structuring of nationality choice by price can be seen in the crewing strategy of a European shipowner with a large fleet of Panamanian-flagged container and ro-ro ships in long-distance trades. Seven of this company's ships appeared in the SIRC 1992–93 survey, and in each of them the officer corps consisted of Italian senior officers and Croatian junior officers. The petty officers and ratings were likewise employed in a consistent pattern of nationality and seniority, except that this part of the crew had a triple-layered price structure. First and second were the "West" and "East" European layers consisting of Italians and Croatians. Third was a developing countries' layer, mainly made up of Malagasies or Western Samoans.

The mainstream nationality patterns revealed by the surveys are, of course, only cross-sectional representations of a particular moment in time. Earlier or later snapshots of the same owners' ships might well show different ensembles of nationalities – as in the case of a large products tanker owned by one of the oil majors. In November, 1992, the ship had European officers and was otherwise manned by Filipinos. By April, 1993, however, the ship had the same officer composition but the Filipinos had been replaced by Sierra Leoneans. Such changes of crew sources within fleets and over a period of time are common, but this does not mean that owners and managers are constantly switching between nationalities. The 1997–2000 SIRC survey found that the oil major mentioned above was still employing Sierra Leonean seafarers six years later. "Experimentation" may well have become the norm, but it does not follow that the labour market is, at any given moment, so anarchic and inconsistent that ships frequently sail with newly invented permutations of crew nationalities. The labour market may be fluid, but it is not characterized by large inflows and outflows over short periods of time. Were this the case, the SIRC surveys would show a very much wider variety of crew compositions than actually apparent.

Figure 3.9 shows the origins of seafarers by world region and rank. In general, it is clear that the world shipping industry has become heavily dependent on crews drawn from Eastern Europe, the Far East and South Asia, with these three regions between them providing 81 per cent of the world's seafarers.

Figure 3.10 shows the national origins and ranks of seafarers from the ten largest labour supply countries, and it is clear that neither of the two principal shipping OECD countries – Germany and Greece – have enough junior officers to replace their seniors. The countries with an equivalent or favourable balance between junior and senior officers are China, India, the Philippines, Romania, the Russian Federation and Ukraine, and it can, therefore, be confidently predicted that citizens of these countries will, within the next decade, be responsible for the day-to-day running of a very large proportion of the world's ships. The impact of these developments will be felt most by OECD shipowners, who will find it increasingly difficult to exercise their current preferences for OECD senior officers.

The global seafarer

Figure 3.9 Seafarers' origins by world region, all ranks, 2000 (percentages)

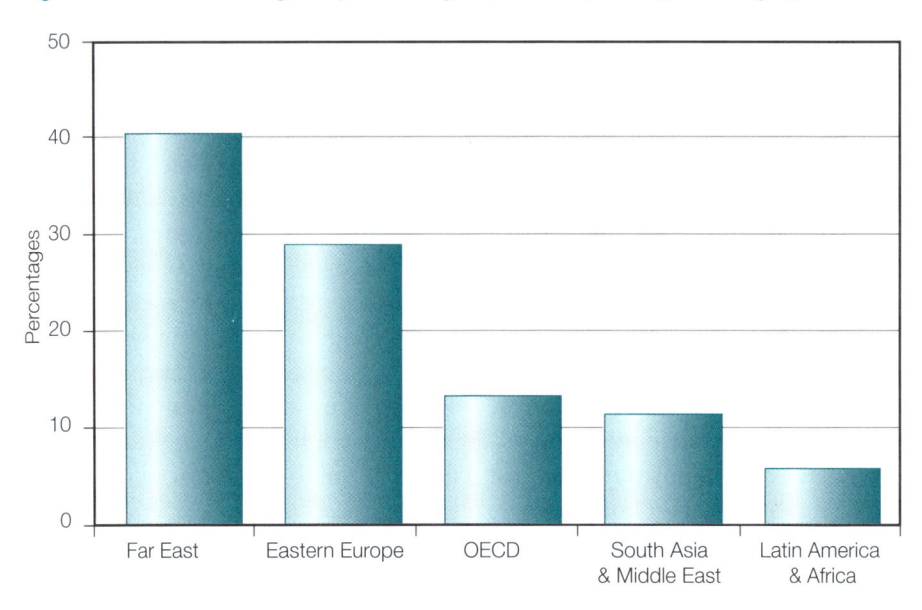

Source: T. Lane et al.: *Crewing the international merchant fleet* (Redhill, Lloyd's Register–Fairplay, 2002).

Figure 3.10 Top 10 labour supply countries for senior and junior officers, 2002

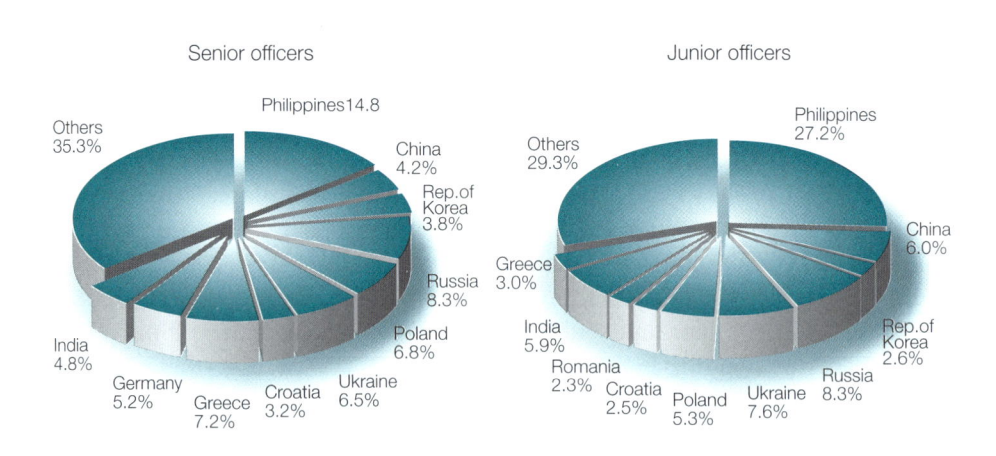

Senior officers

- Philippines 14.8
- Others 35.3%
- China 4.2%
- Rep. of Korea 3.8%
- Russia 8.3%
- Poland 6.8%
- Ukraine 6.5%
- Croatia 3.2%
- Greece 7.2%
- Germany 5.2%
- India 4.8%

Junior officers

- Philippines 27.2%
- Others 29.3%
- China 6.0%
- Rep. of Korea 2.6%
- Russia 8.3%
- Ukraine 7.6%
- Poland 5.3%
- Croatia 2.5%
- Romania 2.3%
- India 5.9%
- Greece 3.0%

Source: T. Lane et al.: *Crewing the international merchant fleet* (Redhill, Lloyd's Register–Fairplay, 2002).

As noted earlier, single nationality crews are now mostly confined to ships owned in developing countries, where the employment costs of seafarers are below those commonly found among internationally trading ships. Although there are many single nationality crewed ships flying FOCs, such as Malta and Panama, large numbers of these ships are owned in countries such as China, the Russian Federation and Ukraine. Such is the competition elsewhere among shipowners and ship managers for well-trained and experienced crews that increasingly they often have little choice but to assemble their crews from different nationalities. Although mixed nationality crews do not seem to have been devised as a matter of conscious policy, there is emerging evidence that, once owners/managers have accumulated experience of them, they find them advantageous (see Chapter 4). Whatever the reasons, the charts of figure 3.11a showing crewing patterns in six principal ship types in 1999 illustrate the fact that crews combining three or more nationalities have become extremely common: almost 50 per cent of oil tankers and 40 per cent of chemical/gas tankers and container ships have crews of this kind. As the labour market begins to stabilize and living standards rise in countries such as China and Eastern Europe, smaller countries from Africa and Latin America are likely to increase their labour market contributions, thus ensuring that mixed nationality crews will become the norm. Figure 3.11b clearly shows that the labour force is already well advanced in this direction.

The organizational structure of the labour supply chain is straightforward. Where shipowners or ship managers operate large fleets, overall manning policies are decided at senior management level and then operationalized by in-house personnel departments through their onward linkages with manning agents and training institutions. For companies with a global reach and operating technically sophisticated ships or less complex ones trading in niche markets, crew recruitment and retention require a high level of investment. Permanent staff need to be employed at both the "metropolitan" and the "peripheral" ends of the business; in-house training programmes have to be run; attractive employment contracts have to be offered to retain key personnel; senior managers need to travel the world to monitor peripheral offices, agencies and training institutions to ensure a flow of suitably qualified new recruits. Box 3.4 gives an indication of what this can involve.

In marked contrast to the systematically organized approach to recruitment taken by the larger shipping and ship-management countries are the small agencies that recruit handfuls of people on a catch-as-catch-can basis. The "labour market" does not normally have a literal, physical existence on any scale. Seafarers' hostels and bars in the very large ports of the world are still places where bodies and jobs are found but not in large numbers. However, in

The global seafarer

Figure 3.11a Mixed nationality crewing patterns by selected ship type, 1999

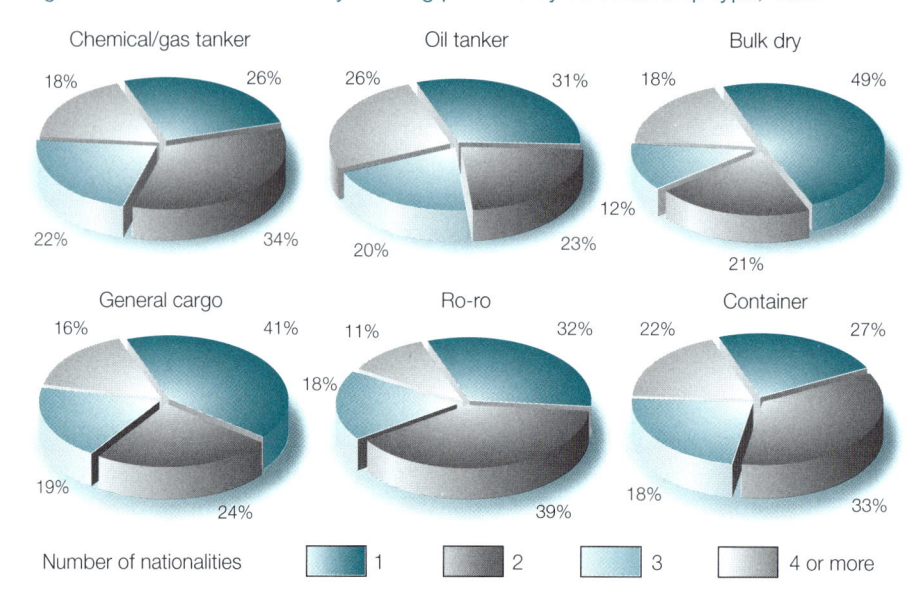

Chemical/gas tanker: 26%, 34%, 22%, 18%

Oil tanker: 31%, 23%, 12%, 20%, 26%

Bulk dry: 49%, 21%, 18%

General cargo: 41%, 24%, 19%, 16%

Ro-ro: 32%, 39%, 18%, 11%

Container: 27%, 33%, 18%, 22%

Number of nationalities: 1, 2, 3, 4 or more

Source: T. Lane et al.: *Crewing the international merchant fleet* (Redhill, Lloyd's Register–Fairplay, 2002).

Figure 3.11b Mixed nationality crewing patterns across all ship types, 1999

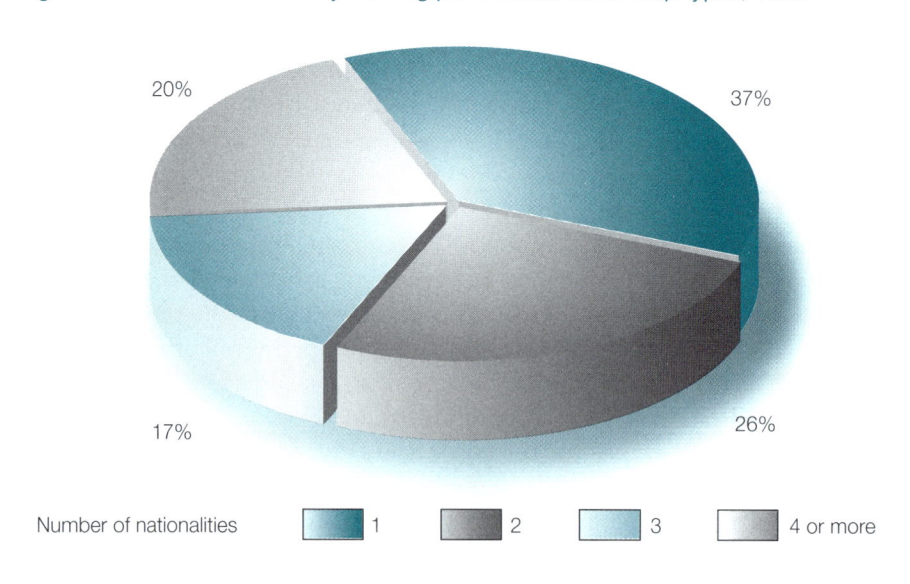

37%, 26%, 17%, 20%

Number of nationalities: 1, 2, 3, 4 or more

Source: T. Lane et al.: *Crewing the international merchant fleet* (Redhill, Lloyd's Register–Fairplay, 2002).

Box 3.4   Barber pushes Polish solution to manning

By Rajesh Joshi, Oslo correspondent

Barber Group, the Kuala Lumpur-based ship-management arm of Norway's Wilhelm Wilhelmsen, claims to have found the perfect solution for the crewing needs of cost- and quality-conscious European shipowners: Polish seafarers. Poland's Solidarity trade union and Barber are equal partners in Polish Manning Services, a Szczecin-based joint venture headed by a Norwegian former master and staffed by English-speaking personnel.

Barber claims to have developed a reliable hold over the market for Polish seafarers, thanks to Solidarity's national standing, Barber's own operational and manning expertise, and Polish Manning Services' close relationship with the Szczecin Maritime University. About 600 Poles already serve as part of Barber's seafarer pool of 5,350 plus. About 170 cadets graduate annually from the Szczecin university, and Barber currently claims to be training 20 cadets, ten each on the deck and engine side.

Poland has never enjoyed the recognition of countries such as the Philippines and India when it comes to affordable seafarer supplies. Barber managing director Petter Larsen in Oslo last week tried hard to rectify this anomaly. He felt Poland stood out as a notable exception in the Baltic region, compared with countries such as Estonia, Latvia and Lithuania, which tended to be small, and Russia, which was seen as somewhat complicated and requiring special effort and treatment. By contrast, Barber's bullishness on Poland was based on the post-communism development of the country itself. "Bureaucracy has been substantially cut. More and more Poles are travelling internationally, and they have an excellent education system," Mr. Larsen said. "Polish seafarers are physically strong and hardworking, which makes them good matches for cold climates. They are always seen immaculately dressed, but more importantly, they come out of the marine academy well-educated and well-trained, and with a basic understanding of big shipping companies."

Mr. Larsen cited the high technical competence of the Poles as another strong factor. The Szczecin university was said to have upgraded its technology, with radar equipment to handle radar observer and automatic radar plotting aid requirements being enhanced by the addition of engine and bridge simulators from Norway's sophisticated Norcontrol. In addition, Polish Manning Services' office was said to function with the aid of a computerized personnel system equipped for all stages, from screening and selection through to crew rotation and client interface.

Mr. Larsen said proficiency in the English language was still a factor when it came to dealings with the 45 plus age group, but was rapidly ceasing to matter among the younger generation, thanks to travel and the popular media. "At a time when there is a scarcity of good people, Poland is a simple solution," Mr. Larsen said. But Barber claimed that the market's awareness of this solution was so limited that last year it was actually forced to run advertisements in the Swedish press seeking suitable employment for its qualified but idle Polish recruits.

Cont./

> Cont./
>
> Polish Manning Services coordinates twice-per-year officer seminars in Szczecin, which are also an installed feature in the Barber Group's operations in India, Norway and the Philippines. The latest such event was held in late November, providing Barber's Polish officers with an opportunity to get updated on the latest developments. In this context, Mr. Larsen identified safety and competence as increasingly important factors in the future. He said that Barber's Polish hand was strengthened by the fact that the Szczecin university's course section had IMO and STCW courses, including courses in tanker safety, advanced firefighting and GMDSS.
>
> Source: *Lloyd's List*, 11 Jan. 1999.

Rizal Park in Manila, the Philippines, there is a daily street market, where several hundreds of people assemble every day in the hope of finding work (box 3.5).

Where the supply of labour greatly exceeds demand, as in the case of ratings and dubiously qualified junior officers, would-be seafarers frequently find there is a gatekeeper's fee payable in cash, services or in a combination of the two. The costs of entry to the labour market incurred by seafarers vary considerably between world regions. Most of the newly qualified seafarers from Eastern Europe were originally trained by the State free of charge, which also applied, in the main, to seafarers from the embedded maritime nations of Europe and Japan. However, the same cannot be said for the new labour supply nations of south and south-east Asia, where, at some stage in the process of entry to the industry, expenses have been incurred by recruits and their families: these can include the costs of training (often in private schools whose standards may not be high), certification and an entrance fee, payable to the manning agent. Of these gatekeeper payments, by far the most prevalent are the fees or percentages paid to manning agents, long-standing practices that are proscribed by ILO instruments.[8] Throughout south and south-east Asia and increasingly in the Russian Federation, the former Soviet bloc nations of the Black Sea rim and Ukraine, entry fees have similarly become routine. Both the existence and the magnitude of the entry costs ensure that the neediest sections of the different populations from the labour market are excluded. They also reflect the high value placed on dollar-earning employment, at levels often impossible to obtain in the indigenous labour markets.

Many agents, especially in Ukraine and other non-English-speaking countries, employ English tests. A maximum age limit and minimum years of service in hotels or restaurants (12 months in most cases) are set to ensure that the industry gets a young, energetic and experienced workforce. Age requirements for women are much stricter than those for men. In the

The labour market for seafarers

> **Box 3.5   Rizal Park, Manila: A daily "labour market"**
>
> Rizal Park, situated in the "crewing capital of the world", is the site of the world's largest seafarers' labour market. Every day, hundreds of seafarers gather there, lingering on the pavements by the park, looking for jobs. Shipowners, managers but mostly manning agents may show up with jobs one day; on another day they may make no appearance at all. Seafarers with various kinds of certificates/qualifications and of various ages can be found here. Most, however, are poorly qualified seafarers of low rank. Many of them are on the Government's watch list or manning agents' black lists, chiefly because of their contact with international trade unions or because they have made complaints about the working or living conditions aboard ship during their employment at sea. There are also women here, although only in small numbers. The women are looking for jobs in the hotel and catering departments of passenger ships. They are young and well educated, with experience of working in hotels or restaurants ashore. Many, however, are barred from entering the labour market by the age limit set by manning agencies, although this doesn't stop them from roaming the park every day. The age limits for cruise ships are set at 40 for men but just 29 for women. To get to this labour market, many of the seafarers have taken long and expensive flights from other islands. The lucky ones stay in Manila with friends or relatives but most have to rent beds, often for months on end before finding themselves a job.
>
> Source: M. Zhao, Nov. 1999.

Philippines, for instance, the ceiling for men on cruise ships is 40 years old; for women, it is 29. It is likely that the age requirements adopted in the West are the same or similar.

The bigger and better regulated crewing agents in Asia and Eastern Europe tend to have a steady pool of seafarers for their main clients or principals (companies that subcontract ship managers). These seafarers are trained or retrained before they sign on ships, and usually face no charges. Many of the crewing agents are, however, small and less scrupulous. They charge seafarers for the paper work they help process, for the training provided and for the jobs to which they have been "introduced". According to a study conducted in 1998 on seafarers employed in a major cruise company based in Miami, in the Philippines it is typical for male and female seafarers to pay an agency fee of 45,000 to 60,000 pesos ($1,200–1,500) to get a job aboard cruise ships. The money is said to cover the return trip airfare with an open return ticket, the seafarer's visa and the medical examination, all of which comes to between $1,100 and $1,300. The rest goes to the agent. Bond money is another device employed by some crewing agents to ensure that the seafarers employed through their service complete the contract to the full satisfaction of the cruise company. There are also cases in which seafarers have been cheated of their money by flying agents, that is, agents who collect fees from seafarers and then disappear without having provided any kind of service.[9]

The rapidly growing cruise sector, which now employs women in up to 30 per cent of ships' complements, engages female crew members according to their national origins. Western women mainly rely on advertisements to find jobs with cruise lines, and only a few are recruited through word of mouth from friends or relatives. In the United Kingdom, for example, the crewing agent's main role is to collect information on job vacancies in the industry and then to sell it in the form of booklets or newsletters to applicants. They do not usually provide training or even conduct interviews with applicants. Their contact with the potential seafarer is primarily by telephone, fax, e-mail or post. Except for the cost of the information they provide, they do not charge individual seafarers for the jobs they help them to find.

The recruitment procedures and training that Asian women have to undergo are significantly different. First of all, they mostly depend on friends and relatives for information and rely heavily on crewing agents not only for recruitment but also for training, which is a thriving business in many Asian countries. Indeed, a recent study found that all cruise companies use crewing agents to recruit their staff and 74 per cent of the companies surveyed use exclusive manning agents, that is, agents who work exclusively for certain cruise lines.[10]

Overall, the participation rate of women in seafaring remains low:[11] according to 1992 IMO data,[12] women represent between only 1 to 2 per cent of the world's 1.25 million seafarers, most of whom come from OECD countries. At the beginning of the twenty-first century, this estimate still seems valid, even though the female participation rates in the seagoing workforce vary greatly by region, country, company and sector. By far the largest numbers of women, both absolutely and proportionately, are found in the hotel staffs of the cruise sector.

Among a group of eight European countries (Belgium, Denmark, Finland, Germany, Italy, Norway, Sweden and the United Kingdom), the average proportion of women in the total seafaring workforce between 1997 and 2001 was found to be 9.15 per cent, although the relatively high number of Swedish and Danish women and the very low number of Italian women seafarers seriously distort this average.[13]

In other parts of the world, women's representation in the seafaring workforce also varies greatly from country to country. For example, their share of the workforce is 5 per cent in Indonesia and Latvia, about 3 per cent in Australia and 0.5 per cent in New Zealand.[14] In 1998, India reported that the country had 43,000 registered seafarers, of whom only three were women.[15]

In the Philippines, the largest supplier of seafarers to the world merchant fleet, only 225 women out of 230,000 seafarers appear on the national seafarers' register for 1983–90,[16] while in Brazil, there are 1,279 women seafarers out of a total of 119,835, that is, 1.1 per cent of the workforce.[17]

Training and certification

The drop in the number of officer trainees is acknowledged to be a serious problem. The BIMCO and the ISF have been publicizing this shortfall through a series of reports commissioned by the Institute of Employment Research (IER) at the University of Warwick in the United Kingdom. Officer trade unions in OECD countries have been campaigning for greater state involvement in officer training, with some effect. The Governments of the Netherlands, Norway and the United Kingdom have all introduced supportive measures and the European Commission is aiming to build a system of integrated national strategies.[18]

In an early evaluation of the economics of flagging out, G. N. Yannopoulos argued:

> The more difficult it is for native skilled seamen from embedded maritime countries to flag themselves out, the greater will be the reliance on unskilled labour from other countries. Because of this difference in the quality of labour employed in the two market sectors, the efficiency of shipping operators in the FOC sector will be lower – other things being equal.[19]

Five years later, in 1993, when the managers of the Standard Steamship Owners' Protection and Indemnity Association (the Standard P&I Club) were, in their own words, assessing "the causes of the claims explosion since 1987", their internal memorandum, "Minimum Standards", spoke of "demoralized and unqualified casual crews with little or no loyalty to their employers". They also noted that a "shortage of qualified crews is only too well known and it is our experience that a high percentage of personal injury claims are caused by fairly serious negligence. [...] One cannot any longer rely on paper qualifications of crew members without giving them additional training."[20]

The training, education and certification of seafarers have become increasingly prominent issues, largely in response to concerns among industry professionals of levels of crew competence. A spate of reports from underwriters, the Salvage Association, shipmasters and maritime administrators in different parts of the world from the mid-1980s onwards have all questioned the adequacy of the new world regime of maritime education and training (MET). Confidence was not enhanced when the maritime authority of one important new supplier of seafarers stated, in 1990, that approximately 50 per cent of Indonesian seafarers had received no formal training. And in the same year, one of the oil majors said that from henceforward it would be expecting chartered shipowners to commit themselves to proper training programmes for staff and crew and to have a clear policy regarding navigation and watchkeeping. A year later, in 1991, the maritime authorities of the then territory of Hong Kong refused to recognize Philippine licences for employment on Hong Kong-registered ships. The ban was lifted once it had been shown that measures had been taken to address corruption in the Philippine examination system (box 3.6).

These issues were brought to a head in 1993 when Andreas Ugland, then chairperson of Intertanko, complained of the wide variation in standards required for certificates of competency, ranging from high to dangerously low. He called for higher requirements in Standards of Training, Certification and Watchkeeping (STCW) certification, greater policing of standards by flag States, better MET and PSC inspections to ensure STCW compliance. The result of the very public airing of these issues, which for long had been the talk of everyday discussion, resulted in the substantial revision of the STCW Convention of 1978 in 1995 (STCW-95), which aims to retrieve the training standards lost in the 1980s. The move offshore in that decade not only led to the recruitment of large numbers of inexperienced crew members, it also resulted in a substantial decline in MET in the embedded maritime nations and a growing reliance on the under-resourced, inexperienced and poorly regulated

---

Box 3.6   Corruption in Philippine maritime training schools

A dramatic fall in the pass rates recorded by the Philippines' maritime training schools has followed a thorough overhaul of the previously corrupt system of examination. [...] Pass rates as high as 100 per cent were being regularly recorded in the early 1980s by some of the 70-odd schools and, although the rates dropped to a more realistic 40–50 per cent in 1986, by the late 1980s they were once again in the 90 per cent and above range. Cheating, bribing and fixing in the exams were endemic. [...] It was well known for some time, both in and outside the Philippines, that licences could be bought, but the biggest impetus for change came in 1991 when the Hong Kong authorities refused to recognize Philippine licences for employment on Hong Kong-registered ships. [...] Elaborate security measures [introduced in 1992] resulted immediately in the overall pass rate falling to 15 per cent. In May last year the pass rates for master mariners were 12 per cent, chief mates 17 per cent, second mates 11 per cent and third mates 3 per cent. Foreign employers of Filipino seamen are still concerned, however, that the exams, although now "tamper-proof and leak-proof", are still of a generally low standard.

Source: *Lloyd's List*, 28 Apr. 1994.

MET colleges found in some of the new labour supply countries. The initial gap in relative standards between the "old" and the "new" sources of seafarers was inevitably large. By 1999, after a period of almost 20 years, the training quality gap had narrowed. Standards advanced most in the more rapidly developing regions and nations of south-east Asia, such as Taiwan (China), and the Republic of Korea, but, and with some irony, they are each taking the path already followed by Hong Kong (China) and Singapore. The latter two, although sites of excellent training standards, have long ceased to be significant suppliers of seafarers. Whereas in 1964, Hong Kong had some 45,000 seafarers, this had declined to 2,088 in 1992, even though Hong Kong owned and managed a fleet of 1,233 ships. For its part, Singapore, with one of the world's largest and most modern fleets, relies almost wholly on Filipinos, Indians, Indonesians, Malaysians and Myanmar nationals to crew its ships. Singaporeans account for less than three per cent of those employed aboard the national flag fleet.

Both the ISF and the ITF made considerable contributions to the shaping of the revised STCW Convention and were active participants in the sessions of the IMO/ILO Joint Committee on Training. Although the globalization of the labour market had made a new international Convention on labour certification standards a necessity, implementation presented the IMO with an unprecedented regulatory task. All maritime administrations that license seafarers were asked by the IMO to submit their specifications regarding institutional and procedural arrangements. This validating procedure delivered what became known as the "white list": a register of administrations deemed to be in compliance with IMO requirements (although it fails to pass judgement on the quality of institutional provision, nor does it include detailed curricula specifications). With the STCW-95 Convention, the global shipping industry now has a clear set of requirements for the types of certificates that seafarers need and the procedures that maritime administrations must carry out. There remain, however, often substantial variations in the standards of supervision, curricula content, the overall quality of training institutions and the extent of fraudulent certification. The potential significance of the latter is revealed in box 3.7, in which a PSC inspector recounts an incident that took place in the Persian Gulf in the early 1990s.

The question of the degree to which ships might be sailing without a proper complement of qualified staff has recently become a policy issue. In 1999, the IMO commissioned research to be carried out into fraudulent certification and the ISF proposed measures to enable Internet checks to be made on the validity of certification. The IMO study, which was reported in 2001, found that the highest number of incidences of fraudulent practice occurred in south and south-east Asia and that there was also cause for

> Box 3.7 A cautionary tale
>
> Whilst working in the Persian Gulf a few years ago, I boarded an 11,000 dwt dry cargo vessel to carry out an inspection. The ship had loaded cargo in Italy and had arrived via the Suez Canal and a few ports in the Gulf. Documentation on board indicated that the crew list as presented to us was the same as it had been while loading in Italy. Deciding to check the documentation further, the master was asked to produce the officers' certificates of competency. This request produced much shuffling of feet and urgent undertones in Arabic. In the end the master produced one certificate – his own. This document appeared to be a 2nd mate's certificate, was printed in English and had been issued by the harbour master's office of a Middle Eastern port some four weeks previously. It was endorsed on the obverse side to the effect that it had been "issued without examination". There were no other certificates of any description on board. No master, mate, second mate, chief or 2nd engineer and, above all, no radio officer, nor anyone on board with any knowledge whatever of how to operate anything except the VHF set on the bridge. In this state, the vessel had been passed by PSC in Italy and had somehow passed through the Suez Canal.
>
> It was decided immediately that the vessel should be detained pending contact through official channels with the maritime authority who had registered the ship and its owners. They were told that the vessel would be detained until such time as they supplied the vessel with a properly certificated officer complement. An extraordinary telex reply was received back along the lines to the effect that the registering authorities, after consultation with the owners, considered that the vessel was adequately manned according to their standards and they demanded the vessel's release. This demand was naturally not complied with and they were told yet again that the vessel would continue to sit in port until they supplied the requisite complement.
>
> Eventually, about two weeks after the date of the original detention, six Greek officers arrived by air, all properly certificated (in particular, we had the radio officer's certificate checked out by a Greek national) and the vessel was finally passed and released. Its progress down the Gulf en route to the Far East was followed by our port radio station with interest. And at a rendezvous point somewhere off Dubai a boat came out and took all six Greek officers off for repatriation. They were not replaced. Thus the vessel continued on its way with the original rogue complement.
>
> Source: *Seaways* (London), May 1996.

concern in Central America, Eastern Europe, the Mediterranean and the Middle East.[21] The study identified maladministration (by maritime administration officials, examiners, training establishments and employers), which allowed fraud to pass undetected, as a main cause of fraudulent practice as well as forgeries of various kinds.

In the IMO survey, 17 per cent said that they had sailed with people they knew to be holding fraudulently obtained certificates and that, of this group, nine out of ten said that they themselves held fraudulent certificates. The general nature of the problem can be seen in the following excerpt taken from a report by the IMO's study team on field research carried out in one of the major labour supply countries, where it was estimated that between 15,000 and 20,000 fraudulent basic safety training certificates were being issued each year:

> The substantial increase over the past few years in the number of private training establishments offering short STCW courses has resulted in the administration [of this country] being unable to maintain effective control of the standards of every single training establishment. Reliable sources within the administration informed the research team that about 20 of these private training institutes issue certificates for safety-related courses without offering any training. [...] Officials within the administration who are genuinely concerned about this situation have reported it to higher authorities. However, their efforts are constrained due to the political patronage enjoyed by some of the owners of these institutes.
>
> There was evidence to indicate that some manning agents have good contacts with sub-standard institutes and, in fact, some of these are owned [...] by manning agencies. Prospective job seekers who approach these agencies are routinely asked to undergo short STCW courses [...] or are provided with [...] certificates without undergoing any training. One of the researchers was offered, by a manning agent, all basic safety training certificates for the equivalent of $300.[22]

There are, as yet, no data compilations of the world's MET institutions in the public domain, although the IMO will be in a position to publish this information when it has received and processed the applications for IMO inclusion on its "white list" of institutions in compliance with STCW-95. However, even though no precise data are available, the trends in MET are well known. The number and range of training establishments in the embedded maritime nations fell substantially in the 1980s and 1990s, while there was considerable growth in south and south-east Asia and, probably, stability or only modest decline in Eastern Europe. The shift of MET from the relatively prosperous northern hemisphere to the less prosperous southern hemisphere has inevitably led to an overall decline in standards.

The developments in the embedded maritime nations of the 1960s and 1970s that aimed to create a highly skilled and professional seafaring workforce at all levels of the shipboard division of labour underwent a steady process of attrition in the face of a collapse of demand for places. Many colleges closed, especially those specializing in training rankings, and now there are also fewer colleges specializing in officer training – those that do have become increasingly dependent on foreign students. For some years, the number of foreign students enrolled in Australian, British and Irish colleges have greatly exceeded those of home students. Indeed, but for the foreign demand for places, more of these officer-training colleges would also have closed. In more recent years, there have been concerted attempts in the Netherlands, Norway and the United Kingdom to arrest the decline in the training of own-nationals, and it is plausible to suggest that there will be an upturn in demand for training places in the embedded maritime nations, at least in Europe. There has been some convergence in wage rates between Europe and the new labour countries, and rising PSC expectations in respect of standards of competence are likely to lead to some rebuilding of the European officer corps. Although European training standards in the 1990s were maintained, further increments would signal a renewed commitment to professionalism and have a knock-on effect in the new labour supply countries, where in some cases there is an urgent need for upgrading.

Recent research commissioned by the EU and coordinated by the World Maritime University (WMU) and the SIRC produced an objective account of training provision and standards in China, India, Indonesia and the Philippines.[23] Unsurprisingly, the research reported that, in general, funding levels are insufficient to match the general level of standards found in the embedded maritime nations. Relatively speaking, these are poor countries and they cannot be expected to provide sophisticated equipment for maritime colleges to train people to work in offshore labour markets. The research does, nevertheless, report high overall training standards in China and India. The situation in Indonesia and the Philippines is very different: most of the training provision comes from private institutions, which are typically inadequately equipped and staffed by people who are poorly qualified, both formally and experientially. Outside the personnel departments of the ship-management companies recruiting seafarers, there is little recent knowledge of current standards in Eastern Europe. The Polish and Baltic States' systems are widely held in high regard and the colleges in Bulgaria, Romania, the Russian Federation and Ukraine also seem to have maintained their high standards.

The shipping industry has never considered it necessary to make any substantial investment in non-officer training except for a brief ten-year period from the late 1960s. However, as trading conditions improved and regulatory requirements increased during the 1990s, there is some evidence of a renewed interest in crewing ships from top to bottom with well-trained multi-skilled professionals. The United Kingdom's Chamber of Shipping, for example, has been expressing views of this kind and similar expressions have been heard in the Netherlands and Norway. The possibilities of transferring the more routine tasks of officers to ratings and upgrading maintenance to ships at sea have often been recognized and, as noted above, some shipowners have taken steps towards doing so. However, the consequences of such changes have been inhibited by the lack of sufficiently skilled ratings and uncertainty as to whether the additional cost outlays can be justified given normal cost-accounting time horizons. On an operational level, the shipping company Concordia managed to realize profits while running ULCCs and VLCCs with crew complements almost double those of the industry norm. However, there is little information on the availability of sufficiently qualified ratings. The BIMCO/ISF labour market studies have consistently highlighted the shortages of well-trained officers and successfully raised awareness of the problem. The most recent of these studies has suggested that the recorded surplus of available ratings might be more apparent than real. An SIRC study on the training and certification of ratings stated:

> While there may be little reason to doubt that the number of persons offering themselves for employment as ratings is in excess of the available number of jobs, there are on the other hand genuine reasons for doubting whether all those offering themselves for employment are suitable for employment in terms of training and experience. These doubts are sustained by the following considerations:
>
> - Substantial variations in the quality of pre-sea and post experience training provision in different countries make it difficult to define "suitability for employment". The problem is compounded by the lack of a universal definition of skills needed by ratings.
>
> - Minimalist manning practices severely curtail the possibilities of on-the-job training and therefore raise questions as to the quality of experiential training.
>
> - The prevalence of fraudulent certification practices at rating levels suggests that many new entrants have had no prior preparation for life and work aboard ship and that watchkeeping certificates have often been issued improperly.
>
> - The lack of adequate labour market data on manning levels in different ship types, on recruitment, on duration of seagoing careers, on educational backgrounds, on age profiles, on the duration of the voyage–leave cycle.[24]

There is no logistically realistic way of determining whether there are sufficient numbers of suitably trained and experienced ratings to crew the world's ships. Appropriate levels of skills and the knowledge ratings need never have been the subject of investigation or codification. The industry has always worked on the assumption that the work done by ratings was best learned on the job and that this would involve new recruits working at the shoulder of experienced shipmates. This approach seems to have worked well when ships had relatively large crews and boy ratings' ranks were an established part of ships' complements. However, given today's minimum crewing levels, there would not seem to be enough time for on-board training, even if young ratings' ranks were to be reinstated. Meanwhile, although cadet training programmes that mix college and seagoing periods have become an almost universal aspect of officer training, similar schemes for ratings are rarely found. The SIRC study on ratings found that, of the training schemes examined in 15 countries and evaluated on 12 criteria, only three countries (Denmark, Romania and Ukraine) satisfied more than half the procedural criteria.[25]

Trade unions and collective bargaining

The existence of well-organized trade unions and national collective bargaining institutions lay at the heart of the labour market regulatory systems of the embedded maritime nations. The rapid decline since the 1970s of the fleets of these countries has, naturally, been accompanied by declining union membership. Trade union influence, however, has remained significant, especially in Australia, Europe, Japan and the United States, where unions have continued to play an important political role in the development of policies aimed at squeezing out sub-standard shipping. Informal and mostly tacit alliances with shipowners, insurers, classification societies and the P&I Clubs significantly contributed to the establishment of effective PSC measures and organizations in the 1990s. The institution of PSC itself may have had little effect on the employment possibilities for seafarers in the embedded maritime nations but it has unquestionably made a major contribution and added to the impetus of the process towards regulating the global labour market.

The trade unions, and the Norwegian trade unions in particular, have also been influential in setting wage rates. Critical to the creation of the NIS in 1987 was the support given to Norwegian shipowners by the country's unions. Part of the quid pro quo for this support was the involvement of the Norwegian unions in setting wage rates and ensuring collective bargaining agreements for foreign seafarers (principally Indian and Filipino) working aboard NIS ships. Because the NIS flag grew so rapidly and employment contracts were subject to some regulation under this flag, thanks to Norwegian trade union influence, Norwegian shipowners rapidly set best practice standards in the Philippines. The impact of this on the Filipino labour market was almost instantaneous: European shipowner employment of Filipino seafarers increased by 83 per cent in 1986–87.

More recently, some of the Danish trade unions have established a similar transnational bargaining role with Danish shipowners concerning DIS crews, although this possibility was not open to British trade unions and the Red Ensign Group: the United Kingdom's national collective bargaining machinery, the National Maritime Board, was dismantled in the mid-1980s. The United Kingdom's ships' officers' union, the National Union of Marine Aviation and Shipping Transport Officers (NUMAST), has company agreements and, now that the union recruits seafarers employed aboard British-flagged ships regardless of their nationality, it follows that non-nationals have been integrated into the United Kingdom's collective bargaining arrangements. The German transport union, Verdi, claims negotiation rights for all seafarers working aboard German second register ships.

The influence of the Norwegian seafarers' trade unions on ship-management company practice has, in general, also been important. Where Norwegian ship-management companies, such as Barber International, commonly have collective bargaining agreements in labour supply countries, others have been obliged to follow in their attempts to attract similarly well-trained seafarers. By 1993, for example, Barber had established an agency in Poland in cooperation with Solidarity. However, not all ship-management companies are keen on union involvement. When BP Tankers flagged out its fleet to Bermuda and the Isle of Man and awarded crew-management contracts to Wallems, Acomarit and the Schulte subsidiary, Dorchester Maritime, in 1986, all three companies refused to set up negotiating rights with NUMAST.

Among the labour supply countries of Asia, India was the only nation to have well-established trade unions, which, like those in Europe and Japan, were also active participants in an intricate tripartite regulatory system. Until the 1970s, much of the Indian union's membership worked aboard British-, Danish- and Norwegian-flagged ships, although since the 1950s growing numbers have been employed in the new state-owned shipping companies. The seafarers' unions of the Philippines and the Republic of Korea only became firmly established when their countries became large suppliers of labour in the 1980s.

The extent to which the trade unions of the labour supply countries are directly involved in collective bargaining machinery at the level of detail typical of the embedded maritime nations is not clear. At least in some cases – and perhaps in many – the presence of collective bargaining arrangements does not extend much beyond the union signifying its agreement to the terms of the employment contract. These agreements are not normally rooted in any permanent or standing procedures capable of dealing with disputes or grievances as they arise or at appropriate moments. Shipboard representational schemes are extremely rare. The ISMA's Code of Shipmanagement Standards does require "procedures for dealing with complaints and/or grievances from or about personnel" but makes no reference to trade union representation, although this does not, of course, preclude the possibility of such machinery nevertheless being provided for. The likelihood of disputes, grievances and so on being dealt with at ports of call by trade union organizations is also low.

The trade unions of the new labour supply countries do not usually have agency arrangements with foreign trade unions. Even the more experienced and organizationally efficient trade unions of the embedded maritime nations were never enthusiastic about ceding representational services to other unions, except in emergencies. Furthermore, rapid turnaround times, out-of-the-way port locations and finding someone with the personal skills to register complaints effectively all place severe restrictions on trade union involvement during the period of engagement aboard ship.

Although there is enough information in the public domain to show the continuing importance of trade unions and collective bargaining, there are no data series listing seafarers' trade unions and their memberships on a world regional or global basis. Neither are there any regular surveys of the extent of collective bargaining. The best available indication of the scale of trade unions can be gleaned by looking at the number of trade unions affiliated to the ITF. In 1999, there were 235 unions from 97 countries with a total declared membership of 660,059, representing approximately 66 per cent of the global workforce. Apart from the absence of the state-controlled trade unions of China, most of the world's eligible organizations are ITF-affiliates.

Between 1994 and 1998, the number of affiliated unions increased by 10 per cent although their combined membership fell by 9 per cent. This tends to suggest a diminution in the size of national maritime unions, a phenomenon that is most apparent in the traditional maritime nations. The ITF also maintains an inspectorate consisting of 105 inspectors in 39 countries. In 1998, 6,187 inspections were carried out, 87 per cent of which were on FOC vessels. The purposes of these inspections are essentially twofold: firstly, to ensure that if a ship has an ITF agreement, it is adhered to; and secondly to attempt to secure an ITF agreement where no other agreements governing a crew's conditions of service are in place.

The ITF is formally a trade secretariat like all the other trade union internationals. That is to say and using the supply chain analogy, it is a hub for receiving and passing on information to and from its affiliated unions. Because the structure of the modern shipping industry makes it impossible for nationally based unions working independently to have a significant impact on their members' employment situation, the ITF has, through its "Special Seafarers' Department" (SSD), become an international trade union in its own right. The SSD also coordinates the industrial side of the ITF's FOC campaign. SSD membership is open to all seafarers who sail on FOC vessels or "other such ships as the FPC [Fair Practices Committee] may decide".[26] In 1996, SSD membership numbered about 10,000.

The ITF has developed an intricate set of arrangements and customary practices allowing it to function globally but in the traditional manner of trade unionism. On the one hand, it aims to regulate the everyday terms and conditions of employment between employers and employees. To this end, it focuses its efforts on the FOC and other offshore fleets. By both constitution and convention, it makes no attempt to regulate national flag fleets, except in circumstances where "local" practices undermine global objectives. On the other hand, the ITF also attempts to secure legislation in those employment matters that are beyond the reach of standard collective bargaining. Through its membership of the International Confederation of Free Trade Unions (ICFTU), the ITF seeks to establish working partnerships with other shipping industry constituencies to create laws and Conventions on matters of health and safety, training and education and so on, all of which contribute to the well-being of seafarers. The industry has the equivalent of a minimum wage, which is periodically negotiated between employers and unions under the aegis of the ILO (see Chapter 4). In a new and significant departure, in 2000, the ITF and the International Maritime Employers' Committee (IMEC) set up permanent collective bargaining machinery and marked it with an agreement on ITF benchmark wages and hours of work for ships on ITF Blue Card agreements.

The ITF has a well-codified policy on FOCs, which has, however, seen various changes since its inception in 1948. Although the ITF has maintained an underlying principle that seeks the reflagging of all FOC vessels to their national flag of beneficial ownership, such policy is now constrained by more pragmatic considerations relating to the effective regulation of the FOC fleet. Therefore, the ITF has, in recent years, been seeking to raise the effectiveness of its FOC campaign by adopting a more robust approach to industrial action against sub-standard ships, while at the same time aiming to enter into a dialogue with all those in the industry concerned with eliminating exploitation and raising standards.[27]

The ITF also has an Actions Department and an Agreements Department. The former unit takes action against vessels that have been the object of complaints from crew members or other interested parties. In 1998, the causes of complaints were: non-payment of wages (56 per cent of cases); sub-standard ships and/or living conditions (15 per cent); abandonment (12 per cent); non-compliance with collective agreements (12 per cent); and "other" cases, including victimization, unfair dismissal, problems with medical treatment, and overtime and delayed allotment issues (5 per cent). FOCs feature among the worst offenders: 75 per cent of crew complaints concerned FOC-flagged vessels (table 3.6).

There are a number of problems that typify trade union activity and collective bargaining in the maritime industry. First, trade unions find it difficult to organize workers because eligibility for membership often

The global seafarer

Table 3.6 Crew complaints handled by the ITF's Actions Department, 1998

Flag	Number of complaints	As a % of all complaints
Panama	274	17
Malta	245	15
Cyprus	226	14
Saint Vincent and the Grenadines	127	8
Bahamas	108	7
Liberia	89	6
Romania	57	4
Singapore	40	3
Belize	38	2
Russian Federation	38	2
Antigua and Barbuda	35	2
Ukraine	32	2
Greece	26	2
Honduras	21	1
GIS	18	1
Cambodia	16	1
NIS	14	1
Turkey	14	1
Malaysia	13	1
DIS	11	1
Others	155	10
Totals	**1 597**	**101**

Note: Flags in italics are FOCs. Percentages have been rounded up.

Source: ITF Actions Department (1998).

commences when a voyage begins, and ends at the termination of that voyage. Second, there is competition in some of the labour supply nations between strong trade unions and more compliant ones. The ITF recognizes that its current rules on representation rights can be used by some unions merely as a means to secure membership and, thus, revenue. Accordingly, the ITF published, in 1997, its *Seafarers' Charter*, which sets out the responsibilities of its affiliates. Third, the employment contract is often made, or mediated, between the seafarer and a crewing agency, rather than with the shipowner directly. This again tends to weaken the ties between worker and union. Such practices are particularly prevalent among FOC crews.

The ITF's rules on union representation rights do not, in themselves, make for a perfectly clear collective bargaining structure. According to these rules, trade unions in the country of beneficial ownership have the right to conclude agreements covering vessels beneficially owned in those countries. In cases where the beneficial ownership is not easy to determine, the trade union in the country where effective control is exercised has negotiating rights, including the right to transfer those rights to the labour supply trade union.[28] In effect, such rules have introduced the concept of the internationalization of trade union membership, albeit in an incoherent fashion.

There has also been some increasing polarization between unions representing officers and those representing ratings, although too much should not be made of this. On certain issues, the unions of ratings and officers inevitably have conflicting interests, although in many countries officers and ratings are members of the same union. Nevertheless, it is true that, while officers' unions have seen the skills of their members in great demand during a period of worldwide shortage, the opposite has been the case for ratings' unions in OECD countries, where there has been downwards pressure on jobs and wages.

It would seem that the collective bargaining power of unions could be enhanced if the relevant Conventions of the ILO were to be accorded the same weight as those concerned with safety and pollution, for example. In particular, on the subject of sustainable employment it would be useful if the provisions of the Continuity of Employment (Seafarers) Convention, 1976 (No. 145), could be inserted into the rubric of the Merchant Shipping (Minimum Standards) Convention, 1976 [and Protocol, 1996] (No. 147), at the earliest opportunity. Such a move would give more stability to the employment structure of the maritime industry as it would enhance the bargaining power of national maritime unions.

Notes

[1] For most of this period, the United Kingdom had the world's largest shipping industry, with up to one-third of its seafarers recruited from British Somaliland, India, Hong Kong, Singapore, West Africa, the West Indies and the Yemen. All these seafarers had British nationality until their countries became independent, at which point they became Commonwealth citizens. Comparable arrangements applied to citizens of the former French and Dutch empires.

[2] BIMCO/ISF: *2000 Manpower Update* (Bagsvaerd, BIMCO Publications, 2000).

[3] T. Lane et al.: *Crewing the international merchant fleet* (Redhill, Lloyd's Register–Fairplay, 2002).

[4] These figures refer to seafarers engaged aboard cargo-carrying ships. Using the assumption adopted by the BIMCO/ISF study that, at any given moment, 40 per cent of the active labour force is on leave or otherwise between ships, the cargo-carrying labour force is estimated to stand at 900,000 seafarers. A further 128,000 employed on cruise ships brings the total to 1.03 million.

[5] A British study of wastage in the 1960s found that 45 per cent of deck cadet entrants had left the industry by the age of 25. See British Parliamentary Papers: *Report of the committee of inquiry into shipping* ("the Rochdale Report"), Paper/Bill number: Cmnd. 4337 (London, HMSO, 1970), paragraphs 869–881.

[6] *Lloyd's List* (London), 4 Feb. and 12 June 1988.

[7] *Lloyd's List*, 31 Aug. 1993.

[8] ILO: *Recruitment and placement of Asian seafarers* (Geneva, 1991); *Seafarers' conditions in India and Pakistan* (Geneva, 1947); *Seafarers' welfare in the Asian region: Report of the regional seminar, Singapore* (Geneva, 1990).

[9] D. C. Goff: *A view of life below deck at Carnival cruise line* (London, ITF, 1998).

[10] J. Scharkosi: "Manning and training in the cruise industry", Paper presented at the LSM [Lloyd's Ship Manager] Asia-Pacific Manning and Training Conference, Manila, Nov. 1999.

[11] Questions concerning the employment of women at sea are discussed at length in ILO: *Women seafarers: Global employment policies and practices* (Geneva, 2003).

[12] IMO: *1992–1996 Medium-term plan for the integration of women in the maritime sector* (London, 1992).

[13] See Belgian Federal Ministry of Employment and Labour: *Belgian pool of seafarers* (Brussels, 1997); C. Keitsch: *Women at sea* (Flensburg, Museum of Shipping, 1997); data on Finnish women seafarers from the SIRC Women Archive (1998); data from the German Ministry of Transport (2001); data from the Federation of Italian Transport Workers' Union (1998); data from the Norwegian Maritime Directorate (2001); Swedish Seafarers' Register (1997); United Kingdom Chamber of Shipping: *Manpower Inquiry, December 2000* (London, 2000).

[14] Effective Change Pty. Ltd.: *Women at sea: Policy discussion paper* (London, 1995).

[15] SIRC/MARCOM Archive (1998).

[16] IMO: *Action programme for equal opportunities and advancement of women in the maritime sector 1997–2001*, Internal document (London, 1997).

[17] SIRC Women Database (2001).

[18] Communication from the Commission to the Council and the European Parliament on the training and recruitment of seafarers, COM (2001) 188 final, Brussels, 6.4.2001.

[19] G. N. Yannopoulos: "The economics of flagging out", in *Journal of Transport Economics and Policy*, 1988, Vol. 22.

[20] The Standard Steamship Owners' Protection and Indemnity Association (Bermuda) Ltd.: "Minimum Standards", Internal memorandum (London, 1993).

[21] IMO: *A study on fraudulent practices associated with certificates of competency and endorsements* (London, 2001).

[22] ibid.

[23] SIRC/WMU: *Study on the MET systems of China, India, Indonesia and the Philippines* (CIIPMET), (Mälmo, 1998).

[24] J. Veiga and T. Lane: *A study of the global supply of suitably trained ratings* (Cardiff, SIRC, 2001).

[25] ibid.

[26] ITF: *Flags of Convenience Campaign Report 1998* (London, 1999).

[27] ITF: *Report of the secretariat*, ITF 39th Congress, New Delhi (London, 1998).

[28] ITF: *Oslo to Delhi: A comprehensive review of the ITF–FOC campaign* (London, 1999).

4

SHIPBOARD LIFE AND WORK – I

A Maldivian at work

Shipboard society

In 1979, S. Roger, a well-known American journalist specializing in labour relations, stood on a quayside with two colleagues, waiting to join the Norwegian ship *Hoegh Mallard*. Roger's mission was to sail with the ship for a period of seven weeks and to consider the impact on crew members of technological and social organizational change. As Roger commented: "Here on the *Mallard* we might catch a glimpse of the future of not only maritime shipping, with the evolution of all-purpose seamen, but what might happen in any workplace."[1]

In consultation with Oslo University's Work Research Institute, Hoegh Lines had been experimenting with life aboard its vessels and had introduced a number of practices contrasting strongly with prevailing conditions aboard American merchant ships. Whole crew dining and recreation were the norm, ships were provided with excellent recreational facilities (the *Mallard* had an indoor swimming pool, among other things) and the labour force was encouraged to upskill and increase its flexibility in terms of work roles. As regards the latter, ratings were given more responsibility for their own work and were said to hold the view that they had "become their own bosuns",[2] and the divide between deck and engine was diminished. There was also an expectation that rigid ships' hierarchies would be eroded as more democratic forms of management were introduced:

> On this trip we expected to be engaged with basic and central workplace issues: the involvement of the worker in decisions about how work was to be organized and carried out, the levelling of a once-rigid and authoritarian hierarchy, the effort to create a more humane and responsive environment within an insulated shipboard culture, and the training of an all-purpose seaman, as much at home on land as at sea.[3]

More than 20 years later, in a new century, hardly any of this vision of the future has materialized in the international merchant marine. Inevitably, the industry has seen some changes, including a reduction in the size of crews. However, the radical changes introduced aboard the *Mallard* have not been noticeably taken up elsewhere. Hierarchies still persist aboard almost all vessels and the divisions of labour between deck and engine crews have generally been maintained. Ships retain a recognizably institutionalized form, accurately reflecting the descriptions and analyses of some of the first social scientists to look at shipboard societies.[4] Social isolation remains a prominent feature of seafarers' lives, even if they concurrently suffer from time to time from a kind of claustrophobia resulting from being confined with their shipmates. It is a strand of continuity that links the lives of the very earliest seafarers with their contemporaries, as Paulo Perez-Mallaina acknowledged in his description of sixteenth-century Spanish mariners:

> A sailor could feel himself separated from the world and at the same time physically crushed by the presence of his comrades; and he could watch thousands of landscapes pass before his eyes and scarcely have occasion to experience any of them. These circumstances constituted, and still constitute today, the character and the burden of a life at sea.[5]

Alongside such consistencies in on-board living and working conditions, however, there have also been significant social changes. These include the large-scale introduction of multinational crews, a revolution in information and communication technologies, and faster ship turnaround in ports.

The sixteenth-century Spanish mariners described by Perez-Mallaina were accustomed to sailing with their own compatriots in single nationality crews. However, many sectors of the merchant marine have used multi-national crews for a long time now. Even where nineteenth-century ships set sail with single nationality complements, crew members that became sick or injured, who died or who simply signed off, were frequently replaced with whomever was available in foreign ports, regardless of nationality. Nevertheless, despite the prevalence of polyglot crews in international shipping since the fifteenth century, Chapter 3 showed that it is only since the 1980s that modern-day practices of international recruitment came to be formalized on a world scale.

Just as technological innovation has not had the radical impact on the shipboard division of labour as expected by Roger and others, so too have changes in the composition of the global seafarers' labour market been accompanied by more continuities than fractures. Changes in the nationality composition of modern-day crews, while significant for a variety of reasons, have not generally had the overwhelming impact that might have been envisaged in terms of life and work aboard.[6] In today's fleet, contractual engagement and occupational culture remain the key to any understanding of everyday life aboard merchant ships. Regardless of crew nationality, a fundamental feature of modern ships is that, although they do not house organic communities marked by population or social network continuities, crews of complete strangers nevertheless find familiar, integrating social mechanisms. The familiar and limited number of shipboard roles, the boundaries of permissible variation in role performance, the simplicity of formal and normative rules patterning shipboard conduct are universal and, therefore, create the essential conditions for making the transfer of people between ships possible – a necessary requirement in the context of discontinuous, casual employment contracts and mixed nationality crews of unpredictable permutations. In these circumstances of employment insecurity and a resilient shipboard occupational culture, national identities are essentially redundant for the purposes of everyday life. Conflicts in the home countries of crew members may, under certain conditions, "reawaken" national identities aboard ship, but there is little evidence of the significance of national identity as a routinely potent source of conflict among seafarers and a good deal of evidence to the contrary.[7] Indeed, one comprehensive study of mixed nationality crews has demonstrated that the vast majority (approximately 80 per cent) of seafarers prefer to work aboard mixed nationality vessels.[8]

Living aboard similar ships, doing similar work, visiting similar places and experiencing a regular stream of encounters with fellow crew members who are also strangers but are nevertheless "people just like us" all support and encourage the maintenance of a viable and "living" occupational culture. The manifestations of the elements of this occupational culture may in themselves seem insubstantial, but they form a powerful compound when taken together. Something of this can be seen in the pervasive practice among seafarers of relating stories to each other of experiences of past ships and shipmates. Regardless of the nationality composition of crews, story-telling remains an important part of life aboard and has not been displaced by the sophisticated entertainment and communication systems found on well-equipped ships. Stories are typically told in those passing moments when there are just minutes to spare but there is a need to assert some social contact. In their content these stories are not necessarily or even often extensive narratives with elaborate plots punctuated by climaxes and denouements. They just tell of bars visited, beautiful women, lively ports, sad shipmates, storms and calms, good and bad captains, devious crewing agents, abominable food, and the like. Such story-telling encourages inclusion because it offers snapshots of moments that everyone can relate to regardless of who they are or where they come from. Such tales have a long tradition and a "solidifying" effect both in the telling and in the enactment of everyday shipboard life. In this, as well as in work content, work routines and the social relations of hierarchy, there is much to demonstrate the continuing existence of strong shipboard occupational cultures in the new era of global crewing.[9]

Ships continue to have formal hierarchical structures, where officers form approximately 40 per cent and ratings 60 per cent of total complements. For a variety of reasons, modern cargo ships are predominantly male environments, which continue to be characterized by occupational hierarchies that are often relatively inflexible. Crews are divided into officers and ratings and within each of these groups further ranks exist, ranging from chief engineer to 4th engineer, from captain to 3rd officer and from bosun to OS. The occupational hierarchy aboard most ships is so important that it is quite usual for crew members to introduce and refer to themselves and others by rank, rather than name. Nicknames can also derive from rank and are often passed from one crew member to their reliever, outliving the tour of duty of any individual. Thus, pumpmen are commonly referred to as "pumps" or "pumpie", radio officers were known as "sparks", electricians as "leckies", and so on. Accommodation and messing arrangements generally reflect this layering, although this has not been the case aboard Chinese vessels, where recent attempts to introduce separate officer and rating dining were thwarted. Aboard the ships of one major shipping line, Chinese crews resisted efforts to introduce separate messing and expressed strong preferences for dining with colleagues from within their "department". Thus, deck ratings and officers share a table, engine-room staff dine together as do catering staff.[10] Elsewhere in the world fleet, there are ships where officers and ratings eat in the same space, but in general officer/rating separation is normal and off-duty social interaction between higher and lower ranks is infrequent.

Although on genuinely multinational ships nationality does not have a strong impact on social or working relations, different patterns can sometimes be seen aboard ships with only two or three nationalities. Where ships have fewer nationalities, transnational solidarities may be weak and sometimes have a "colonial" character, especially where ratings are from less economically developed countries and officers are from relatively prosperous countries. Aboard these ships, divisions between officers and ratings can be reinterpreted along nationality rather than occupational lines. Thus, aboard one ship, everybody beneath the rank of 2nd officer and chief engineer may be counted as a "rating" because they belong to the same nationality, while aboard a different vessel everybody from fitter upwards might be given access to officer facilities on the grounds of nationality.[11] Aboard ships with these crewing patterns, discriminatory practices are likely to be more frequent. The best available evidence of discrimination on the grounds of race/nationality comes from a poll conducted for the ITF in 1996 by the MORI polling group. In response to the question of whether in the last year respondents had experienced "unfair treatment because of my race/nationality?", some 66 per cent said "not at all", 20 per cent replied "sometimes", 5 per cent said "frequently" and 9 per cent had "no opinion". These responses, however, were not analysed on the basis of crew nationality composition and, therefore, it is not possible to identify the extent to which "crew nationality mix" had an impact on the MORI findings.[12]

It has been suggested that cultural differences might have an impact on initiative, submission to authority and rule following,[13] and in the 1990s such views gained wide support within some sectors of the industry. However, more recent and comprehensive data collected from observation studies aboard multinationally crewed ships[14] suggest that such cultural generalizations are misleading and unhelpful. Sometimes they are sustained by literature provided by well-intentioned crew managers and shipowners and designed to "inform" seafarers of one ethnic group about the culture of others. Unfortunately, some of this literature inadequately differentiates between cultural habits/norms and variations in individual behaviour, and so end up reinforcing stereotyped beliefs and prejudices rather than reducing them. Once seafarers of different nationalities have had a significant amount of contact with one another, they become aware of the inaccuracy of many stereotypes and generalizations. Only where their exposure to a particular nationality is limited do seafarers show a tendency to fall back on stereotyped views of others.[15]

Although the available evidence indicates relatively low levels of discriminatory practices aboard mixed nationality crewed ships, there are some accounts of discrimination by officers towards both officers and ratings of other ethnic groups. Discrimination and prejudice have also been reported among ratings.[16] Wherever such attitudes and practices exist, they produce unwarranted divisions and impede the safe and effective running of ships. Two issues spring to mind regarding appropriate policies: the extent to which all employers have effective anti-discriminatory procedures in place and the quality and reliability of the STCW human relationships model course component of the basic safety training certificate. As discussed in Chapter 3, fraudulent practice in basic safety training certification is widespread.

As in all work situations where men outnumber women, it is common for women seafarers to experience institutional discrimination. Sexual harassment may also be commonplace, although it is less likely to be an institutional practice. More and more employers, especially those in the cruise sector where women form a large and growing proportion of crews, have formal policies in place that are specifically aimed at combating sexual harassment. However, if these policies simply define proscribed behaviour, then sexual harassment is not likely to be eliminated. Indeed, there is ample evidence of harassment.[17] In cruise ships this may sometimes be masked in the ambiguous badinage often found in mixed gender workplaces, but when it is experienced aboard cargo ships, sexual harassment can appear more menacing. Women who have sailed aboard these types of ships have almost invariably reported instances that applied to themselves or to others known to them – to the extent that they felt obliged to lock their cabin doors at night to keep out predatory males.

The occupational hierarchies that are sometimes quite formally observed aboard ship can cause problems and dangers, regardless of the national make-up of the crew. The levelling of the shipboard management and decision-making process envisaged by Roger[18] has generally failed to materialize. Many ships continue to be run along strictly hierarchical lines by masters who discourage "challenges" to their authority. The inevitable transient nature of working on deep-sea vessels and the associated isolation of crew members place severe limits on the visibility of shipboard power relations and, therefore, the ability of shore-based managers to influence directly the regulation of ship society. The social and physical distance of the ship from its managers can sometimes have dangerous consequences. The loss of the *MV Green Lily* off the Shetland Islands in the United Kingdom and the associated death of a helicopter winchman in 1997 is a case in point, although there are many other incidences that are talked of privately among shipowners and managers. In the case of the *Green Lily*, the vessel's master, chief engineer, 2nd engineer, 3rd engineer, chief officer and 2nd officer were all Croatian nationals. The United Kingdom's Marine Accident Investigation Branch (MAIB) report into the incident suggested that the junior officers were unwilling to challenge the decision of the master to sail in very poor weather conditions, despite their belief that he was making an error of judgement. The report concluded that the master's autocratic style of management was a causal factor in the accident.

Transnational crews are very rarely assembled simultaneously. Hence, crews are made up of strangers who become shipmates, which means that the social aspect of seafarers' employment, taken together with its casual nature, is experienced as a series of discontinuous and discontinued encounters. Casual employment for all ranks is the norm wherever seafarers are engaged through third parties. Only where the shipowner is a direct employer is there a possibility of an employment contract extending beyond the current engagement. These aspects of employment are registered in the commonplace seafarer remark that "a friendship ends at the gangway". Aboard ship, there are surprisingly few team-building routines and rituals to help counter these discontinuities. And few officers receive proper instruction in team-management during their professional training.

Perhaps partly as a consequence, social life aboard merchant ships is subject to considerable variation, and much depends on the individual ship's workload and trade. Aboard many vessels there simply isn't the time or space for recreational activities, and seafarers often experience many months of monotony broken only by the demands of heavy workloads. However, existing data suggest that the attitude of the master is the single most important factor influencing the "happiness" of seafarers aboard ship, a factor that has long been recognized.[19] Where masters actively encourage recreational activities, they can take a variety of forms: birthday celebrations; regular barbecues; darts or table tennis tournaments; bingo, card games, maj jong; and "horse racing". Aboard many ships, seafarers occasionally have the opportunity to play basketball, practise their tennis or golf techniques, play music, sing karaoke, box, or work out in the gym. However, in ships where masters disapprove of such activities, even when schedules and facilities allow for a reasonable range of social activities, seafarers tend to withdraw to their separate cabins and mix little with their colleagues.[20]

An additional factor influencing the social life of seafarers on board ship relates to alcohol consumption. In 1979, Hoegh Lines introduced crew bars aboard their vessels,[21] in recognition of the importance of fostering drinking habits linked with sociability rather than those encouraging isolation and introspection. Other companies promptly followed suit, and separate officer and crew bars came to be incorporated into the design of many new vessels. However, in recent years many firms have responded to international concerns about health and safety by introducing complete bans or strict limits and restrictions on the consumption of alcohol. As a result, some shipboard bars are now underused spaces – a forlorn reminder of happier times. Such international and company-based restrictions on alcohol generally have a negative impact on seafarers' social lives. Not only do complete bans discourage the scheduling of communal events such as barbecues and so on, they also encourage solitary drinking behind closed (cabin) doors, which promotes social isolation and can endanger mental health.[22] It also inhibits the development of team relations and marks a significant break with many of the traditions associated with mariners' lives.

With or without the assistance of alcohol, a large part of the social interaction aboard ship involves telling jokes and using joking strategies. Making jokes is frequently risky, since it relies on a fairly sophisticated understanding of the "rules" of social interaction and an ability to implement such "rules". Seafarers are generally not regarded by their land-based contemporaries as having good social skills and, indeed, mariners are often thought of as "loners" – except, of course, when seen ashore by outsiders. However, their skilled use of jokes and their ability to maintain cordial relations with colleagues, with whom they may have little in common, during stressful, tiring and highly confined months aboard ship imply that the contrary is true. Multinational crews are particularly impressive in their ability to overcome cultural barriers and uncertainties well enough to be able to use humour aboard, although crew members with poor language skills may avoid making jokes and thereby miss out on an important aspect of a crew's social life.[23]

The decision to avoid joking with fellow seafarers or the inability to participate in social banter and tell jokes is likely to contribute to a seafarer's sense of isolation. This can be a serious problem aboard modern-day vessels, which often spend very little time in port. Recent studies have highlighted the disproportionate levels of suicide among seafarers in comparison with other occupational groups.[24] These and general mental health problems, such as depression and those that result in addictive behavioural patterns, can thrive in an environment of social isolation.[25]

While there is no evidence to suggest that the exposure rates of women seafarers to general mental health problems are higher than those for men, it is certainly possible that women seafarers, especially those working in the cargo sector where women crew members number at most one or two, tend to be more isolated. The 2001 SIRC paper on women seafarers reported that women working in otherwise all-male environments often find themselves "spending excessive amounts of time in their cabins pursuing solitary activities" as a way of avoiding the gossip apt to develop if they engaged in socializing with male crew members in their cabins. The report quotes a woman captain as saying: "You can't go to somebody's room and just sit down, because [...] all the crew are men. [Since] I was a captain, you can imagine how miserable it was."[26]

The ability to communicate in such an isolated and independent context is crucial. Yet, on many of the vessels in the modern international fleet, the stated common working language of the ship is English, which is usually a second language for everyone on board. Communication difficulties can, therefore, pose a major challenge to mixed nationality crews. Many seafarers have expressed the view that, although there are benefits to working with other nationalities, the negative side of working in multinational crews is that it is much harder to communicate effectively.[27]

Sometimes miscommunication can cause work-related problems. Whether classified as merely irritating or actually hazardous, such problems tend to be exacerbated by the unwillingness of individuals to admit to any difficulties in understanding or communicating. The working culture of most ships probably does not help much in this respect. Senior officers exercise a considerable amount of power over juniors and even more so over ratings. Closed reporting systems and practices of "blacklisting" seafarers combine to create a certain amount of fear among all but the most senior ranking, and most seafarers are consequently afraid of being seen as less than competent in any aspect of their job, including their fluency in English.

Occasionally, incidents occur that might have serious consequences for seafarers and the environment. In such cases, the circumstances in which communication takes place are relevant. The conditions on board ship, the environment in which the work is being carried out and the communications equipment employed all increase the risk of errors being made, whichever language is being used and regardless of the linguistic competence of the seafarers. Even a native English speaker can find it difficult to understand what is being said on a VHF radio aboard a noisy vessel, let alone above the noise of the engine room.

The ability to communicate not only depends on a technical grasp of the language but also on a facility to understand accents and new and particular forms of language. The maritime English taught in nautical schools is one such new form of the language. Aboard vessels with multinational crews, you can also come across Chinese English, Filipino English, German English and Singaporean English. Words and expression from several of these languages can then find their way into the vocabulary of stable and long-established crews. The development of such individualized ship languages appears to reinforce other integrative mechanisms aboard and adds to the social cement binding many crews together. However, situations in which such ship-based "languages" can develop are becoming increasingly rare.[28] The global labour market and the drive for cheaper labour sources militate against establishing crews who serve together for significant lengths of time. Once company mergers, acquisitions and bankruptcy are added into the equation, it is easy to see why seafarers rarely find familiar faces among the crews they join on returning to work after a period ashore. Such fluidity means that, in practice, seafarers are constantly having to adapt to the language and accents of their newly encountered, fellow crew members, a process that can be stressful and which is not helped by fears of being misunderstood.

Turnaround and voyage cycles

A number of studies have highlighted the monotony of working and living aboard modern cargo ships, and structural changes within the industry can be said to have exacerbated the boredom and social isolation that have always

The global seafarer

been a feature of a seafarer's working life. Containerization has meant that such ships now "turn around" much faster than they did in the cargo liner trades 20 years ago and a recent study has demonstrated that all ships spend considerably less time in port than 30 years ago.[29]

In 1998, 27 per cent (number = 428) of the ships visiting the port of Sandmouth[30] (a middle-sized port in the United Kingdom, with a cross-section of trades) spent less than 12 hours in port (figures 4.1 and 4.2), whereas only 11 per cent of ships visiting the port in 1970 had a port stay of less than 24 hours. Forty-five per cent (n. = 707) of the 1998 arrivals spent 13 to 24 hours in port and this made up the largest category of ship turnaround times. The data show that, in 1998, seven out of ten ships turned around within 24 hours and only 4 per cent (n. = 58) of the ships stayed in port for more than three days.

This dramatic change in turnaround times has occurred even though there has been a substantial increase in tonnage. Between 1970 and 1998, the tonnage of ships calling at Sandmouth increased fourfold, but, despite this increase in ship size, turnaround times decreased ninefold. Table 4.1 shows the comparative turnaround times for ships with different cargoes.

Ships are places where displaced people come together and form occupational communities, which are themselves isolated from wider society. This isolation has been exacerbated by the ongoing and immense reduction in turnaround times since 1970. In theory, no matter how short turnaround time

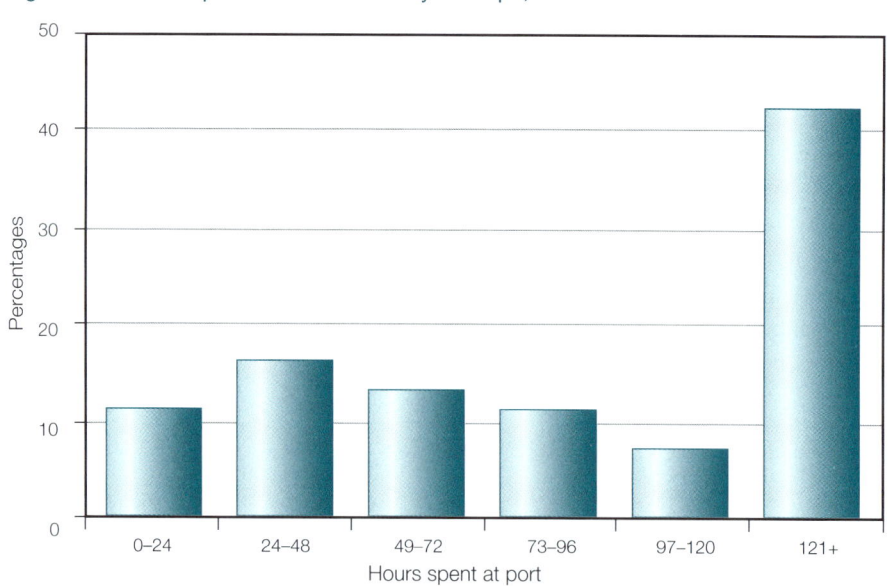

Figure 4.1 Hours spent in Sandmouth by all ships, 1970

Shipboard life and work – I

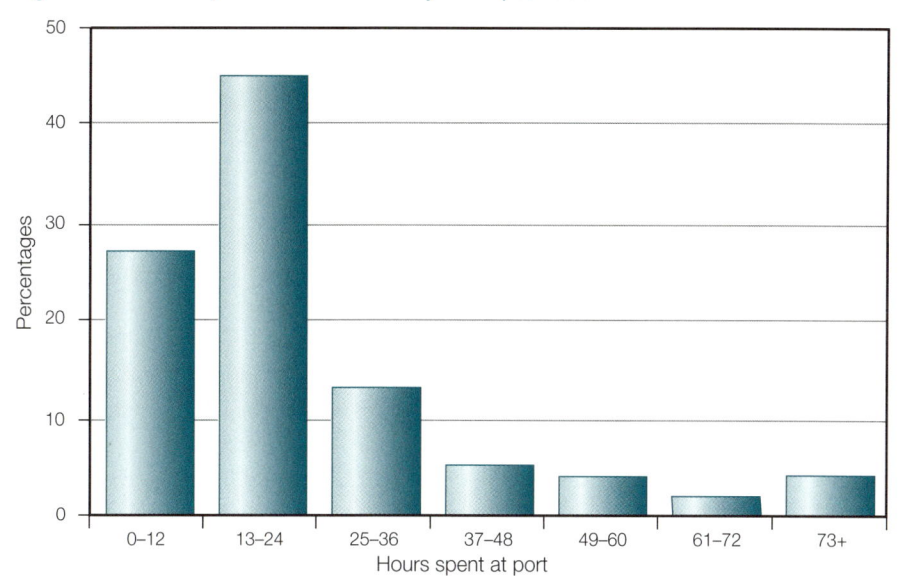

Figure 4.2 Hours spent in Sandmouth by all ships, 1998

Table 4.1 Comparative turnaround times, 1970 and 1998

Type of cargo/ship	Average hours/minutes spent	
	1970	1998
All ships	138.30	15.49
Dry bulk	150.37	48.36
Cars	207.00	13.19
General cargo/containers	150.37	11.23
Liquid bulk	58.22	17.07
Petroleum products	35.04	20.48
Forest products	263.00	28.38

is, it should still be possible for seafarers to be granted shore leave. However, in practical terms this is extremely difficult, since there are a number of additional factors that contribute to making it difficult for seafarers to go ashore:

- intense workload while ships are in port;
- a decline in crewing levels;
- port locations and environments;
- security measures.

The global seafarer

On top of the normal everyday routine work on board for all crew members, there is also additional work that has to be undertaken in port, mainly by senior officers. This includes dealing with visitors (that is, immigration and customs officers, PSC inspectors, cargo surveyors, flag State and class surveyors and so on), loading/unloading cargo, lashing and unlashing cargo, dealing with cargo plans, bunkering, crew changes, taking stores as well as the many additional engine and maintenance tasks that can only be done while the ship is stationary and in port. Furthermore, modern ports frequently work 24 hours a day, which means that pressure only begins to ease when the ship returns to sea. Security restrictions imposed in the United States in the aftermath of the events of 11 September 2001 have made it impossible, at least for the foreseeable future, for many seafarers to take shore leave while their vessels are in port there.

In addition, during the past 20 years or so, there has been a reduction in the size of crews. In the early 1970s, a typical 10,000 grt bulk cargo carrier would have had approximately 40 crew members. Today, a much larger (that is, 30,000 grt) bulk carrier is likely to have only 18 to 25 crew members on board. The same crew-size pattern applies to cargo-carrying ships of all kinds. The decline in the size of crews also makes it difficult for seafarers to be given shore leave. Smaller crews mean that labour is intensified, with seafarers working longer hours and performing flexible tasks. These issues are illustrated by the following quotations taken from interviews with seafarers visiting Sandmouth, ITF inspectors and port welfare workers (boxes 4.1, 4.2 and 4.3).

Box 4.1   "To go ashore, you had to be super-human!"

There aren't crew members like captain's boy, mess boy, second cook, oiler or wiper any more. This ship's captain does the chief officer's job as well. We have two ABs, but that's not enough for this ship. This ship used to have 16 crew, but there are only six now. We do more work. We have no time to go ashore.

Lithuanian bosun

My seafaring career lasted 20 years and I've experienced big changes, working on fast turnaround ships, ro-ros and containers, where we had full crew complements of 26/27 men, a three-watch system, with good time off. So even on a fast turnaround ship, when we didn't have much time off duty, you had adequate rest periods and you had time off ashore because you had enough manpower and you benefited from very good leave periods – nearly one-for-one leave periods. Towards the end of my seafaring career, though, the manpower was reduced, so there were fewer people to perform more work. Instead of a three-watch system, you were doing a two-watch system, so you were either working or sleeping. To go ashore, you really had to be super-human!

Apostleship of the Sea worker and former seafarer

> Box 4.2   Ports are "far away from anything"
>
> With containerization, you need a lot of room. And you need room where it's cheapest to build a container terminal. So this is out in the hinterland and it's very difficult and very expensive to go anywhere. As the industry has changed, the terminal facilities have changed, it's all changed with containerization. In San Francisco, we had the Embargendero, which is the street that runs along the waterfront, which used to be full of ships. And now that's all gone and the ships are 15 to 20 miles away. They're not just far away from San Francisco, they're far away from anything – no municipal transport because there's no people nearby other than the people involved in the terminals on shore who drive where they're going and drive home. There's no reason for the municipalities to put in a bus service. So these guys lead very isolated lives.
>
> ITF Northern Californian inspector
>
> Recently, the environment around ports has changed a lot. In the old days, when there were European – German, English, Swedish – crews, we used to spend money. There were girls and many pubs around the ports. For example, the Swedish ports were busy with girls and drinks. Porto was the same. Now these ports are barely recognizable. The cheap labour crews don't spend money. When the foreign [non-European] crews come to port, they can only buy one can of beer. They have no money to go out with girls.
>
> German captain

Traditionally, ports were located near city centres; these ports, such as Liverpool, San Francisco and Yokohama, are now regarded as historical ports and docks. By contrast, modern port development generally takes place some distance away from residential and shopping areas. These ports are automated, unpeopled, steel-framed and are not served by public transport (box 4.2).

Fast turnaround times have limited the possibilities for seafarers to have any form of social contact beyond the shipboard community, while the reduction in crewing levels has diminished both the extent and the quality of social contact at sea. Of course, cargo ships are not built primarily to accommodate seafarers, but these are places where many everyday activities (such as working, eating, sleeping and socializing) take place in a restricted environment characterized by vibration, sea motion and engine noise. Lack of shore leave means that many seafarers are trapped in this environment, often with a set of people of different nationalities and cultures for months at a time. There is, therefore, increasing concern that lack of shore leave is having a detrimental effect on the mental and physical well-being of seafarers as well as reinforcing isolation, fatigue, depression and stress.

The global seafarer

Box 4.3   "By the end, a certain madness attacks some crew members"

It's a major problem. There's no social life when you go to sea, it's total isolation. You could say that the cabin crew of an aeroplane do something similar, but a seafarer might go from, for example, I've done runs from, say, Singapore to the Philippines to New Zealand and back to western Australia. So, for maybe 15 weeks you get no mail, you do not go ashore, and by the end, a certain madness attacks some crew members. Very small things become very big things. Things like insomnia: many of the crew will be pacing the alleyways at 3 o'clock in the morning. Alcoholism can rise a great deal if alcohol's available. Many seafarers are on different types of medication – Valium and that kind of thing and anti-depressants. Much higher than the regular population.

Former seafarer of Australian origin

Working on the feeder container vessels, some calling at three ports in 24 hours (that is, Tilbury–Zeebrugge–Tilbury) would mean that, after three weeks on board, people's behaviour became automatic. Occasionally, I used to go from Tilbury to Zeebrugge or Rotterdam. One of the vessels didn't have a regular ship's agent and I would turn up at all times of the day or night with parcels ordered from the previous trip plus the mission bus to take the seafarers to the mission. I once visited a vessel at 7.30am in Zeebrugge, but when they asked me to take them to the mission, I refused, which surprised them. Apparently, because I had turned up, the crew assumed that the ship had to be in Tilbury. When I said, "Look out of the porthole", they were amazed that they were not in Tilbury but in Zeebrugge. Throughout my 28 years as a chaplain, I've seen increasingly smaller crews, less time spent in port, more abuse and welfare and justice cases, and the growth of FOC flag vessels. There has also been an increase in workload. This also increases stress – it's a killer. That is something I have seen over the years. Of course, working for some companies is better than for others, but stress is so obvious, I can comment on that – it is getting worse.

Mission to Seafarers' chaplain

Seafarers' lives, even in the best situation, are very grim, very lifeless and very devoid of any *joie de vivre* – it's just work. They work tremendous hours and they have nowhere to go, either at sea or in port. One of the big innovations since I started going to sea is video tapes, but after you've seen *Terminator 3* for the fourth time, I'm sure that it gets to them.

American ex-seafarer

Being in this ship all the time gets to you. The ship is damp; it's sometimes cold. The food isn't fresh. There's noise and vibration. When the ship goes, it vibrates. We are always on board. I work here, eat here, sleep here. Sometimes it creates psychological problems. You're away from your home. No news from your country.

Bulgarian chief officer

Wages and conditions of employment

The global character of the shipping industry means that the nature of the decisions that present themselves to those within it differ qualitatively from those made in other industries, no matter how global their organizational span may be. If a manufacturing plant is to be built in second or third countries, for example, the wage component of the calculation involved in deciding which country to build it in is a once-and-for-all decision. A cheaper and adequately skilled supply of labour in a fourth of fifth country may become available subsequently, but given the location of the newly established plant, this potential labour supply may be prohibitively expensive and politically impossible to import for employment. Either the plant has to be relocated or the owner has to circumvent national laws concerning the use of foreign labour. None of these limitations applies to shipowners. As seen in Chapter 3, the composition of the labour force can easily be changed.

As there is a large global pool of sufficiently skilled and mobile labour in the shipping industry, the wage and employment market is highly competitive and sometimes volatile. The fact that employers drive the labour market and that intervention by national States and para-national organizations is minor makes employment contracts and practices highly variable. In a labour market consisting of many nationalities and far more numerous employers spread across sectors with different labour standards requirements and operating in quality-stratified freight markets, it is, unsurprisingly, difficult to assemble data on wages and conditions. Accordingly, it is only possible to give the most general overview of these issues.

The ISF conducts regular surveys of wage rates, and these show large variations between the average monthly earnings of ABs of various nationalities. The 1992 survey found that the average monthly earnings of a German AB ($5,758) were 19 times higher than the earnings of a Bangladeshi AB ($305), while average earnings in Hong Kong and the United Kingdom were similar to the level of average earnings for all countries surveyed ($1,762). All nationalities earning above the international average were from either Western Europe or other developed parts of the world (Australia, Japan, New Zealand and the United States).

The ISF's 1995 survey showed that the nationalities earning above-average wages were more or less the same as in 1992, except that Sri Lankan and Taiwanese seafarers had joined those earning more than the international average. The 1995 data also revealed the appearance of new, low-paying labour supply countries in the global market. The gap between the lowest and highest average earning countries remained, with the average earnings of Japanese ABs ($9,349) being 41 times higher than the lowest paid – Bangladeshi seafarers on

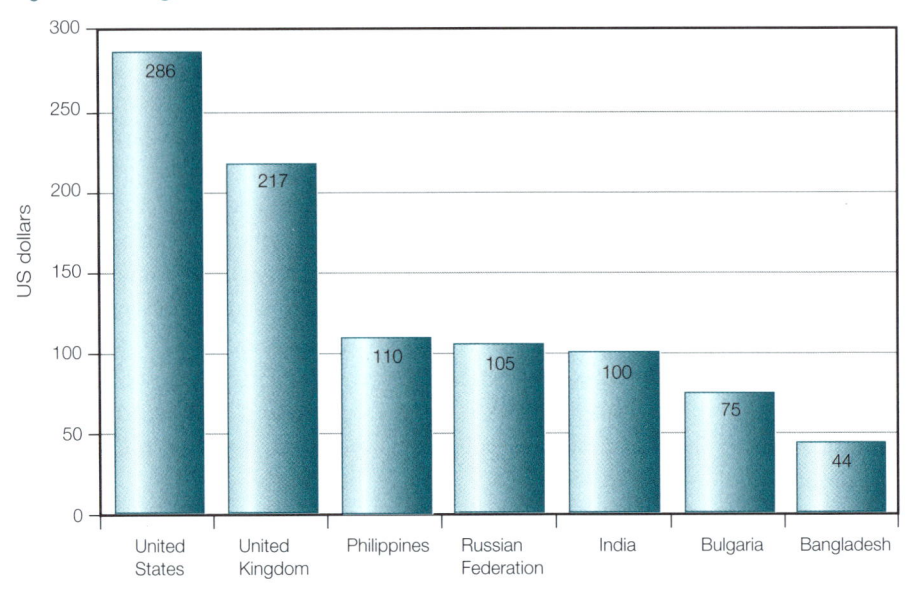

Figure 4.3 Wage costs of ABs, selected nationalities, 1999 (in US dollars)

Country	US dollars
United States	286
United Kingdom	217
Philippines	110
Russian Federation	105
India	100
Bulgaria	75
Bangladesh	44

Source: ISF (London, 1999).

$227. The 1999 survey showed the average earnings of ABs to be $1,318, or three-quarters of the 1992 average. The downward movement of the overall average in this period almost certainly reflects the continuing displacement of relatively expensive OECD seafarers by those from the new and more established labour supply countries of Asia and Eastern Europe. Figure 4.3 shows the comparative wage costs for ABs in 1999.

In the period 1992–99, supply fell short of demand in the global labour market for officers, which led to an upward pressure on wages. The ISF surveys of chief officer wage rates confirm this situation: the rates of pay in the major officer supply countries rose steadily from 1993.

An analysis of these data by nationality shows that average pay rates for Filipino chief officers increased by 1.6 per cent in 1993–94, by 4 per cent in 1994–95 and by 14 per cent in 1995–96. The average rates of pay for Polish officers also increased by nearly 50 per cent in the same period. By contrast, average pay rates for chief officers in the United Kingdom fell by nearly 10 per cent; currently there appear to be a number of Indian and Polish chief officers being paid above the rates of their lowest paid British counterparts. Comparisons of this kind need to be made with caution to ensure that due account is taken of the fact that chief officers of different nationalities may not hold positions that are comparable in terms of type of ship and market sector, while the movements in United States dollar exchange rates can

Table 4.2 Average monthly wages of seafarers, 1996

Monthly wage band (in $)	Number of seafarers	As a %
Less than 300	258	5
300–499	645	13
500–699	702	15
700–899	499	10
900–1099	505	11
1 100–1 299	385	8
1 300–1 499	259	5
1 500–1 999	606	13
2 000–2 499	371	8
2 500–2 999	234	5
3 000–3 499	221	5
3 500–3 999	107	2
More than 4 000	5	0
Totals	**4 797**	**100**

Note: Percentages have been rounded up.

Source: ITF/MORI: Seafarers' Living Conditions Survey (London, ITF, 1996).

enhance or diminish purchasing power according to the currency of the seafarer's native State.

The most recent and most reliable data source on wage rates comes from the 1996 ITF/MORI survey, which drew 6,504 responses from seafarers of various nationalities.[31] It classified the monthly wages of seafarers into 13 bands, as shown in the analysis of responses in table 4.2. The analysis has been simplified here by breaking down the categories into "Low" (less than $300 to $499), "Medium" ($500 to $2,999) and "High" ($3,000 to more than $4,000).[32] On this basis, 18 per cent of seafarers fall in the low category, 75 per cent in the medium and 7 per cent in the high category, although it should be noted that these wage levels are strongly influenced by the seafarers' nationalities and ranks and the type and flag of vessel.

Where a ship's flag is concerned, some 10 per cent of seafarers employed aboard FOC-flagged vessels fall within the high earnings band; aboard nationally flagged vessels 15 per cent receive high earnings. Aboard the nationally flagged vessels of Greece, the Philippines, Romania and the Russian Federation, the figures for the low band are 26 per cent, 27 per cent, 28 per cent and 29 per cent respectively. Nationality is, of course, the most important determinant of wage levels; unsurprisingly, seafarers working aboard the nationally flagged vessels of low-wage countries receive low pay. Forty per

Table 4.3 The effect of rank on wages, 1996

Rank	% falling within low wage bands	% falling within low wage band
Master	7	37
Senior deck officer	9	20
Junior deck officer	7	7
Senior engine officer	4	39
Junior engine officer	6	7
All officers	6	17
Catering ratings	12	10
Deck ratings	28	3
Engine ratings	24	2
All ratings	21	5

Source: ITF/MORI: Seafarers' Living Conditions Survey (London, ITF, 1996).

cent of seafarers from Ukraine fall into the low wage band, 31 per cent from Africa and the Middle East, 30 per cent from Croatia and 27 per cent from China. Table 4.3 shows how rank affects monthly wages. Apart from the obvious distinction between officers and ratings, there are considerable differences within rank groups – another indication of the importance of nationality. Where vessel type is concerned, the lowest paid seafarers are most commonly found on general cargo and bulk carriers, the highest paid on tankers and passenger vessels.

Aboard cruise ships, officers and managers are among the highest paid personnel within the shipping industry, mainly because these positions attract bonuses that are given either at the end of the voyage, the end of the season or the end of the year.[33] In the hotel and catering departments, seafarers are divided into wage earners and tip earners. Tip earners are primarily those who provide direct services to the passengers, such as waiters/waitresses and stewards/stewardesses. In this case, the crew members receive a small monthly payment from the company and are expected to make up the rest of their monthly wages from tips or gratuities given by the passengers. Most cruise lines advise their passengers that they are expected to tip at a specified minimum rate per day. Pay levels and pay methods vary from company to company and, more importantly, according to the region in which the ship operates. In the Caribbean, the Bahamas and other regions where most of the passengers are from the United States, seafarers typically receive a monthly wage from their company of $50. This payment is nominal.

Cruise lines operating in Asia and Europe tend to pay service seafarers fixed monthly wages, principally because European passengers are less generous tippers than North American passengers. Asian passengers also rarely give tips. These variations presumably reflect differing assumptions about service sector payment systems. Wage levels vary greatly, from $270 to $2,400 per month for the same or similar positions. Variations are due to several factors, of which nationality is the most important. For example, waitresses from France, Germany and the United Kingdom are paid more than double the wages paid to waitresses from Indonesia, the Philippines and Thailand on a top-market cruise ship operating worldwide. Similar patterns are found in ships operating in the Asia-Pacific region.

The geographical area within which the ship is operating also contributes to the way in which tips are given. In Asia and Europe, companies advise passengers to pay tips at the end of the voyage, although this advice is not given as strongly as on American-based ships. In Asia, tips are collected by the management and shared among the crew rather than paid to the service seafarers who have had direct contact with the passengers.

In recent years, some cruise lines have introduced a system of security bonds, the purpose of which is to ensure that seafarers provide proper service and complete their contracts. The most widely adopted practice is to deduct a certain amount of money, usually $100, from a seafarer's wages every month. The money is kept until the end of the seafarer's contract, when it is paid as "leave pay". However, this practice is generally not applied to tip-earning seafarers, nor does it seem to be applied to seafarers employed from industrialized countries.

Wage regulation in various forms is well-established in the shipping industry but its impact is uneven and fragmented. There are two quite different wage regulatory practices: one derives from the ILO, under whose aegis employers and trade unions periodically meet to set a minimum benchmark wage; the other originates with the ITF, which aims to regulate wage payments aboard FOC ships.

There are several competing definitions and interpretations of what is known as the ILO minimum wage. The mechanism for setting the minimum wage is provided by the ILO Seafarers' Wages, Hours of Work and the Manning of Ships Recommendation, 1996 (No. 187). In 2000, the ILO minimum wage standard stood at $435 per month for an AB, based on a maximum 48-hour week. However, the ITF and the ISF each use this figure as an indicative minimum rather than as a substantive level and, accordingly, make additional calculations and arrive at divergent sums: in 2000, the ISF calculated the minimum wage standard as $563 per month and the ITF as $823.

There seem to be two issues concerning the ILO account of minimum wages. Firstly, the substantive content of the Recommendation itself; secondly, the legal status of the agreed Recommendation. With regard to the former, the

ILO minimum wage, and the interpretations based on it, are only set for an AB. The Recommendation does not provide any means of calculating wage levels for other ranks. Secondly, the ILO instrument only provides a definition of the rate at which overtime should be paid (1.25 times the hourly rate of pay), without referring to the number of overtime hours that may be worked.

The legal status of Recommendation No. 187 is weakened owing to its status as a Recommendation rather than a Convention. International labour Recommendations are not mandatory for signatories, unless a government chooses to make them so through its own legislation. Furthermore, derogation is permitted through collective bargaining where it is formally recognized by a government. As a result, discrepant interpretations of the ILO minimum wages agreements are inevitable. The content, status and effective downplaying of the Recommendations by PSCs have rendered this "legislation" almost wholly ineffective as a regulatory instrument. On the other hand, the vigorous conduct of negotiations at the ILO when the minimum wage is due for revision suggests that it has more than symbolic significance for real wage rates.

Compared with the shrouded meanings surrounding ILO minimum wages standards, the ITF standards set out in the "Standard" and "Total Crew Cost" (TCC) Agreements have the form and content of conventional contracts. The 1998 ITF Standard Collective Agreement sets $934 per month (based on a 40-hour week) as the acceptable wage standard for an AB, and, as with Recommendation No. 187, defines the rate of overtime without giving maximum weekly hours. By contrast, the ITF Uniform TCC Collective Agreement rate for an AB is $1,204 per month, based on a 40-hour week and a guaranteed overtime of 103 hours per month paid at an hourly rate of $3.94. This explicit coverage of overtime has the advantage of providing strict conditions for the length of the working month. The TCC Agreement also covers a whole range of other contractual issues, such as allotments, disability compensation, repatriation, sick pay, paid leave and so on. In 1999, 5,255 vessels were covered by ITF agreements, a 15 per cent increase on 1998. These agreements covered approximately 116,000 seafarers, of which some 90 per cent were on TCC agreements. The ITF estimates that about 35 per cent of all seafarers on FOC vessels are covered. Many ITF national affiliates now spend much of their time and resources negotiating and enforcing ITF agreements for FOC vessels, rather than negotiating with national shipowners. Some FOCs also have a higher percentage of their vessels covered by these agreements than some national flags. Table 4.4 gives a general indication of ITF agreement coverage on variously flagged ships.

In 2000, the ITF and the IMEC set up permanent machinery for the negotiation of the TCC rate for ABs. The joint committee, known as the IMEC–ITF at the time of writing, agreed to an annual increase of $50, to run

Table 4.4 Vessels under ITF agreements, by flag, 1998

Flag	ITF-covered	Fleet size	% of fleet covered
Panama	1 938	4 834	40
Liberia	918	1 599	57
Bahamas	564	1 070	53
Malta	442	1 312	34
Cyprus	314	1 533	20
GIS[1]	274	535	51
Antigua and Barbuda	192	501	38
Saint Vincent and the Grenadines	142	885	16
Marshall Islands	99	129	77
Singapore	67	968	7
Bermuda	50	96	52
Isle of Man	43	159	27
Vanuatu	43	85	51
Cayman Islands	31	51	61
Netherlands Antilles	21	104	20
NIS	19	674	3
Madeira	15	114	13
Honduras	12	612	2
Belize	10	509	2
Barbados	9	59	15
Cambodia	9	98	9
Sri Lanka	7	26	27
Hong Kong, China	7	268	3
Kerguelen Islands	6	77	8
Lebanon	6	99	6
Tuvalu	5	13	38
*Myanma*r	3	55	5
Luxembourg	2	37	5
Malaysia	2	495	*
Mauritius	2	18	11
Philippines	2	935	*
Gibraltar	1	18	6
Totals	**5 255**	**17 968**	**29**

Note: Flags in italics denote FOCs as defined by the ITF. [1] The figure used here for fleet size is the ITF estimate. If the correct figure of 547 (as supplied to the SIRC by the German Maritime Administration) is used, then the percentage of vessels covered equates 50 per cent. * Indicates less than 1 per cent.

Source: ITF (1999).

from 2001 until 2005. The initial scope and influence of the joint committee was limited by the number of shipowners and managers affiliated to the IMEC, but the rise in numbers of affiliated employers in late 2002 and early 2003 has helped to solidify this important development in international collective bargaining.

An important characteristic of seafarers' work is that, for the most part, it is contracted for the voyage only. Income does not flow steadily and can change according to the seafarers' good fortune in getting the next contract or, contrarily, by the flow of labour from lower wage labour supply countries displacing them. As previously noted, seafarers are employed on a casual basis. And even though shipmasters and chief engineers of proven experience are unlikely to be without work, more often than not they have periods without contracts. However, a more prominent concern for shipmasters and chief engineers is likely to be the duration of the contract. European shipmasters in some trades can reasonably expect contracts of three months on voyage and three months' leave. Shipmasters of Eastern European nationalities, by comparison, are more likely to have contracts requiring longer periods at sea and shorter periods at home. Contracts as well as wages are stratified by nationality and this applies to all ranks.

For ratings, a typical contract for Filipinos lasts nine months, 12 months for Sierra Leoneans and six months for Eastern Europeans. Typical senior Western European officers' contracts are three to four months in length compared with six to nine months for their Filipino and Indian counterparts. A survey of 4,525 seafarers, conducted under the auspices of the ILO, found that in more than 50 per cent of cases, the longest contract period worked by seafarers was over one year in duration.[34] Without a proper relief system, it is inevitable that ratings will be pressurized into staying on board for longer periods than the specified length of their contracts.

The ITF/MORI survey showed that the most common length of contract is between six and 12 months, although, as with wages, this varies with flag, vessel type, nationality and rank. In contrast to wages, the employing agency appears to be a significant factor when it comes to contracts of employment as distinct from voyage contracts. Overall, 12 per cent of seafarers indicated that their current contract was for more than 12 months. For all national flags, this rises to 17 per cent, but for FOCs it is 8 per cent. With regard to vessel type, the extremes of contract length are even more apparent. While 12 per cent of all contracts are over 12 months in length, for seafarers on passenger vessels this rises to 37 per cent, but for chemical carrier crews it is only 5 per cent. With regard to crewing agencies, union recruitment offers the most secure employment, with 25 per cent of seafarers employed through this route having contracts of employment of over 12 months in length. Those employed by private crewing agencies have contracts of this duration in only 6 per cent of cases.

Contracts are sometimes used to limit seafarers' access to benefits, additional remuneration and/or trade union representation rights. In Sri Lanka, for example, the Standard Crew Agreement made under the provisions of the Merchant Shipping Act Number 52 of 1971 specifically states that representations in the event of any dispute over terms and conditions may only be made to the owner or master and to no other organization. Similar practices were reported by the Greek seamen's union, which discovered in 1986 that Polish seamen working aboard Greek-flagged ships were in some cases required to sign letters of loyalty "undertaking that they will never seek any additional payment or benefits over and above the terms of the contract". The letter states:

> This applies especially to the possible event that the owner and/or captain of the vessel should be forced by the ITF anywhere to pay a higher wage or extra salary to me or granted to me any additional condition which should be a disadvantage to the mutual employment contract for the owner and/or captain of the vessel. I especially confirm that in such above case I will consider this extra payment as advance payment, which the owner and/or captain is entitled to deduct at any time from my subsequent wages.[35]

Where the length of the working week or month is concerned, there is a wide variety of stipulations. The ITF Uniform TCC Collective Agreement specifies that the ordinary hours of duty of all seafarers shall be eight hours per day, Monday to Friday inclusive. The standard Filipino employment contract requires that normal working hours be eight hours in every 24 hours, midnight to midnight, Monday to Sunday. The Sri Lankan standard contract specifies that the normal working week should be 44 hours, while the Collective Agreement for Cypriot seafarers aboard Cypriot-flagged cargo and tanker vessels states that the hours of monthly compulsory employment are 173.

Actual hours worked, including overtime, are frequently very high compared with most shore jobs. This can be seen in the hours of work reported by some seafarers in the ITF/MORI survey.[36] The 1996 survey revealed that, overall, 24 per cent of respondents had a typical working day of up to eight hours; 62 per cent worked eight to 12 hours; 11 per cent worked 12 to 18 hours; and 3 per cent of seafarers worked a typical day of more than 18 hours. As with length of contract and wages, these hours varied according to flag, ship type and crew nationality. The effects of rank and employing agency are less obvious. In respect of flag, 4 per cent of seafarers reported a typical working day in excess of 18 hours on FOC-flagged vessels; aboard nationally flagged vessels 2 per cent reported working these hours. In terms of

The global seafarer

vessel type, long hours were most often reported on passenger ships and ro-ro ferries, while seafarers on reefers and bulk carriers reported shorter working days. Where nationality is concerned, Filipinos, Indonesians and North Americans were among the seafarers most likely to report working days of more than 18 hours, with 9 per cent, 8 per cent and 5 per cent respectively doing so.

In the late 1990s, the ITF conducted its own survey of working hours, collecting questionnaire responses from 2,500 seafarers of 60 different nationalities, serving under 63 different flags.[37] The results showed working hours were often in excess of the requirements of the ILO Seafarers' Hours of Work and the Manning of Ships Convention, 1996 (No. 180). Overall, 3 per cent of seafarers had an average working day of less than eight hours; 65 per cent worked eight to 12 hours; 27 per cent worked 12 to 15 hours; and 5 per cent had an average working day of more than 15 hours. There was also evidence that seafarers work consistently long hours on a regular daily basis. Sixty-two per cent of seafarers said they worked more than 60 hours per week and 24 per cent said they worked more than 80 hours per week. Additionally, 60 per cent of seafarers indicated that their working hours had increased in the past five to ten years, despite the fact that 64 per cent of seafarers said they were aware of international regulations on working hours.[38]

Although wages are a fairly obvious focus for attention, there are other important factors to consider when examining the living and working conditions of seafarers. These include food, accommodation and welfare provision as well as standards of health and safety, all of which are looked at in the next chapter on shipboard life and work.

Notes

[1] S. Roger: "American seamen on the *Hoegh Mallard*", in Schrank, R. (ed.): *Industrial democracy at sea: Authority and democracy on a Norwegian freighter* (Cambridge, MA, MIT Press, 1983).

[2] ibid.

[3] ibid.

[4] W. Aubert: *The hidden society* (Somerset, NJ, Transaction Publishers, 1965); N. Perry and R. Wilkie: "Social theory and shipboard structure: Models, metaphors, and ships", in *Maritime Studies and Management*, 1974, Vol. 1, No. 3; T. Lane: *Grey dawn breaking: British merchant seafarers in the late 20th century* (Manchester, Manchester University Press, 1986).

[5] P. E. Perez-Mallaina: *Spain's men of the sea: Daily life of the Indies fleets in the sixteenth century* (Baltimore, Johns Hopkins University Press, 1998).

[6] E. Kahveci, T. Lane and H. Sampson: *Transnational seafarer communities* (Cardiff, SIRC, 2002).

[7] ibid.

[8] ibid.

[9] Three recent books, each covering different periods within the past 70 years, show the continuities of seafaring culture, despite the large variations in types of ship and trading patterns. See E. Newby: *Learning the ropes* (London, John Murray, 1999); H. Schulenburg: *Bilder aus den Alben eines Seefahrers 1958–1965* (Allersberg, Jacob-Gilardi-Verlag, 1995); Captain A. W. Kinghorn: *Away to sea* (Abergavenny, Wales, P. M. Heaton Publishing, 1996).

[10] M. Zhao: Interviews with Chinese crews undertaken for the SIRC in May 2002.

[11] Kahveci et al., op. cit.

[12] ITF/MORI: Seafarers' Living Conditions Survey (London, ITF, 1996).

[13] D. Moreby: "Communication problems inherent in a cross-cultural manning environment", in *Maritime Policy & Management*, 1990, Vol. 17, No. 3, pp. 199–205.

[14] Kahveci et al., op. cit.

[15] ibid.

[16] ibid.

[17] ILO: *Women seafarers: Global employment policies and practices* (Geneva, 2003).

[18] Roger, op. cit.

[19] J. de Hartog: *The captain* (New York, Atheneum, 1966); M. G. Sherar: *Shipping out: A sociological study of seamen* (Cambridge, MA, Cornell Maritime Press, 1973).

[20] Kahveci et al., op. cit.

[21] Roger, op. cit.

[22] H. Sampson and M. Thomas: "Health and safety at sea: Social factors a neglected dimension", in *Proceedings of the International Symposium on Human Factors on Board* (Bremen, 2002).

[23] H. Sampson and M. Zhao: *Jobs, jokes and jibes: Communication and the operation of ships with multilingual crews*, unpublished paper presented at the 2000 WOME [Workshop on Maritime English] 2 China Conference (Qingdao).

[24] S. Roberts: *Occupational mortality among merchant seafarers in the British, Singapore and Hong Kong fleets 1981–1995* (Cardiff, SIRC, 1998).

[25] Sampson and Thomas, op. cit.

[26] ILO, op. cit.

[27] Kahveci et al., op. cit.

[28] H. Sampson and M. Zhao: *World Englishes*, 2003, Vol. 22, No. 1, pp. 31–43.

[29] E. Kahveci: *Fast turnaround ships and their impact on crews* (Cardiff, SIRC, 1999). In the 1970s, general cargo ships carried a wide variety of small quantities of loose items, such as boxes, bags, packing cases and drums. Later, containers came to dominate the transport of general cargo.

[30] The name of this port has been changed for reasons of confidentiality.

[31] ITF/MORI, op. cit.

[32] These categories are used purely for comparison purposes and are not intended to imply any value judgements as to the levels encapsulated within the bands.

[33] Occasional bonuses used to be employed by some companies as incentives for seafarers, but this came to an end in the mid-1990s for seafarers in lower positions. Currently, in the interests of cost reduction, only supervisors receive bonuses.

[34] ILO: *Seafarers' welfare in the Asian region: Report of the regional seminar, Singapore* (Geneva, 1990).

[35] *Lloyd's List*, 21 July 1986.

[36] The ITF/MORI figures include overtime and so should be treated with caution.

[37] ITF, undated, c. 1997.

[38] This figure should be treated with caution, since the relevant question only asked if they had "any" knowledge of relevant international regulations.

5

SHIPBOARD LIFE AND WORK – II

A ship's cook of Indian nationality

Food, diet and accommodation

Food in residential institutions often takes on a particular significance, and this is particularly true for ships' crews.[1] As seafarers are denied many of the pleasures of their shore-based contemporaries, food can be more important to them than simply satisfying hunger. Food is addressed by the ILO Food and Catering (Ships' Crews) Convention, 1946 (No. 68), which considers issues such as supplies, storage and preparation facilities, the training and qualification of catering crew and "the provision of food and water supplies which, having regard to the size of the crew and the duration and nature of the voyage, are suitable in respect of quantity, nutritive value, quality and variety" (Article 4). The Convention also requires that competent authorities provide a system of inspection that includes "the qualification of such member of the catering department of the crew as are required by laws or regulations to possess prescribed qualifications".

The number of seafarers working in galleys has decreased considerably over recent years, reflecting cost-cutting efforts and a general trend towards a reduction in crew size. Ships sailing with small crews, such as those mainly employed in the coastal trades, often have no crew member employed specifically as cook and, therefore, it is common for shipmasters to buy supplies in supermarkets and to take turns with other crew members in cooking the meals. Although cooks are invariably employed in larger ships, training is not always adequate. A syllabus from a British college that meets

> Box 5.1   A British college's syllabus for ships' cooks
>
> **Certificate of Competency Part 1**
> **Course Content**
>
> This course is intended to provide candidates with the basic skills and knowledge in cookery and bakery production for use on board ship. Candidates will demonstrate the making of: basic breads (white and brown doughs); basic cake sponges (assorted biscuits and scones, choux pastry goods); various pastries; and simple hot and cold desserts. The candidate will produce basic meals from a variety of ingredients using various methods of cookery, including stews, casseroles, deep fried foods, roasts, breakfast dishes, etc.
>
> **Certificate of Competency Part 2**
> **Course Content**
>
> This course is intended to provide candidates with more advanced skills and knowledge in cookery and bakery production for use on board ship. Candidates will demonstrate the making of: advanced breadmaking using a variety of ingredients and techniques producing brown, white, wholemeal and wheatmeal doughs, also some speciality breads (multigrain, French, brown-ale). The doughs will be made into a variety of shapes including baps, loaves, rolls, bloomer, etc.; various cakes, such as Madeira, cherry, fruit, etc.; pastries; and advanced hot and cold desserts. Advanced cookery using a variety of ingredients and methods of cookery will be used to produce meals suitable for a variety of consumers.
>
> **Higher Certificate**
> **Course Content**
>
> This course is intended to provide experienced candidates with advanced skills and knowledge in complex cookery and bakery production for use on board ship. Candidates will demonstrate the making of: complex bread and doughs, e.g. brioche, Danish pastries; complex hot and cold desserts; cold buffet work is essential, using whole hams, salmon, etc; the making of galantines and the decoration of these items with chaud froid, aspic and a variety of garnishes; complex game dishes will be produced using pheasant, hare, rabbit, pigeon, etc.; complex meat, poultry and fish dishes using a wide variety of cooking methods; complex vegetable and salad dishes including hot and cold hors d'oeuvres.

present (British) requirements for standards of training and course content for ships' cooks conspicuously lacks any provision for training in nutrition, healthy food preparation and hygienic storage, focusing instead on a limited range of, predominantly, baking skills (box 5.1). In the United Kingdom, the MCA has been reviewing the certification of ships' cooks and it is likely that, under new proposals, all those involved in the storage, preparation and presentation of food will be required to hold certification in food hygiene.

The question of food and diet has been given some attention in the cruise sector of the industry, although this has mainly centred on the problems of gastrointestinal disorders and food poisoning outbreaks among passengers.[2] There has been no scientific research on the spread and consequences of food-borne diseases among ships' crews or on the diet of seafarers. The limited data available do, however, suggest that there are considerable problems with diet and nutrition. Studies of Danish (male) seafarers report that those over the age of 34 years are significantly more likely than men in the general population to be defined as "grossly obese", that is, having a Body Mass Index (BMI) of 30 or above: in the age group 45–54 years, 30 per cent of the seafarers sampled had a BMI of 30 or above, compared with 6 per cent of men in the general population.[3] The results of British medical examinations taken throughout 1998 show that obesity is the second most common reason for seafarers to be issued a restricted certificate and the fifth most common reason for failing a medical examination.[4]

Seafarers who are issued with a restricted certificate or who have failed a medical examination because of obesity may go on a "crash diet" in order to lose weight rapidly. However, crash dieting can be dangerous to a person's health and the effects are unlikely to be long lasting. Obesity itself also has severe health consequences: it can lead to hypertension and an increased risk of coronary heart disease. It is possible that obesity among seafarers has become an occupational problem. In a study carried out in Australia, seafarers expressed concern over the large amounts of fried foods in their diet and the absence of low-fat products on some ships.[5] The study also showed that seafarers consume significantly more sugar and fat at sea than when they are ashore, which may reflect a lack of choice and autonomy: the range of food available to seafarers is subject to decisions made about supplies, as well as the knowledge, skills and competencies of the cook (if, indeed, there is a cook at all). Weight problems may also reflect seafarers' more sedentary occupational demands, owing to increased automation and increased administrative duties, along with restricted opportunities for physical exercise while aboard. It is also unclear to what extent "unhealthy choices" reflect a paucity of knowledge when it comes to nutrition and health. Shore-based research shows that many men rely on their partners for food purchase and preparation and hence the provision of a nutritionally balanced meal.[6] However, knowledge is useless if it cannot be operationalized and, as noted earlier, seafarers often have little choice in the matter.

The choices seafarers make about what they eat may also reflect more complex issues, such as changes in eating patterns related to working shifts. A consistent finding of research with shiftworkers in shore-based occupations is that they complain more than other workers of gastrointestinal digestive symptoms.[7] Working shifts has been found to have an effect on the regularity and number of meals eaten,[8] and night shiftwork has also been associated with increases in "snacking" and "nibbling".[9] Research with ferry-workers working irregular shift patterns shows that they are often dissatisfied with their eating patterns and have problems adjusting meal routines to changes in shift.[10] For those seafarers with longer tours of duty, problems can be exacerbated by the lack of autonomy associated with the range of food, preparation and availability while aboard. Those seafarers who are working traditional watch hours and, therefore, missing conventional meal times, may find their choices limited to what is available at their breaks. Long irregular working hours may also affect eating habits. Research with shore-side workers in Japan has shown that there is a positive correlation between working extra overtime and increases in BMI and waist circumference.[11] Thus the very nature of seafaring work patterns while aboard may be detrimental to healthy eating, with the subsequent implications for health.

Food consumption also has social implications. Shared meal times provide a crucial opportunity for social contact at sea. Now that almost all ships have small crews and operate to tighter deadlines, seafarers frequently experience periods of isolation and loneliness. Modern seafarers often work alone or in conditions that prohibit conversation. After work they may be too tired to take advantage of whatever opportunities to socialize exist. Research with Finnish seafarers has shown that the most common leisure activity while aboard is reading, with less than 40 per cent reporting "chatting with friends" as a way of spending their free time.[12] Communal meals can be one of the few opportunities that seafarers have to spend time together, thus promoting social solidarity and a sense of camaraderie, which is so vital for emotional well-being. Reductions in crewing levels have led to suggestions that communal meals prepared by specialist galley crews should be replaced with self-service meals to be taken according to individual needs and work patterns. Aside from the nutritional implications of such proposals, the repercussions on social contact aboard and the subsequent effect on seafarer well-being could be considerable.

The importance of seafarers' working conditions in respect of recruitment and retention,[13] social cohesion and welfare on board[14] and crew efficiency[15] has been recognized for some time, and it has been argued that standards of shipboard accommodation need to be "very much in advance" of those ashore to attract sufficient numbers of people to a seafaring career.[16] Naval architects have asserted that shipowners are "morally obligated" to ensure that accommodation aboard offers seafarers a "high standard of comfort" and that "there is a responsibility on people who proscribe the conditions in which others live to give careful attention not only to their safety and comfort but also to the state of mind which an environment inculcates".[17] Reduced crewing levels and single-person tasking have minimized opportunities for social contact aboard, accommodation structures that include separate leisure areas for different crew members have compounded this. Designs that maximize casual interaction between seafarers while also providing private space for individuals have been regarded as desirable.[18] Such favourable accommodation and leisure facilities on board have been seen to play an important role in the social organization of the ship and subsequently on its operational efficiency.[19] Indeed, it has been claimed that capital outlay which improves efficiency through crew contentment should be regarded as a contribution to economic success.[20]

Despite the recognition in the literature of the importance of high-quality accommodation, standards vary considerably from ship to ship. At best, ships have single-berth accommodation for all crew members, with en suite bath and toilet facilities, adequate space for storage, desks or tables, comfortable seating, air conditioning/heating, good lighting and ventilation. Officers are allocated larger rooms or a suite of two rooms with separate living or sleeping areas and refrigerators. Laundry facilities include a sufficient number of washing machines, dryers and irons. The minimum standards of accommodation are laid down in a number of international labour Conventions: the Food and Catering (Ships' Crews) Convention, 1946 (No. 68); the Accommodation of Crews Convention (Revised), 1949 (No. 92); and the Accommodation of Crews (Supplementary Provisions) Convention, 1970 (No. 133); and certain Recommendations.

Ships that are owned and/or managed by shipowners of the north European States (Nordic ships are particularly likely to fall into this category), Japan, the Republic of Korea and the United States tend to have high standards of accommodation. Although newer ships are generally considered to have better leisure and recreational facilities, the age of the vessel is not necessarily an accurate guide to standards of accommodation or other facilities. There are reports, for example, that some newer ships have poor sound insulation between rooms, use cheaper and less robust materials in accommodation areas and suffer from excessive and continuous vibration.

It is difficult to make generalizations on the quality of accommodation. There is, however, some evidence that reefers, tankers and container ships are more likely to have reasonable standards of accommodation than ferries, cruise ships and bulk carriers. The reasons for this relate not only to notions of benevolence or "good" and "bad" employers but more to market and operational considerations. To some extent, container ships that operate on fixed routes are protected from competition because they have grouped themselves into conferences, which operate rather like cartels. They are consequently under less pressure to cut costs than, for instance, bulker owners. They can, therefore, afford to offer seafarers better standards of accommodation. Owners of ferries and cruise ships, which, like bulkers, also operate in a highly competitive environment, are particularly concerned with limiting the space (and therefore the facilities) available to seafarers because of its opportunity cost. Even the most luxurious of the cruise industry's vessels provide relatively poor standards of crew accommodation. In some vessels, cabins can be hot and noisy, with exposed pipework running along deck-heads. Seafarers have little space and furniture: sometimes just one small fixed locker per person in cabins for up to four people.

Whatever their motivation, many shipowners and designers have taken the provision of high standards in accommodation and recreational facilities seriously and appreciate that, as one author has pointed out, "an essential prerequisite to a seaman's health, in addition to his personal comfort, dignity and welfare, is that he has adequate accommodation".[21] Nevertheless, some seafarers continue to live in poor conditions. In too many ships, cabins are cramped and shared, badly lit and ventilated, and often infested with pests, such as cockroaches. There are frequently no recreational facilities (apart from a television perhaps), toilet facilities are shared and basic standards of hygiene are not met. These ships are more likely to be ferries, older generation bulk carriers and general cargo ships that do not operate on international routes. However, there are also many vessels operating internationally that fail to conform to the relevant ILO standards (tables 5.1 and 5.2).

Despite the provisions of Conventions Nos. 68 (Article 5) and 92, which are included in the Appendix to the Merchant Shipping (Minimum Standards) Convention, 1976 [and Protocol, 1996] (No. 147), and later supplementary provisions on accommodation of crews in Convention No. 133, standards of food and accommodation have not been always a priority of PSC inspectors. With the adoption of Convention No. 147 in 1976, ratifying States could apply the standards of Conventions No. 92 and Article 5 of No. 68 to all ships visiting their ports, regardless of their origin or "flag". For the first time, sub-standard vessels could be detained for failing to comply with international minimum labour standards. Following the signing of the Paris MOU on PSC, issues relating to food and accommodation were accorded greater attention. In particular, a three-month concentrated campaign of inspectors was carried out in the autumn of 1997; during this period, nearly 4,000 vessels were inspected for living and working conditions. Although 54 per cent of deficiencies concerning accommodation and a 120 per cent rise in deficiencies concerning food and catering were reported, the number of detentions remained low: it is still unusual for a ship to be detained on the grounds of deficiencies in accommodation and catering alone. The value of inspections should not, however, be underestimated. Deficiencies have to be put right and increasing the number of follow-up inspections should result in improvements being made on ships.

Although most ships are not detained solely on the grounds of sub-standard food and accommodation, there are numerous examples, in almost any given month, of vessels that are detained for these reasons among others. The Saint Vincent and the Grenadines-flagged 12,000 grt bulk carrier, *Leader*, was detained in Aberdeen, Scotland, in 1996 for 101 days for structural deficiencies and "unsanitary conditions in accommodation". In November 1995, the 39,865 dwt Maltese-flagged, *Atlantic Sea*, was detained in Milton Haven, England, with a number of deficiencies, including "severe cockroach infestation" and "rotten food". The 1976-built, 70,633 gt Liberian-flagged tanker, *Mystras II*, was detained on 19 October 1999 by the United States PSC for numerous deficiencies, including "accommodation spaces infested with roaches, and numerous toilets, showers and sinks ... [that were] inoperable".[22] An examination of the declarations from PSC published in *Lloyd's List* highlights the extent of the problem: in the randomly selected month of July 1999, the details of the following vessels detained by the PSC for reasons including poor (usually unsanitary) accommodation and catering provisions were printed:

- *Heng Ya*, a 1,691 gt Belize-flagged general cargo ship, built in 1993;
- *Mailicia*, a 7,142 gt Cyprus-flagged reefer, built in 1980;
- *Marmara*, a 3,712 gt Ukraine-flagged general cargo ship, built in 1973;
- *Osman Er*, an 8,400 gt Turkish bulk carrier, built in 1980;
- *Swan*, a 1,865 gt Honduras-flagged general cargo ship, built in 1964.

Given the likely under-reporting of deficiencies in accommodation and food and the reluctance of PSC inspectors to detain ships, it is perhaps surprising to find as many ships detained on these (among other) grounds. However, other sources also suggest that there is still a significant problem in terms of food and accommodation, which needs to be addressed by the industry. Of 9,324 vessels detained in 1997, 406 were detained for deficiencies in accommodation (table 5.1, column C).

Table 5.2 shows the number of deficiencies for ILO-related matters found in four years by the Paris MOU States. On average, about 10 per cent of all deficiencies (not all the categories have been listed in the table) are related to crew and conditions of work, and of these approximately half are concerned with issues of accommodation and food and catering. It should be noted, however, that issues such as articles of agreement, employment contracts and other matters that PSC authorities do not verify have not been included, although they are part of Convention No. 147.

The global seafarer

Table 5.1 Main categories of deficiencies per flag, 1997

Flag	A	B	C	D	E	F	G	H	I	J	K	L	Total
Algeria	4	2	7	14	16	8	4	5	10	4	5	3	82
Antigua and Barbuda	5	10	8	40	29	29	8	12	22	9	12	9	193
Bahamas	21	18	10	51	56	52	16	20	33	14	37	13	341
Barbados	3	4	7	12	13	11	8	3	8	2	6	0	77
Belize	6	0	2	13	16	9	9	9	9	3	8	2	86
Bulgaria	31	32	14	82	58	63	40	23	65	28	36	15	487
Cambodia	0	1	3	13	11	8	6	8	7	2	2	1	62
Cyprus	73	58	52	198	190	176	93	93	152	57	109	32	1283
Egypt	7	3	8	25	24	29	9	15	18	13	7	1	159
Estonia	3	1	1	5	7	9	3	2	5	3	1	0	40
Honduras	34	30	23	70	60	61	37	9	51	32	32	18	457
Lebanon	10	11	7	32	18	18	11	8	17	11	8	3	154
Liberia	15	16	14	59	70	48	33	13	26	8	22	12	336
Libyan Arab Jamahiriya	1	1	3	8	11	9	1	1	8	5	8	3	59
Malta	47	55	55	196	193	172	89	77	125	56	82	18	1165
Marshall Islands	2	1	2	6	6	8	2	1	7	3	6	2	46
Mauritius	4	2	4	6	7	2	5	1	4	2	2	1	40
Myanmar	1	1	0	4	4	5	1	4	1	3	2	1	27
Panama	100	110	33	308	294	228	132	104	191	72	134	57	1763
Romania	17	9	23	37	40	43	16	31	37	18	21	4	296
Saint Vincent and the Grenadines	53	31	38	127	123	132	70	42	90	38	61	20	825
Syria	13	13	23	46	33	36	21	8	37	16	12	3	261
Turkey	35	50	69	207	158	133	77	42	147	68	76	23	1085
Totals	485	459	406	1559	1437	1289	691	531	1070	467	689	241	9324

Key: A: ships' certificates; B: crew; C: accommodation; D: life-saving appliances; E: fire-fighting equipment; F: safety in general; G: load lines; H: propulsion and auxiliary machinery; I: navigation; J: radio; K: marine pollution; L: operational deficiencies (SOLAS).

Source: Paris MOU on PSC (1998).

The data collected by the Mission to Seafarers in the United Kingdom confirm that significant numbers of seafarers are unhappy with their living conditions. Of 1,549 complaints received between 1994 and November 1999, 123 (that is, 7.9 per cent) were concerned with living conditions (table 5.3).

Table 5.2 Deficiencies recorded by the Paris MOU, 1996–99

Selection of deficiencies	1996	1997	1998	1999
Crew				
Certificate of competency	699	810	835	670
Number/composition	346	276	222	251
Medical certificate	231	262	227	213
Other	93	104	120	98
Total crew	**1 369**	**1 452**	**1 404**	**1 232**
Accommodation				
Cleanliness/parasites	226	274	272	265
Ventilation/heating	52	97	78	75
Sanitary facilities	255	521	483	440
Drainage	13	23	36	25
Lighting	154	211	154	167
Pipes/wires/insulation	18	30	17	28
Sick bay	85	206	151	144
Medical equipment	462	530	488	522
Other	152	291	252	223
Total accommodation	**1 417**	**2 183**	**1 931**	**1 889**
Food and catering				
Galley/handling spaces	510	955	705	625
Provisions	96	324	223	187
Fresh water/piping/tanks	29	84	63	36
Other	51	145	114	106
Total food and catering	**686**	**1 508**	**1 105**	**954**
Working spaces				
Ventilation/heating	26	31	34	36
Lighting	278	311	338	354
Others	104	163	146	117
Total working spaces	**408**	**505**	**518**	**507**
Accident prevention				
Personal equipment	84	107	132	157
Protection machines/machinery parts	218	330	341	386
Pipes/wires/insulation	121	174	186	202
Other	261	300	349	591
Total accident prevention	**684**	**911**	**1 008**	**1 336**
Totals of columns	**4 564**	**6 559**	**5 966**	**5 918**
Totals of all deficiencies	**53 967**	**53 311**	**57 831**	**60 670**

Source: Paris MOU on PSC (1999).

The global seafarer

Table 5.3 Complaints by seafarers to port chaplains, 1994–99

Reason for complaint	Frequency of complaints	As a % of total
Abandonment	48	3.1
Contractual problems	206	13.3
Discipline	59	3.8
Illness	118	7.6
Living conditions	123	7.9
Other	185	11.9
Safety	173	11.2
Termination	77	5.0
Unknown	26	1.7
Wages	527	34
Unspecified	7	0.5
Totals	**1 549**	**100**

Source: Mission to Seafarers (1999).

It would seem reasonable to conclude, therefore, that there are significant numbers of ships that fail to provide even basic standards of accommodation and catering to their crews and that there are many more ships, which, while their provisions may not be particularly hazardous to health, do not provide reasonable standards of food and/or accommodation to seafarers. Although there has been a great deal of speculation within the industry about whether or not the transfer of ships to open registries has led to a decline in standards, the limited evidence available here suggests that the flag of the ship is not necessarily an indication of the standards of food and accommodation aboard. In 1950, an ILO report on conditions aboard Panamanian ships considered that ownership was, in fact, a better guide to standards, and it appears that little has changed:

> The conditions of safety and employment in the ships it saw depended largely on the owners, agents and masters. There are owners who, because of their national traditions or their sense of responsibility, see to it that their ships are seaworthy and comply with good standards of safety and employment conditions. There are others who are apparently irresponsible and looking solely for quick profits and are prepared on that account to take risks as to the safety of passengers and crew and apply the lowest standards of employment that the crew (often in the grip of circumstances and prepared to accept any job rather than be unemployed) will tolerate.[23]

Table 5.1 shows that many detentions apply to a number of flag States of all types, including national flags. In fact, many companies with reputations for high standards have flagged out, but nevertheless continued to maintain excellent standards of food and accommodation on their ships. With regard to food, catering and accommodation, it might be appropriate for PSC inspectors to target those fleets of owners who are recurring offenders and submit them to frequent inspections. Where ships have been detained, follow-up inspections should be made to ensure that deficiencies have been corrected.

Occupational safety

Seafaring remains a high risk occupation: for example, fatal injuries and drownings among Danish seafarers from 1986 to 1993 were 11.5 times higher than average rates among the Danish male workforce ashore.[24] Similarly, in England and Wales, the latest available official statistics on work-related fatalities show that seafarers' mortality rates for water transport accidents are higher than train drivers' rates for railway accidents and truck drivers' rates for traffic accidents, despite the likely undercounting of some British seafarer deaths occurring outside British waters on non-British registered ships. Among transport workers, only aircraft flight deck officers have higher fatal accident rates.[25] A 1986 ILO survey of 1,600 seafarer fatalities in 30 countries over a 12-month period estimated that at least 36 per cent of those deaths were occupationally related.[26]

Although an International Ship Information Database has recently been set up within the IMO, there is at present no shipping equivalent of the International Civil Aviation Organization's regular published analyses of global aviation industry deaths. A method for analysing casualties was finally agreed by the IMO at the end of 2000, but reports depend on casualty investigations being conducted by the flag State, not all of whom have the capacity or are willing to conduct thorough, professional investigations. Although the IMO database may well become an important research resource in the future, at present most of the (limited) research evidence on work-related fatalities and non-fatal injuries relates to seafarers from the developed world: the fragmentary research evidence from the developing world points to significantly higher fatality rates. Thus, a comparison of occupational mortality over 15 years in the British-, Hong Kong- and Singapore-registered merchant fleets showed that Asian seafarers had occupational accident mortality rates 2.4 times (in the case of the Singaporeans) and 2.0 times (in the case of the Hong Kong crews) greater than those of seafarers on British-registered ships,[27] with many more Asian deaths due to foundering and grounding.

In the absence of any comprehensive international reports, the best international dataset is probably that provided by the United Kingdom P&I Club's ten-year analysis of major claims,[28] since the club's membership accounts for 20 per cent of the world's deep-water fleet and covers all major ship types. However, the P&I Club analysis of personal injuries and fatalities is, of course, limited to claims data and to those claims exceeding $100,000. Over the period 1987–97, an initial rise in claims in the late 1980s was followed by a fall in the number of major claims over the 1990s, with claims due to "ship failure" falling more rapidly than claims due to "human error". Some types of ship are over-represented in claims: not surprisingly, passenger ships accounted for a disproportionate number of personal injury claims, as did rig and supply ships, but the incidence of claims from the latter is falling. Data on cargo-carrying vessels from the Lloyd's Register of Shipping *World Casualty Statistics* show that 5,962 seafarer lives were lost at sea in the ten-year period 1989–99.[29] Considering these data in conjunction with world fleet crewing data,[30] evidence suggests that fatality rates vary by ship type. For example, in 1998, 20 per cent of the world's seafarers were employed on oil tankers, yet only 1.2 per cent of fatalities in this period occurred on vessels of this type. The United Kingdom P&I Club's analysis found ship failure to be greatest among a cohort of ships built between 1973 and 1978 and among ships from certain flag States (the Bahamas, Cyprus, Malta, Panama, Romania, the United States and, since 1993, the Russian Federation).[31] A British study of mortality showed that 40 per cent of British seafarers' deaths on FOC ships were due to occupational injuries and maritime disasters, whereas on British-registered ships such deaths accounted for only 15 per cent of the total.[32] "Human error" should not imply blame-worthy behaviour where it arises out of commercial pressures, falling crewing levels and turnaround times, inadequate training, excessive hours, fatigue and so on (see the section on occupational health below). Major claims of the United Kingdom P&I Club due to "human error" fell in the 1990s; the fall was especially steep in respect of crew and deck officer error, the likely reason being the downward trend in numbers of officers and crew in the same period, with a consequent overall reduction in personal injury.[33] "Human error" claims were disproportionately high in respect of medium-sized bulk carriers, probably reflecting trading patterns (with a greater likelihood of shorter voyages and more frequent berthing, discharging and loading).[34] A 1993 Japan Maritime Research Institute (JAMRI) report suggested that 53 per cent of casualties from grounding and 38 per cent of casualties from collisions were due to "less alert lookouts" and "dozing off during navigation";[35] in the United Kingdom, the Donaldson inquiry[36] suggested that fatigue was the primary, or a major contributory, cause of 70 to 80 per cent of marine pollution-causing accidents.

National occupational accident reporting schemes are subject to under-reporting and reporting bias, but analyses of such data can nevertheless be instructive. Hansen et al.[37] analysed the data on more than 2,000 reported accidents aboard Danish-registered merchant ships: fatal accidents and those causing permanent disabilities are most common on coasters and ro-ros, occur

> Box 5.2   The near grounding of the *Kotuku* tanker (off Cape Kidnappers, North Island, New Zealand, November 1997)
>
> While the ship was in Wellington Harbour, extra work was created by the need to change berths before discharging was completed. On leaving Wellington, the ship ran into heavy seas. The 02:00 hours position of the ship was misread and wrongly plotted on the chart by the 2nd officer, who had been on duty for 11 hours in the previous 24–hour period; he did not check the position independently. On the next watch, the 1st officer perpetuated this mistake every half hour for the next four hours; he did not check the position independently. The 1st officer had been suffering from tonsillitis for the past year. An operation to remove his tonsils had been scheduled for the previous week but had been postponed because the tanker company was unable to find anyone to relieve him. In the 24 hour period prior to the incident, the 1st Officer had been on duty for 15 hours. The day before that, he had been on duty for 12 and a half hours out of the 24. The officer on the next watch obtained a radar echo of land on the starboard side of the ship and brought it to the attention of the master, who altered course. In an interview immediately after the incident, the 1st officer said that he "was tired and the watch seemed like being in a fog". The investigator recommended that the certificates of the 1st and 2nd officers be suspended.
>
> Source: abridged from the *Report of the Maritime Safety Authority of New Zealand* (1997).

more frequently to ratings than to officers, and most frequently during the earlier part of the seafarer's trip (suggesting that unfamiliarity with tasks or environment may play a role in occupational injuries).

Fatigue can be attributed to many factors: the voyage cycle, the sea state, noise, vibration, climate, functional shipboard role and crewing levels (box 5.2). Changes in technology may also be contributing to a new source of seafarer fatigue: crews operating catamaran-designed fast ferries report additional fatigue (owing to the uneven acceleration to vertical and lateral movement) and drowsiness (owing to the fact that they are regularly taking medication to counter motion sickness).[38] Fatigue is likely to be less of a problem on long-haul ships and more of a problem on near-sea trade ships with their short passages, numerous port calls and small crews. The fact that at least one oil major will not hire any ships where the master keeps a watch may well exemplify a widespread problem in near-sea traders. A recent review of the literature on fatigue, health and injury among seafarers found that the risk of accidents occurring was greatest during the early hours of the morning; that environmental factors were related to sleep disturbances, fatigue and stress; that motion adversely affected cognitive and psychomotor performance; that seafarers reported higher levels of anxiety, greater workload, dissatisfaction with shift levels and sleep problems; and that circadian adaptation could only partially be achieved, at best, on four-on/eight-off shift patterns.[39]

Equipment failure was estimated to cause around 20 per cent of accidents to seafarers in an earlier ILO review.[40] In some areas of shipboard activity, the proportion of accidents attributed to equipment failure is very much greater: an international survey conducted by the ICS and the OCIMF found that 70 per cent of accidents associated with the lifeboat drills and launchings were caused by equipment failure.[41] On British-flagged ships alone, in a ten-year period there were 12 deaths and 87 injuries involving lifeboats and their launching systems.[42] One area in which equipment currently appears to be inadequate is that of wharf/gangplank/vessel perimeter barriers. National data from Australia,[43] Denmark[44] and the United Kingdom[45] all show very high rates of off-duty fatal injuries (the crews of British-registered vessels appear to suffer higher rates of fatal injuries off duty than on), but the most common cause of off-duty fatalities is that of falls into docks and rivers when returning to a berthed vessel from shore. Many of these falls are alcohol-related, but they only had fatal consequences because of inadequate and hazardous access arrangements. Fatal shipboard falls into holds and so on occur frequently, but many fatal and non-fatal injuries are sustained by falls down stairways in ship accommodation and engine-room areas. It is likely that falls are exacerbated by the steepness of ships' stairways, which typically have had steeper angles of inclination than the domestic and industrial norm (despite regulatory changes).[46] Poor physical working conditions (excessive noise, vibration and heat) contribute to accidents[47] as well as fatigue brought about by long working hours and disturbed patterns of sleep due to shiftwork.[48]

Injuries caused by exposure to chemicals remain common among seafarers. A total of 177 such injuries and fatalities were reported to the Danish maritime authorities between 1988 to 1996, from a fleet of approximately 800 ships crewed by about 9,500 seafarers. Eye injuries were particularly common, especially those due to exposure to caustic soda and cleaning detergents.[49]

Occupational health

Health surveys of workforces tend to show lower levels of morbidity (the incidence or prevalence of a disease or diseases in a population) than surveys of general populations. This is known to epidemiologists as the "healthy worker effect" and is a consequence of unhealthy and incapacitated individuals leaving the workforce or being prevented from joining it. Effective health surveys require the long-term follow-up of a cohort of seafarers over time, including those leaving the shipping industry; no such longitudinal surveys, however, exist.

The healthy worker effect can be expected to be strong in an occupation such as seafaring that has mandatory periodic medical examinations designed to screen out people with incapacities or chronic health problems: in 1998, 25,438 seafarers underwent medical examinations conducted by the United Kingdom's approved medical examiners, of which 672 seafarers failed their medicals and 2,172 seafarers were issued with restricted certificates; in the same year, there were 90 appeals but only 11 of these resulted in the seafarer being declared fit.[50] Similarly, analyses of death certification data by the occupation of the deceased tend to understate deaths to those in physically demanding jobs, since unfit people tend to leave such occupations early to take up more sedentary jobs before their deaths; in the case of seafarers, death certification data are also thought to be subject to a degree of undercounting, since a certain number of deaths occur abroad.[51] All these reasons would lead one to assume that seafarers' morbidity and mortality rates would be relatively low; in fact, reported levels are surprisingly high.

In respect of morbidity, the United Kingdom P&I Club reports rising numbers of repatriation and illness claims (with costs per claim averaging between $10,000 and $25,000),[52] and enhanced medical surveys of seafarers detect substantial morbidity among many seafarers who would probably have been passed fit at the standard examination. An enhanced examination was conducted on 977 Filipino crew in 1996/7, utilizing tests for blood count, liver function, hepatitis B, malaria, lung function and an electrocardiogram (ECG), at a cost of $80: it was found that 9.6 per cent of the crews were unfit, mostly because of abnormal liver function, hepatitis B or high blood pressure.[53] In a study of 135 Finnish pilots aged over 45, the results of physical examinations (mimicking the periodic medical examination) were compared with an enhanced examination using blood analyses, chest X-rays and exercise-ECG: many more cases of cardiovascular disease were detected in the latter examinations and the authors concluded that "the current periodic health examination does not seem to effectively prevent a person with a possible health defect from working as a sea pilot".[54] A major difficulty here is the fact that in most countries the approved medical practitioners who conduct these periodic examinations are typically general practitioners who have no direct access to specialized equipment or laboratories. For example, ILO/WHO guidelines lay down minimum in-service hearing standards: at least 30 decibels (dB), unaided, in the better ear and 40 dB, unaided, in the other ear within the frequencies 500, 1,000, 2,000 and 3,000 Hz, at distances of 3 metres and 2 metres respectively.[55] However, audiometric testing requires a soundproof room, to which general practitioners rarely have access. Nevertheless, substantial levels of serious morbidity are going undetected under the present system. Of the 672 seafarers who failed their British examinations in 1998, for example, 98 had hypertension, 62 had ischaemic heart disease, 54 diabetes, 32 asthma, 24 were alcohol dependent, 14 suffered from acute psychosis and 15 suffered from loss of hearing.[56]

In respect of mortality, Britain's *Occupational Health Decennial Supplement* data for 1995 can be taken as typical of seafarers' mortality data in the developed world, with British seafarers having high mortality rates for cancers (of the oral cavity, the pharynx, the liver and larynx), cirrhosis, pancreatitis and "other alcohol-related diseases". The editor commented that the findings were consistent with those in previous decennial supplements and "reflect unusually high consumption of alcohol among seafarers".[57] However, it should be pointed out that, although alcohol consumption undoubtedly plays a part, the possible role of hepatitis B and C in generating high rates of liver disease among seafarers has not yet been properly examined, although fragmentary data are already available showing high prevalences of hepatitis B in some national seafaring populations.[58] Cardiovascular diseases can be expected to be a common cause of death among seafarers in the developed world, although cardiovascular deaths are also common among some developing world seafaring populations, such as Indian ratings.[59] Suicide rates are reported to be high among seafarers from some OECD countries such as Britain[60] and Denmark,[61] compared with other occupational groups, although suicides are not confined to the crews of the industrialized world: for example, 14 of 449 recorded deaths of Indian seafarers in the period 1990–96 have been attributed to suicide.[62]

Exposure to toxic and carcinogenic materials is also responsible for a significant number of deaths and acute and chronic illnesses. The Norwegian Cancer Research Institute has found that mesothelioma deaths are six times more common among Norwegian ships' engineers and engine ratings than among the general population,[63] as a likely consequence of the crew being exposed to asbestos in the past. Shipping companies are now reported to be facing a flood of claims as a result of negligence in exposing employees to asbestos dust in the 1950s and 60s.[64] Seafarers have also been found to have a significantly greater risk of getting gastric cancer, which has been attributed to over-exposure to certain chemicals, including nitrogen oxides and mineral dusts.[65] Among Danish seafarers, cancers are more common among the engine than deck crew.[66] Research has also shown increases in the incidence of skin cancers among younger seafarers.[67] Tanker crews are known to have particularly high rates of lung cancer, urogenital cancer[68] and leukaemia[69] because of their exposure to various carcinogenic agents, most notably benzene, but also to polycyclic aromatic hydrocarbon (PAH) compounds and organic lead compounds. Although new international regulations and technological improvements have undoubtedly reduced exposure to chemicals among tanker crews, shipboard studies indicate that levels of benzene exposure may still be too high.[70] Benzene exposure may also affect the central nervous system; central nervous system symptoms reported by individuals have been associated with high benzene exposure levels among tanker crews.[71]

Seafarers are also exposed to physical hazards to their health, particularly noise and vibration but also excessive heat and cold and harmful radiation from sunlight. The 1993 Joint ILO/WHO Committee on the Health of Seafarers stated that engine-room noise levels sometimes exceed 100 dB and living quarters noise sometimes exceeds 60 dB,[72] which can have an impact on a person's hearing, alertness and mental health. Measured noise levels on a range of Polish merchant ships have been shown to exceed acceptable levels for engine crews by an average of 1–2 dB, while audiometric testing at the beginning and end of voyages has revealed statistically significant temporary shifts in hearing thresholds, with the shift being more pronounced among engine-room crews.[73] Furthermore, shipboard performance testing has shown that crews subjected to high noise levels demonstrate slower reaction times and more lapses of attention.[74]

Ergonomic hazards increase the risk of injury and of musculo-skeletal disease. Seafarers are particularly susceptible to back injuries: the motion of the ship is counteracted by movement in the lumbar region, and back strain can also be exacerbated by holding and lifting loads in pitching seas.[75] The uneven acceleration rate in fast ferries results in a specific type of ship movement which induces a high level of sea-sickness and extreme physical tiredness.[76] Crews on such vessels have been reported to take large doses of sea-sickness medication, often for prolonged periods. Little is known about the health consequences of taking high levels of such medication long term; however, the short-term effects of drowsiness and lethargy are well-documented[77] and have been reported by fast ferry crew, along with subsequent concerns regarding a lowering of performance levels, particularly in emergency situations.

Seafarers are susceptible to infectious diseases, both as a result of shore and shipboard exposure. It is claimed that seafarers from industrialized countries have the highest prevalence of infectious diseases. Like other transport workers, and migrant workers, seafarers have high rates of sexually transmitted diseases (STDs): a 1991 review of studies on STDs among seafarers showed that rates of gonorrhoea in different national groups of seafarers were between five and 20 times as great as national average prevalences for males.[78] Prior infection with STDs (such as gonorrhoea and chancroid) is known to increase the risk of human immunodeficiency virus (HIV) transmission.

A recent paper on the sexual health of women seafarers aboard cruise ships reported that heterosexual relationships are a common feature of shipboard life but that restricted, and frequently non-confidential, access to ships' doctors is possibly making it difficult for women to obtain prescription contraceptives and for STDs to be diagnosed and treated. It was recommended that preboarding induction courses on sexual health and on the sexual risks for crews be introduced.[79]

Lifestyle studies show that seafarers are more likely than the general population to engage in a range of unhealthy behavioural habits. For example, a recent study of 1,806 Australian seafarers[80] showed that, compared with surveys of the Australian general public, seafarers smoke and drink more, exercise less and consume more sugar and fat. Danish seafarers have been found to smoke considerably more than the general population and those aged over 34 years are significantly more likely to be obese.[81] Female Danish seafarers have been found to adopt the same lifestyle of their male colleagues: they have a high risk of fatal accidents and suicide and an increased risk of dying of lung cancer and heart diseases, both of which probably reflect high tobacco consumption.[82]

Only comparatively recently has the mental health of seafarers started to receive the attention it deserves. High seafarer suicide rates have already been mentioned, but poor mental health can manifest itself in much less dramatic ways. Among the seafarers in the 1997 Australian study, 60 per cent reported moderate to high stress levels and 70 per cent reported poor quality sleep at sea, with masters, mates and pilots reporting higher incidences of stress, and pilots reporting the worst sleep quality.[83] Direct measurement (using wrist-worn actimeters) of sleep quality at sea and on shore among the crew of a European passenger ferry showed that seafarers working split shift patterns experienced the worst sleep disturbances.[84] The irregular shift patterns of marine pilots have been found to lead to stress-related difficulties, including social and domestic problems.[85] Ferry crews working to erratic schedules have been reported to take significantly more days off sick, have poorer sleep patterns and more consultations for insomnia than those working more predictable schedules.[86] High levels of stress have been reported by crews on vessels in the Finnish merchant fleet. Stress was found to be most strongly connected to work-related factors, including noise, occupation on board and unfair distribution of workload. An important predictor of both stress and depression was worry about loved ones ashore (box 5.3).[87] In the Australian study, the "home–work interface" was the highest ranked source of stress for all seafaring groups,[88] while a parallel Australian study of the wives and families of Great Barrier Reef pilots found that pilotage work had an impact on the mental health of the pilots' wives, with 14 per cent being assessed as having

Shipboard life and work – II

> Box 5.3 "I could have quite easily jumped over the side"
>
> I used to cry on the ship. I used to sit there, I used to lie there and I used to work out what I was going to say. You know, when I get home this time, I'm going to tell them [the children], I'm going to explain it and I used to cry on the ship. I knew I couldn't do it. I was quite suicidal a couple of times. I could have quite easily jumped over the side on a couple of occasions, I was so, I was so down. [. . .] Once I mean, you know, I walked down to the end of the ship and I was just standing on the end and I, it was about 10 o'clock at night, nobody would have noticed. I'd gone to bed. You know, we'd had a few drinks in the bar. I'd gone up to the cabin. Nobody would have missed me.
>
> British chief engineer talking about his feelings on his divorce while aboard ship
>
> It's very easy when you're working in an engine room. There are two points in the day where you actively have to come back and that's for a smoke at 10 o'clock and at 3 o'clock, so at those points that's all there is. No one has to know, it's very easy to sit there and cry your eyes out if you wanted to. There are so many spaces where people don't go to very often. The engine room is very noisy, so you can scream your head off and somebody standing next to you would still have a job hearing you.
>
> British junior engineer

high anxiety levels and 9 per cent being depressed, higher prevalences than would be found in a normal population sample.[89]

The medical examination for seafarers includes an assessment of mental health. Acute psychosis, persistent alcohol abuse (dependency), a history of drug or substance abuse in the past five years and chronic or recurrent neurosis all lead to a seafarer being assessed as permanently unfit for sea duty.[90] Seafarers suffering from neuroses that are neither chronic nor recurrent can be assessed as temporally unfit, and this assessment is reviewed after a number of weeks.[91] The data from the 1998 medical examinations of British-based practitioners showed that mental health problems accounted for approximately one in ten medical examination failures: 70 of the 672 failures in this period were due to mental disorders. It is unclear how effective the medical examination is at screening for psychological health. However, the high rates of suicide among seafarers suggest that a significant number of mental health problems may still be going undetected.

Changes in working conditions can effect the psychological well-being of seafarers. In particular, reduced crewing levels and the rise in single-person tasking can lead to isolation problems.[92] Research has shown that marginality is a central feature of a seafarer's lifestyle.[93] A study of Danish seafarers found that nearly half (47 per cent) of those working on cargo ships and almost a third (28 per cent) of those working on passenger ships experienced a feeling of loneliness "often" or "sometimes". This can also extend to leisure time while aboard. Research on the free-time leisure activities of Finnish seafarers aboard cargo ships showed that most of the seafarers spent their leisure time alone, the most popular activity aboard being reading. Those seafarers who pursued "sociable" activities aboard were found to be less likely than others to suffer from anxiety or depression.[94] Problems of social isolation may be exacerbated for female seafarers in the predominantly male domain of cargo shipping, where sexual harassment is a common problem.[95]

The traumatic nature of many incidents at sea, whether these relate to vessel casualties, acts of piracy, accidents and injuries or the death of a crew member, is scarcely acknowledged in the literature or research. It is likely, however, that witnessing or experiencing such incidents can potentially have a negative impact on a person's mental health. It has been suggested that shipping companies would benefit from adopting a model of critical incident stress debriefing (CISD), a method successfully used to reduce suffering from stress-related ailments such as insomnia, depression and anger.[96]

Shipboard medical care is normally provided by fellow seafarers who have undergone paramedic training courses. Although some trainees receive training of a high standard, an international investigation of training standards has shown considerable cross-national variations in standards.[97] Furthermore, the prescribed international training standards were not being effectively enforced, and it was believed that seafarers were not receiving the same quality of care as people in land-based occupations. Access to health care can even be restricted for those crews sailing with qualified medical professionals. Research with seafarers on cruise vessels has found that access to the ship's doctor can be limited, particularly for lower ranking crew.[98] Concern has also been expressed about the range of medical supplies aboard ship, and the absence of basic equipment and drugs for life-threatening emergencies on passenger ferries.[99] Reduced access to professional medical care and supplies can have dramatic consequences. An analysis of the records held by the Singapore Mercantile Marine Office on death by disease on board Singapore ships found that radio medical advice was sought in only two of the total 69 cases. Eight of those who had died on board had seen a doctor and been declared fit, which suggests deficiencies in port medical services or pressures on port doctors to avoid costly repatriations.[100]

Notes

[1] P. H. Fricke: *The social structure of crews of British dry cargo merchant ships: A study of the organization and environment of an occupation* (Cardiff, University of Wales Institute of Science and Technology, Department of Maritime Studies, 1972).

[2] N. A. Daniels et al.: "Travellers' diarrhoea at sea: Three outbreaks of waterborne enterotoxigenic *Escherichia coli* on cruise ships", in *Journal of Infectious Diseases*, 2000, Vol. 181(4), pp. 1491–1495; D. Koo, K. Maloney and R. Tauxe: "Epidemiology of diarrhoea disease outbreaks on cruise ships", in *Journal of the American Medical Association*, 1986, Vol. 275(7), pp. 545–547.

[3] H. L. Hansen et al.: "Lifestyle, nutritional status and working conditions of Danish sailors", in *Travel Medicine International*, 1994, Vol. 12(4), pp. 139–143.

[4] MCA: *Doctors' Annual return of medical examinations of seafarers: 1 January 1998–31 December 1998*, MC/18/3/069/17 (Southampton, 1999).

[5] A. W. Parker et al.: *A survey of the health, stress and fatigue of Australian seafarers* (Canberra, Australian Maritime Safety Authority, 1997).

[6] S. Mennell, A. Murcott and A. H. van Otterloo: *The sociology of food, eating, diet and culture* (London, Sage, 1994).

[7] A. Meers, A. Maasen and P. Verhaegen: "Subjective health after six months and after four years of shiftwork", in *Ergonomics*, 1978, Vol. 21, pp. 857–859; J. Rutenfranz, P. Knauth, and D. Angersbach: "Shiftwork issues", in L. C. Johnson et al. (eds.): *Biological rhythms, sleep and shift work* (London, Spectrum Publications, 1981); D. I. Tepas: "Do eating and drinking habits interact with work schedule variables?", in *Work and Stress*, 1990, Vol. 4, pp. 203–211; S. Wyatt and R. Marriot: "Night work and shift changes", in *British Journal of Industrial Medicine*, 1953, Vol. 10, pp. 164–172.

[8] J. C. Duchon and C. M. Keran: "Relationships among shiftworker eating habits, eating satisfaction, and self-reported health in a population of US miners", *Work and Stress*, 1990, Vol. 4, pp. 111–120.

[9] A. Reinberg et al.: "Cicadian and ultracicadian rhythms in the feeding behaviour and nutrient intakes of oil refinery operators with shiftwork every three to four days", in *Diabète et Métabolisme*, 1979, Vol. 5, pp. 33–41.

[10] P. J. Sparks: "Questionnaire survey of masters, mates and pilots of a State ferries system on health, social and performance indices relevant to shift work", in *American Journal of Industrial Medicine*, 1992, Vol. 21, pp. 507–516.

[11] K. Nakamura et al.: "Increases in body mass index and waist circumference as outcomes of working overtime", in *Occupational Medicine*, 1998, Vol. 48(3), pp. 169–173.

[12] H. Saarni and J. Pentti: "Free-time activities among seafarers on board Finnish cargo ships", in *Bulletin of the Institute of Maritime and Tropical Medicine in Gdynia*, 1996, Vol. 47, pp. 33–43.

[13] A. D. Duckworth: "Crew accommodation for the improved type of dry cargo vessel", in *The Royal Institute of Naval Architects*, 1956, Vol. 98, pp. 432–442.

[14] J. G. D. Cain and M. R. Hatfield: "New concepts in the design of shipboard accommodation and working spaces", in *The Royal Institute of Naval Architects*, 1979, Vol. 121, pp. 251–266; M. Meek and N. Ward: "Accommodation in ships", in *The Royal Institute of Naval Architects*, 1973, Vol. 115, pp. 201–218.

[15] E. Holmes: "Crews' accommodation in merchant ships", in *The Royal Institute of Naval Architects*, 1947, Vol. 89, pp. 394–399.

[16] Duckworth, op. cit.

[17] Meek and Ward, op. cit., p. 208.

[18] Cain and Hatfield, op. cit.

[19] ibid.

[20] Holmes, op. cit.

[21] C. Hill: *Maritime law* (London, Lloyd's of London Press, 1995, 4th edition).

[22] *Lloyd's List* Archive.

[23] ILO: *Conditions in ships flying the Panama flag* (Geneva, 1950).

[24] H. L. Hansen: "Surveillance of deaths on board Danish merchant ships 1986–93: Implications for prevention", in *Journal of Occupational and Environmental Medicine*, 1996, Vol. 53(4), pp. 269–275.

[25] Office of Population Censuses and Surveys: *Occupational health decennial supplement*, Series DS No. 10 (London, HMSO, 1995).

[26] ILO: *Health protection and medical care for seafarers*, Report III, Preparatory Technical Maritime Conference (Geneva, 1986). Quoted in Joint ILO/WHO Committee on the Health of Seafarers: *Occupational accidents among seafarers resulting in personal injuries, damage to their general health and fatalities*, Working Paper No. 1 (Geneva, 1993).

[27] S. Roberts: *Occupational mortality among merchant seafarers in the British, Singapore and Hong Kong fleets 1981–1995* (Cardiff, SIRC, 1998a).

[28] United Kingdom P&I Club: *Analysis of major claims: Ten-year trends in maritime risk* (London, Thomas Miller P&I Ltd, 1999a).

[29] Quoted in OECD: *The cost to users of sub-standard shipping* (Paris, Directorate for Science Technology and Industry, 2001).

[30] T. Lane et al.: *Crewing the international merchant fleet* (Redhill, Lloyd's Register–Fairplay, 2002).

[31] United Kingdom P&I Club, 1999a, op. cit.

[32] S. Roberts: *Occupational mortality among British merchant seafarers: A comparison between British and foreign fleets 1986–89* (Cardiff, SIRC, 1998b).

[33] United Kingdom P&I Club, 1999a, op. cit.

[34] ibid.

[35] Quoted in A. Selander: "Working at sea: Safety and health considerations", in *Seafarers' safety and health: Conference proceedings* (Cardiff, SIRC, 1995).

[36] Lord Donaldson inquiry into the prevention of pollution from merchant ships: *Safer ships, Cleaner seas* (London, HMSO, 1994).

[37] H. L. Hansen, D. Nielsen and M. Frydenberg: "Occupational accidents aboard merchant ships", in *Occupational and Environmental Medicine*, 2002, Vol. 59(2), pp. 85–91.

[38] D. Grewal: *Report on fast ferry operations in Australia* (Cardiff, SIRC, 2000).

[39] A. Collins, V. Matthews and R. McNamara: *Fatigue, health and injury among seafarers and workers on offshore installations: A review*. Technical Report Series No. 1 (Cardiff, SIRC/Centre for Occupational and Health Psychology, 2000).

[40] Joint ILO/WHO Committee on the Health of Seafarers, op. cit.

[41] D. Dearsley: "Working at sea: A shipowner's view", in *Seafarers' safety and health: Conference proceedings* (Cardiff, SIRC, 1995).

[42] *Lloyd's List* (London), 7 Mar. 2001.

[43] C. Mayhew: *Work-related traumatic deaths of British and Australian seafarers: What are the causes and how can they be prevented?* (Cardiff, SIRC, 1999).

[44] Hansen, op. cit.

[45] Office of Population Censuses and Surveys, op. cit.

[46] D. M. Anderson: "From accident report to design problems: A study of accidents on board ship", in *Ergonomics*, Vol. 26(1), 1983, pp. 43–50.

[47] Joint ILO/WHO Committee on the Health of Seafarers, op. cit.

[48] L. A. Reyner and S. D. Baulk: *Fatigue in ferry crews: A pilot survey* (Loughborough, Sleep Research Group, 1998).

[49] H. L. Hansen and G. Pederson: "Influence of occupational accidents and deaths related to lifestyle on mortality among seafarers", in *International Journal of Epidemiology*, 1996, Vol. 25, pp. 1237–1243.

[50] MCA, op. cit.

[51] Office of Population Censuses and Surveys, op. cit.

[52] United Kingdom P&I Club: *The UK Club's crew fitness project* (London, Thomas Miller P&I Ltd., 1999b), available at: http://www.ukpandi.com/ [22.08.2003].

[53] ibid.

[54] H. Saarni et al.: "Is there a need for change of health examinations for sea pilots?", in *Bulletin of the Institute of Maritime and Tropical Medicine in Gdynia*, 1992, Vol. 43, pp. 25–34.

[55] ILO/WHO: *Consultation on guidelines for conducting pre-sea and periodic medical fitness examinations for seafarers* (Geneva, 1997).

[56] MCA, op. cit.

[57] Office of Population Censuses and Surveys, op. cit.

[58] United Kingdom P&I Club, op. cit., 1999b; H. L. Hansen, H. K. Hansen and P. L. Andersen: "Incidence and relative risk for hepatitis A, hepatitis B and tuberculosis and occurrence of malaria among merchant seamen", in *Scandinavian Journal of Infectious Diseases*, 1996, Vol. 28, pp. 107–110.

[59] B. L. Barnes: *The acquisition and analysis of global statistics on serious injuries and fatalities of seafarers as a result of accidents on board ship: An Indian perspective* (Cardiff, SIRC, 1997).

[60] Mayhew, op. cit.

[61] L. P. A. Brandt et al.: "Mortality among Danish merchant seamen 1970–1985", in *American Journal of Industrial Medicine*, 1994, Vol. 25, pp. 867–876.

[62] Barnes, op. cit.

[63] Sigmond Eriksen, personal communication.

[64] *Lloyd's List*, 6 Feb. 2001.

[65] P. Cocco et al.:"Occupational exposures as risk factors for gastric cancer in Italy", in *Cancer Causes and Control*, 1994, Vol. 5(3), pp. 241–248.

[66] Brandt et al., op. cit.

[67] E. Pukkala and H. Saarni: "Cancer incidence amongst Finnish seafarers, 1967–1992", in *Cancer Causes and Control*, 1996, Vol. 7, pp. 231–239.

[68] B. E. Moen, R. Riise and A. Helseth: "Cancer among captains and mates on Norwegian tankers", in *APMIS*, 1990, Vol. 98, pp. 185–190.

[69] R. Nilsson et al.: "Symptoms, lung and liver function, blood counts and genotoxic effects in coastal tanker crews", in *International Archives of Occupational and Environmental Health*, 1997, Vol. 69, pp. 392–398.

[70] B. E. Moen et al.: "Exposure of the deck crew to carcinogenic agents on oil product tankers", in *Annals of Occupational Hygiene*, 1995, Vol. 39, pp. 347–361.

[71] ibid.

[72] Joint ILO/WHO Committee on the Health of Seafarers, op. cit.

[73] C. Szczepanski and B. Otto: "Evaluation of exposure to noise in seafarers on several types of vessels in the Polish merchant navy", in *Bulletin of the Institute of Maritime and Tropical Medicine in Gdynia*, 1995, Vol. 46, pp. 13–17.

[74] A. Smith: "Offshore fatigue: A study of ships in the offshore oil industry", in *Symposium 2001 Proceedings* (Cardiff, SIRC, 2001).

[75] C. Torner et al.: "Working on a moving surface: A biomechanical analysis of musculo-skeletal load due to ship motions in combination with work", in *Ergonomics*, 1994, Vol. 37(2), pp. 345–362.

[76] Grewal, op. cit.

[77] See, for example, T. E. Brown and D. L. Eckberg: "Promethazine affects autonomic cardiovascular mechanisms minimally", in *Journal of Pharmacology and Experimental Therapeutics*, 1997, Vol. 282(2), pp. 839–844.

[78] P. Vuksanovic and A. Low: "Venereal diseases and AIDS among seafarers", in *Travel Medicine International*, 1991, Vol. 9, pp. 121–123.

[79] M. Thomas: "Sexual health of women working aboard cruise ships", in *Health Education Journal*, 2003, Vol. 62(3).

[80] Parker et al., op. cit.

[81] Hansen et al., op. cit.

[82] H. L. Hansen and J. Jensen: "Female seafarers adopt the high risk lifestyle of male seafarers", in *Journal of Occupational and Environmental Medicine*, 1998, Vol. 55(1), pp. 49–51.

[83] Parker et al., op. cit.

[84] Reyner and Baulk, op. cit.

[85] A. W. Parker, A. Clavarino and L. M. Hubinger: *The impact of Great Barrier Reef pilotage work on wives and families* (Canberra, Australian Maritime Safety Authority, 1998).

[86] Sparks, op. cit.

[87] A. Elo: "Health and stress of seafarers", in *Scandinavian Journal of Work and Health*, 1985, Vol. 11, pp. 427–432.

[88] Parker et al., 1997, op. cit.

[89] Parker et al., 1998, op. cit.

[90] MCA, op. cit.

[91] ibid.

[92] C. J. Forsyth and W. B. Bankston: "The social psychological consequence of a life at sea: A causal model", in *Maritime Policy & Management*, 1984, Vol. 11(2), pp. 123–134.

[93] ibid.

[94] Elo, op. cit.

[95] ILO: *Women seafarers: Global employment policies and practices* (Geneva, 2003); M. Zhao: *Women seafarers in the EC: A preliminary report based on German and UK case studies* (Cardiff, SIRC, 1998).

[96] H. Saarni, S. Saari and U. Hakkinen: "Critical incident stress debriefing (CISD) in a shipping company", in *International Maritime Health*, 1999, Vol. 50 (1–4), pp. 49–56.

[97] T. Patel: *An analysis and evaluation of international maritime medical training standards* (Cardiff, SIRC, 1998).

[98] ILO, op. cit.

[99] M. S. J. Reilly: "Safety at sea: A forgotten frontier?", editorial in *British Journal of Industrial Medicine*, 1987, Vol. 44, pp. 1–6.

[100] D. Nielson et al.: "Deaths due to disease of seafarers on board Singapore ships", in *International Maritime Health*, 2000, Vol. 51(1–4), pp. 20–29.

6

SEAFARERS' FAMILIES

An absent father's instructions to his young daughter

Introduction

>A seafarer is a peculiar animal. He is a stranger when he comes ashore and is the odd man out in almost any situation. We cater for the loneliness of the seafarer – that might sum the whole thing up. When you come home, you stick out like a sore thumb – the world has gone on without you and it is not going to stop to fit you into it. Often, this is part of the loneliness of seafarers. A man goes to sea, he begins to look forward to coming home. He begins to wish his time away at sea; that's a dangerous thing for a man to do. He is in danger of losing his soul, I would say – his sense of being. He comes ashore and it's fiesta time for him and nobody else. All too often the leave you look forward to falls flat on its face.
>
> Padre in charge of a Seaman's Mission[1]

One thing all seafarers have in common, regardless of rank, nationality or trade, is the fact that their work separates them from their families. Seafarers' families are an important but neglected aspect of seafaring. Family members, including parents, siblings, partners, children and extended family, can all have an impact on the experiences of seafarers and on the decisions they make during their maritime career. Families can have a significant effect on a person's entry into the industry. For example, research on women seafarers has found that, for many, the decision to embark upon a career at sea was precipitated by having a seafaring relative.[2] Some families provide initial financial assistance for maritime education and training and may economically facilitate a seafarer's departures to sea.[3] When the seafarer is at sea, families can give a sense of purpose and meaning to a seafarer's life and work aboard ship.[4] They provide seafarers with an important source of contact and communication during long tours of duty and a base to return to during their leave periods. Families can also play a decisive role in a seafarer's length of service: separation from family has been found to be one of the most stressful aspects of a seafarer's life and can have a strong influence on whether a seafarer stays at sea or not.[5]

Despite the evidence of the importance of the family in seafarers' maritime careers, seafarers' family relations, the role of the family and the experiences of seafarers' partners and family members have largely been neglected as a topic of maritime research and literature. Drawing on the little research there is as well as accounts of seafarers and their families, this chapter looks specifically at these issues. It begins with an examination of the experiences of seafarers and their families, both when the seafarer is at sea and ashore. It then goes on to consider the impact of intermittent separation on seafarers' health and safety and on the health of their partners. Social isolation and the importance of the family as a means of social support are then looked at, followed by a discussion of ship–shore communication and its role in promoting and sustaining family life. The final section of this chapter examines company policies and their impact on the career and family life of seafarers.[6]

Seafarers and their families

The demands of paid employment invariably (although not exclusively) require workers to be separated from their families. Seafarers are not unusual in this. However, such separations can become significant when considerable portions of time are spent away from partners and families. For seafarers, ratios of leave to work vary, but even under the most favourable employment conditions seafarers are likely to spend at least six months of any year at sea. For seafarers in weaker labour market positions, spending ten months or more working aboard ship, with only a couple of months (unpaid) leave before returning to sea, is not unusual. Such patterns of work inevitably have an impact on family life, while prolonged absences from families correspondingly affect seafarers' experiences of their work.

The stresses suffered by seafarers as a result of being away from home and their families have been documented in the research literature (see the section in this chapter on health and safety).[7] These strains can, in part, reflect the emotional consequences of being separated from close family members. Seafarers can also be anxious about matters relating to family members, such as worries about chronically ill loved ones, the sexual fidelity of a partner, or the problematic behaviour of a disruptive child. Such anxieties can take on increased significance when the seafarer is physically absent for considerable periods of time, and may be heightened by restricted opportunities to communicate frequently enough with those ashore (see the section on ship–shore communication). In addition, seafarers may be worried about their family's general well-being and the day-to-day running of practical household matters in their absence. Seafarers recognize the demands of such periods of separation on their partners and on the importance of having a "good seafarer's wife" (typically described as "independent" and "able to cope"), who can manage the home and family for prolonged periods alone. As one senior officer commented:

> If she's the sort of wife who has to ask her husband [...] about everything, you will never succeed.[8]

The absences of seafarers inevitably have an impact on their partners and families. Women speak of missing the companionship of their partner as well as the physical intimacy, affection and practical support in household and family matters.[9] Research carried out on the partners of seafarers in India and the Philippines found that many suffer from considerable levels of anxiety associated with the absence of the seafaring partner. These worries were predominantly related to the seafarers' health and safety, but women additionally reported being concerned about their partner's sexual fidelity.[10] Research carried out in Australia on seafarers' wives found that nearly half (42 per cent) the women felt that their relationship with their partner was greatly at risk because of the seafaring lifestyle, with 25 per cent believing that their partner was having or had had an affair.[11]

Periods of separation can be particularly demanding for couples with young children: seafarers miss their children, and their partners have to cope with the demands of parenthood and all its associated decisions on their own.[12] Some seafarers' wives seem to find that their social lives are more restricted when their husbands are absent, feeling that many events are inappropriate without their partner;[13] additionally, some are concerned that they might attract unwanted sexual attention were they to attend events unaccompanied.[14]

However, life on returning home isn't automatically rosy. Prolonged separations can have a dramatic impact on the lives of families, with children scarcely knowing their absent parent and partners feeling that their lives are more "normal" when their "other half" is at sea.[15] Some partners become so adept at managing the home and family alone that, on their return home, seafarers can become disillusioned on the realization that their family has functioned successfully in their absence. As one seafarer commented: "I always felt, not as if I wasn't important, but that they could survive without me."[16]

The problems mentioned above are similar to those found in research carried out on military personnel. A study that included British Royal Navy wives found that, as the women became more experienced at coping alone, tensions moved from coping with the absence of the partner to reintegrating them into the household on their return home.[17] More practised naval wives were said to feign helplessness when their husbands were home in order to minimize the tension caused by husbands' feelings of emasculation as a result of their partners' evident competence.[18] Similarly, earlier research into the family lives of trawler men also reflected this dilemma: husbands were reported to want their wives to be independent and good managers, but if they became too self-reliant, the men felt that they were loved only for their pay packets.[19]

There are other factors that can lead to problems during seafarers' periods of leave. Their intermittent presence at home can make it difficult for them to develop and maintain shore-based friendships, which can result in loneliness or high levels of dependency on partners and immediate family for social contact. Even where friendships are maintained, the work patterns and commitments of people in shore-based employment often mean that seafarers still spend a significant amount of their free time alone. Indeed, some seafarers can find themselves looking forward to returning to sea because of long and unstructured periods of leave.[20]

Problems associated with seafaring work patterns can peak during the transitional periods from ship to shore and from home back to sea.[21] On their return home, seafarers have to make the difficult adjustment between the dramatically different worlds of work and home, while their partners have to get used to having another adult in the household again.[22] Tensions develop when seafarers first return home and unwind and adjust to family life again.[23] Increased workloads because of reduced crewing levels and less job security have led to a rise in the levels of stress and fatigue,[24] which have an impact on both work and family life.[25] Seafarers may return home physically exhausted, emotionally tense and unable to relax and "switch off" immediately from their shipboard responsibilities.[26] Conflict can also occur as seafarers attempt to assume the position of "head of the household".[27] The period before a seafarer's return to sea can also be fraught with tension as couples anticipate the departure and seafarers become anxious about completing practical tasks and meeting social obligations before returning to sea.[28]

Health and safety

Research suggests that seafaring work patterns and the associated intermittent absences of seafarers from their families can have detrimental consequences on both health and safety. A study of Australian seafarers found that the "home/work interface" was reported to be the greatest source of stress for them, regardless of rank,[29] findings that have been reiterated by studies of workers in the offshore industries.[30] These findings reflect earlier research with Polish trawler crews and seafarers, where again, periods of separation from family and friends were found to be the most frequently cited stress factor associated with their work (ranked highest by 84 per cent of fishermen and 59 per cent of seafarers, respectively).[31] Research work carried out on harbour physicians in Rotterdam, the Netherlands, identified three main psychological problems among seafarers: loneliness, homesickness and "burn-out" syndrome. These problems were primarily caused by long periods away from home, the decline in the number of seafarers per ship and increased automation.[32] The stress associated with frequent absences from home can become particularly acute when there is a family crisis. Such anxieties can be especially difficult for seafarers to deal with while at sea, since many seafarers find it difficult to speak about emotional domestic problems and seafarers cannot draw on shore-based social networks, which they might normally turn to for support.[33] Living with family problems while at sea can have severe consequences: investigations into suicide at sea have identified the role of marital and family problems as a contributory factor.[34]

In addition to affecting a seafarer's health, anxieties about family members and loneliness caused by prolonged separations and the lack of opportunity for any contact can have an impact on work performance, which may have significant repercussions on safety in the workplace. Research carried out on airline pilots has suggested that domestic stress and other major life events can have a detrimental effect on a pilot's judgement and well-being.[35] The importance of the spouse as a social support system, enabling the pilot to cope with stress, has been acknowledged by the aviation industry, along with the specific problems associated with a marriage where one partner is frequently absent.[36] Indeed, even where there are no perceived problems in family relations, the emotional deprivation associated with prolonged absences from partners and loved ones can lead to psychological deterioration and increased rates of emotional tension, which, in turn, may lead to a rise in stress levels, emotional alertness and aggression, all of which threaten individual and workplace health and safety.[37] Behavioural changes as a result of family and relationship problems have frequently been reported in research on British seafarers.[38] As one senior officer recalled:

> Another guy actually comes to mind – he's another engineer. He was just really obnoxious and nasty to everyone for quite a while and then we sort of found out – he got violent one night with the second mate after a night of drinking in a port – that his missus was sort of carrying on behind his back, you know. And

he didn't talk about it at all until, "That bitch, I've divorced her", that sort of thing. So yeah, but I mean that was the way that guy reacted, you know. He didn't tell anyone at all – he was just, like, sort of miserable and sort of horrible.[39]

Finally, although seafarers' partners do not have the pressures of physically having to leave their homes and families, there is some evidence to suggest that their partners' intermittent absences can have a detrimental effect on their own health: the rates of depression and anxiety among seafarers' partners are higher than in the general population.[40] An Australian study of seafarers' wives found that 83 per cent of the respondents reported some degree of stress when their partners were due home or about to return to sea, with nearly one in ten (8 per cent) reporting that they took medication to help them cope.[41]

Social isolation aboard and ashore

The relationships between couples and families have become increasingly important in meeting the emotional and social needs of individuals,[42] and are arguably of particular importance to seafarers working in the industry today. Historically, seafarers were known to have a workplace culture that promoted strong, solidary friendships.[43] However, reduced crewing levels, fast turnaround times, increased automation and longer working hours mean that seafarers are forming fewer on-board friendships, which is leading to concerns that many are leading increasingly isolated lives.[44] Modern crewing patterns, including small crews (reflected in single-person tasking), employment by contract, unsynchronized leave periods and geographical separation can mean that close friendships are difficult to instigate and maintain. Research carried out on British seafarers suggests that friendships on board are typically restricted to working relationships of the nature of "on-board acquaintances" as opposed to close, confiding relationships. As one junior officer explained:

> You know them, but you don't really know them. [...] You have nothing to do with them outside work – basically it's like any job. Unless there are a couple who are really on the same wavelength as you.[45]

Officers can find developing good friendships particularly problematic, since they may feel that they need to keep their distance from junior colleagues in order to maintain respect and authority. Women seafarers on cargo vessels also find themselves socially isolated owing to the huge gender imbalance on board.[46]

Not only can seafarers find it difficult to form close, long-term friendships while at sea, many find that maintaining shore-based friendships is far from easy; long absences and the cost of ship–shore communication do not facilitate close friendships. Seafarers, therefore, tend to rely to a very large extent on their partners and immediate family as a means of social support and as a link to wider social networks.[47] As Fricke has noted: "The wife provides the vicarious link with society ashore for the married officer through the provision of home and a network of friends."[48] In this context, the consequences of a relationship breakdown can be particularly severe.

Ship–shore communication

Opportunities to communicate ship–shore can potentially have a considerable impact on the experience of separation for both seafarers and their partners. Regular contact can be crucial in maintaining good relationships with the family and shore-based life;[49] too little contact can lead to the decline and eventual breakdown of relationships.[50] Contact with home is important for a number of reasons: to allay fears; to maintain close relationships; to improve seafarers' morale; as a way of relieving stress (on board and at home); and to maintain good relationships with children. For unmarried couples whose marriages are being arranged, ship–shore communication can be vital, not just to sustain the relationship but for the couple to get to know each other in the first place. An Indian wife of a seafarer commented:

> He kept on ringing me up from every port, every port. There's no money but it didn't matter. He just kept talking. I said, "It's becoming expensive." But he said, "No, no. You keep on talking to me." Then he called his mother and his father. He kept on talking to them. After all that, I got to know him. Because initially, we didn't know each other at all.[51]

The importance of being able to get in touch with family can increase at various points within a voyage and at certain times in a seafarer's career. For example, making contact can become particularly important when family members are ill, a situation that can lead to a dramatic rise in stress levels for the seafarer.[52] Furthermore, many seafarers are now working in conditions that make it difficult to instigate and maintain shipboard relationships, and consequently rely more and more on networks at home for social support.

The range of communication facilities available to seafarers includes faxes and satellite telephone calls. However, research suggests that traditional letter writing continues to be an important means of keeping in touch. Letters are valued for their tangible nature and for the fact they can be "revisited", that is, re-read. Indeed, in the routine, monotony and isolation of shipboard life, the arrival of mail aboard ship can take on a considerable degree of significance,[53] as a junior officer explained:

> It's a very big, very big part of keeping the morale up in the ship – the mail thing. [...] It's another means of communicating with home and you're thinking, "Well, are they, the office, committed in sending it?" I don't know if they realize how important it is. But you do see a new change sort of thing, if mail comes or if mail doesn't come.[54]

Advances in communication technology have undoubtedly increased opportunities for seafarers and their families to make contact on a more regular basis. Indeed, such developments have been found to be of considerable significance in the lives of work-separated couples.[55] Email and access to cheaper international telephone calls (on coastal routes) via mobile phones have been particularly welcomed by seafarers and their families, and valued, among other things, for the immediacy of contact and relatively low cost.[56] It has been found that communicating by email and mobile phone allows seafarers to keep up with the small everyday events that might not necessarily be reported in a letter or mentioned on their return home. Retaining a sense of "participating" in home life can considerably reduce the stress of intermittent absences on both seafarers and their partners and can be vital for seafarers when dealing with the transition between ship and home. In a study of seafaring and family life, two British senior officers commented:

> [I'm] constantly in touch with her by email, so it's like I'm away but I'm not away.

> And, it [email] does help that period when you come home, because you do know what's going on.[57]

Despite the potential to improve communication opportunities for seafarers, the shipping industry has, in general, been slow to utilize computers and telecommunication facilities, particularly on board vessels.[58] Indeed, research into the communication patterns of seafarers has shown that INMARSAT communication services, which are often extremely expensive, are widely used in ship–shore communications.[59] For those seafarers on both coastal and deep-sea routes, email is an inexpensive and easy way to keep in touch. However, email access continues to be limited – it is often restricted to officers – and is impeded by the fact that many seafarers may not be computer-literate and that family and friends ashore may also lack access.[60] Developments in telephone technology mean that seafarers can phone home using mobile phones in national and international waters as long as the ship is in port or within close range of land. However, for those on deep-sea routes, this service is limited and access is also restricted because of cost. Modern technology can be expensive: in addition to everyday running expenses, the initial purchase of equipment can involve a large financial outlay. However, research seems to suggest that seafaring families have higher rates of ownership of personal computers and mobile phones than the general population.[61]

Company policies and their impact on family life

The effect of seafaring work patterns on family life is not uniform: conditions of service can dramatically influence the experience for both seafarers and their families. The length of tour of duty and the ratio of shore to sea-time can vary considerably between seafarers. For those seafarers employed by voyage, leave time can be marred by the fact that no money is coming in as well as concerns about getting another contract.[62] Access to cheaper communication facilities, shorter tours of duty and opportunities for families to sail together can all help seafarers and their families maintain good relationships and reduce the disruption of a seafaring career on family life.

As the shipping industry has become increasingly regulated, so the demands made on seafarers to ensure that they meet industry training standards (such as STCW-95) have grown. Since they are unable to attend courses while at sea, seafarers often have no choice but to complete prerequisite courses during their periods of leave. Such training courses can be substantial in duration (some can last up to three months)[63] and in financial cost to the seafarer. In the context of a leave period of perhaps eight weeks, even relatively short courses can present a significant encroachment on leave time and on the time available with partners and families, as a second engineer's wife in China bemoaned:

> It is an ocean-going vessel and the voyage lasts for a minimum of 11 months; normally it lasts for more than a year. Last year he was on the ship for more than 13 months (he only came back this April) and a month and a bit later he was called back by the company to do a 48-day training scheme. The scheme was in Guangzhou. During the four months when he was back, he was home for less than half that time. Then he did the training course. After that he was home for less than a week, then he was called to go back aboard the ship.[64]

Tightening global regulation also has implications for seafarers unable to obtain appropriate certification. Such seafarers may find that their employment opportunities are severely restricted and, when they do get work, they may be limited to sailing on sub-standard ships for low wages and under generally poor employment conditions. These seafarers and their families can find themselves in a spiral of debt, as seafarers may have to borrow money to secure employment on vessels, only to be paid wages that are insufficient to meet the costs of repaying loans and supporting their families.[65] To counteract the detrimental effect on family life of requisite training courses and certification, companies could contribute to the cost of necessary courses and compensate for any loss of leave time because of training.

Companies could support seafarers and their families by occasionally allowing their partners and, where possible, their children, to sail with them. Opportunities for couples to sail together vary within companies and according to rank. Many companies restrict this invitation to officers or senior officers only. Rarely are the partners of ratings offered the chance to sail and, even if they were given the opportunity, the costs of travelling to join the vessel would probably be prohibitive. However, the benefits can undoubtedly be great: women who have sailed with their partners have said that they enjoyed being able to spend more time with their partners and that it helped them to obtain a better understanding of their partner's work and life at sea.[66] The children of seafarers could also profit from visiting ships or sailing as these opportunities would break up long periods of separation and allow family bonds to be maintained. This could be particularly important in the case of younger children, who can change considerably over the period of a tour of duty and consequently have difficulty recognizing and remembering their seafaring parent. As one adult child of a seafarer explained:

> Oh [sailing with him] definitely did help. [Seeing] what his cabin was like, the size of the cabin, you know, how many other people he lived with, where he ate, his routine, his isolation and the loneliness that he probably felt as well at times.[67]

In some countries, such as China, where women have traditionally not been allowed to sail with their husbands, it is more usual for the wives of seafarers to visit their husbands on board when the ship is in port. Women have been reported making long and arduous journeys in order to spend some time with their husbands.[68] In the past, when turnaround times were longer, women could spend several days with their partner while the ship was operating in port. By contrast, it is now much less common for women to spend several days travelling to meet their husbands to spend only hours, rather than days, together. The wife of a Chinese second officer explained:

> He was at sea when our child was born. Our child is 8 months old now. Three months ago, when his ship was calling at Qingdao, I took the child and my parents to visit him there. He was missing us so much that he said that he would be happy if he could only have a look at the baby. Otherwise, he would have to wait for another few months when our child would be 1 year old. So I agreed. I had a painful arm; I had to take my parents to help me on the way. It was a long journey, from

Nanyang to Qingdao – 29 hours by train. By the time we arrived there, it was already 5 o'clock in the afternoon and the ship was due to sail at 10. We met for only four hours. I was really sad. [...] I wish he could have stayed longer. But the ship had been loaded and unloaded so quickly that I had to take my baby and leave the ship after being with him for only four hours![69]

Giving partners the opportunity to sail has obvious benefits for couples' relationships, reducing the length of time between separations, and providing partners with a greater understanding of life and work at sea. Having a partner who has sailed may be particularly advantageous to seafarers, who often rely heavily on their partners for emotional support and for advice on problems and events that occur on board.[70] Partners who have sailed become familiar with shipboard life and working conditions and may, therefore, be able to offer more encouragement to their seafaring partners in their careers.[71]

The accessibility of two-way contact between companies and families can vary greatly. Research carried out on seafarers' families has shown that getting in touch easily in times of emergencies or crises is extremely important.[72] A number of companies have policies of repatriation for their crew in the event of the death or serious illness of a close family member. However, this is not extended to all seafarers and, within companies, can depend on rank. Even where free repatriation is available, seafarers who are employed on single-voyage contracts may be reluctant to be repatriated owing to uncertainties about their next job opportunity. Such worries may be exacerbated if seafarers find themselves responsible for medical costs associated with the death or illness of the family member. Similarly, some seafarers who have been repatriated return to their ship prematurely because they are worried that extended leave periods will be viewed negatively or unsympathetically by their employers. Without their usual (shore-based) social support networks, seafarers who remain at sea or return to sea after an insufficient period at home can experience a rise in stress levels.

Being able to make contact is particularly important when accidents or emergencies occur at sea. Inefficient communication between companies and families can aggravate an already distressing situation. Some companies take steps to inform families of the relevant details of incidents, including, as far as possible, an explanation as to how and why certain events occurred. However, it is not unusual for families to find out about shipboard incidents and emergencies through less direct means, such as television news broadcasts or newspaper reports,[73] which can be extremely upsetting.[74] In some cases, seafarers may also be the sole earner for large extended families, and the emotional grief at their injury or death may be compounded by concerns about how the family is to survive financially. Evidence suggests that the P&I Clubs' methods of handling injuries and death claims for seafarers and their families are questionable.[75] While not easing the emotional distress of loss of life or severe injury, adequate compensation for the families of seafarers involved in an accident can certainly help to alleviate the distress caused by economic anxieties.

The unique situation of seafaring families can make support from and contact with other seafaring families important. However, opportunities to do this vary greatly by country. The Seafarers' Wives Associations, organized by the Apostleship of the Sea, assists Filipino seafarers and their families, while the wives of Chinese seafarers have the support of the Seafarers' Wives Committee, an organization introduced by the trade unions of shipping companies under the supervision of each company's Party Committee,[76] with the aim of "uniting seafarers' wives at the home-front and providing support for seafarers at sea".[77] Seafarers' wives and families in other countries may not be so fortunate: sometimes small in number and geographically dispersed, many are offered little in the way of outside support and rely instead on the networks of family and friends.[78] While at sea, seafarers have to turn to visiting chaplains or utilize (increasingly limited) periods in port to visit seafarers' welfare centres such as Missions to Seafarers.

Notes

[1] Quoted in J. M. M. Hill: *The seafaring career: A study of the forces affecting joining, serving and leaving the merchant navy* (London, Centre for Applied Social Research, Tavistock Institute of Human Relations, 1992).

[2] ILO: *Women seafarers: Global employment policies and practices* (Geneva, ILO, 2003).

[3] G. M. Lamvik: *The Filipino seafarer: A life between shopping and sacrifice*, Ph.D. thesis (Trondheim, Norway, Department of Social Anthropology, Norwegian University of Science and Technology, 2001).

[4] ibid.

[5] *NUMAST Telegraph*, Nov. 1999.

[6] To date, the literature and research on seafarers and their families have focused on male seafarers and their female partners, which is why, in this chapter, seafarers are taken to be of the male sex and their partners, female. However, the authors recognize that there is a growing number of women seafarers with male partners and also that both male and female seafarers may have same-sex partners. It is also recognized that couples are not always married and hence are not "wives" or "husbands". In this chapter, the choice of language reflects the characteristics of those who participated in the studies from which the discussion has been drawn.

[7] G. Agterberg and J. Passchier: "Stress among seamen", in *Psychological Reports*, 1998, Vol. 83, pp. 708–710; J. Horbulewicz: "The parameters of the psychological autonomy of industrial trawler crews", in P. H. Fricke (ed.): *Seafarer and community: Towards a social understanding of seafaring* (London, Croom Helm, 1973); A. W. Parker et al.: *A survey of the health, stress and fatigue of Australian seafarers* (Canberra, Australian Maritime Safety Authority, 1997); V. J. Sutherland and R. H. Flin: "Stress at sea: A review of working conditions in the offshore oil and fishing industries", in *Work and Stress*, 1989, Vol. 3 (3), pp. 269–285.

[8] M. Thomas: *Lost at sea and lost at home: The predicament of seafaring families* (Cardiff, SIRC, 2003).

[9] ibid.

[10] E. Kahveci, T. Lane and H. Sampson: *Transnational seafarer communities* (Cardiff, SIRC, 2002).

[11] A. W. Parker, A. Clavarino and L. M. Hubinger: *The impact of Great Barrier Reef pilotage work on wives and families* (Canberra, Australian Maritime Safety Authority, 1998).

[12] Thomas, op. cit.

[13] Kahveci et al., op. cit.; Thomas, op. cit.

[14] Thomas, op. cit.

[15] E. Kahveci: "Husband, father and stranger", in the ITF's *Seafarers' Bulletin* (London), 2001, No. 15; Kahveci et al., op. cit.

[16] Thomas, op. cit.

[17] J. Chandler: *Women without husbands: An exploration of the margins of marriage* (London, Macmillan, 1991).

[18] ibid.

[19] J. Tunstall: *The fishermen* (London, MacGibbon and Kee, 1962).

[20] J. Seale and D. Hawkins: "The dilemma", in *Tinig ng Marino* (Philippines), July/Aug. 1997; M. F. Virtudazo: "When the honeymoon is over . . . (or when reality creeps in)", in *Tinig ng Marino*, Sep./Oct. 1997.

[21] Parker et al., 1997, op. cit.

[22] ibid.; Thomas, op. cit.

[23] Parker et al., 1997, op. cit.

[24] NUMAST: *All in good time* (London, 1995).

[25] Thomas, op. cit.

[26] ibid.

[27] Kahveci, op. cit.; Kahveci et al., op. cit.

[28] Thomas, op. cit.

[29] Parker et al., 1997, op. cit.

[30] Sutherland and Flin, op. cit.

[31] Horbulewicz, op. cit.

[32] Agterberg and Passchier, op. cit.

[33] H. Sampson and M. Thomas: *Lonely lives? Social isolation and seafarers*, Paper presented to the IV International Symposium on Maritime Health (Manila, Philippines), 5–8 Nov. 2001.

[34] S. Roberts: *Occupational mortality among British merchant seafarers: A comparison between British and foreign fleets 1986–1995* (Cardiff, SIRC, 1998).

[35] P. M. McCarron and N. H. Haaksoson: "Recent life change measurement in Canadian forces pilots", in *Aviation, Space and Environmental Medicine*, 1982, Vol. 53, pp. 6–12.

[36] M. Karlins, F. Koh and L. McCully: "The spousal factor in pilot stress", in *Aviation, Space and Environmental Medicine*, 1989, Vol. 60, pp. 1112–1115.

[37] Horbulewicz, op. cit.

[38] Thomas, op. cit.

[39] ibid.

[40] Parker et al., 1998, op. cit.

[41] D. Foster and R. Cacioppe: "When his ship comes home: The stress of the Australian seafarer's partner", in *Australia and New Zealand Journal of Family Therapy*, 1986, Vol. 7 (2), pp. 75–82.

[42] L. Jamieson: *Intimacy: Personal relationships in modern societies* (London, Polity Press, 1998).

[43] The term "comradeship" is said to originate from the Spanish word *camaradas*, which refers to the shared sleeping "chamber" of sixteenth-century Spanish mariners, who survived their epic voyages, if at all, thanks to the mutual aid of their fellows. See P. E. Perez-Mallaina: *Spain's men of the sea: Daily life of the Indies fleets in the sixteenth century* (Baltimore, Johns Hopkins University Press, 1998).

[44] C. B. Chapman: *Trouble on board: The plight of international seafarers* (Ithaca, New York, ILR Press, 1992); C. Groth: *Psychological opinion: Results of a socio-psychological investigation into the feasibility of one-man bridge manning at night.* Exemplary findings of work experience on the basis of two expert reports and own experience. Submitted to the Federal Ministry of Transport Marine Department, Hamburg, 1987. Commissioned by the German transport union, ÖTV; Sampson and Thomas, op. cit.

[45] Thomas, op. cit.

[46] ILO, op. cit.

[47] Thomas, op. cit.

[48] P. H. Fricke: "Family and community: The environment of the ships' officer", in P. H. Fricke (ed.): *Seafarer and community: Towards a social understanding of seafaring* (London, Croom Helm, 1973).

[49] A. J. Davies and M. C. Parfett: *Seafarers and the Internet: Email and seafarers' welfare* (Cardiff, SIRC, 1998).

[50] M. Argyle: "Social relationships", in M. Hewestone et al. (eds.): *Introduction to social psychology* (Oxford, Blackwell Publishing, 1990).

[51] M. Thomas, H. Sampson and M. Zhao: "Finding a balance: Companies, seafarers and family life", in *Maritime Policy & Management*, 2003, Vol. 30, No. 1, pp. 59–76.

[52] Parker et al., 1997, op. cit.

[53] Thomas et al., op. cit.; Thomas, op. cit.

[54] Thomas, op. cit.

[55] J. Robertson: *The effects of short-term work-related separation on couple relationships: Army servicemen, merchant seamen and commuters compared*, M.Sc. thesis (London, Institute of Psychiatry, Kings College, 2001); Thomas et al., op. cit.; Thomas, op. cit.

[56] Thomas et al., op. cit.; Thomas, op. cit.

[57] Thomas, op. cit.

[58] Davies and Parfett, op. cit.

[59] ibid.

[60] ibid.

[61] Thomas, op. cit.

[62] Thomas et al., op. cit.

[63] ibid.

[64] Thomas et al., op. cit.

[65] Kahveci et al., op. cit.

[66] ibid.; Thomas et al., op. cit.

[67] Thomas, op. cit.

[68] Thomas et al., op. cit.

[69] Thomas et al., op. cit.

[70] Thomas, op. cit.

[71] Kahveci et al., op. cit.

[72] Thomas et al., op. cit.

[73] ibid.

[74] ILO: Joint IMO/ILO Ad Hoc Expert Working Group on Liability and Compensation Regarding Claims for Death, Personal Injury and Abandonment of Seafarers (Geneva, JMC/29/2001/4, bis, 2001).

[75] ibid.

[76] The Party Committee is a body of the Communist Party of China; most companies have their own Party Committee. See M. Zhao, T. Feng and X. Shi: *Political commissars and their shipmates* (Beijing, China Social Sciences Archives Publishing House, 2003).

[77] Zhao, personal communication.

[78] Thomas et al., op. cit.

7

SUB-STANDARD SHIPS AND ABANDONED SEAFARERS

Seafarers of the Turkish-owned OBO Basak, *abandoned in Dunkirk, France, in 1997*

Introduction

Abandoned crews and sub-standard ships tend to travel together. As one speaker at the 1999 International Union of Marine Insurance Conference remarked, "Owners who cannot afford (or do not wish) to spend money maintaining their ships tend not to spend money on their crews either".[1] It is, on the other hand, not necessarily true that owners of sub-standard ships will, at some time or other, abandon their crews, and neither is it true that abandoned crews are always engaged aboard sub-standard ships. Large numbers of crews were abandoned in the course of the Adriatic Tankers collapse in 1995–96, but many of the ships were structurally in reasonable condition.[2] In the case of the abandoned crew of the *OBO Basak*, dealt with in some detail in this chapter, the physical condition of the ship was not an issue. These considerations suggest that a definition of sub-standard based on both social and physical structural criteria would be useful, and the aim of the following discussion is to establish a case for doing so. Accordingly, this chapter begins by evaluating the terms and issues conventionally raised in shipping industry debates on sub-standard ships and then addresses questions of definition and regulatory responsibility. The second and larger part of the chapter assesses seafarers' exposure to abandonment, using case studies to illustrate typical instances, and examines the social and economic costs incurred by abandoned crews. A section on ILO and IMO Conventions and other international treaties on abandonment concludes the chapter.

Defining and identifying the sub-standard ship

The debate in maritime circles about sub-standard ships is as old as the modern industry – "coffin-ships" was the term widely used in the nineteenth century – but not until very recent decades has the question reappeared as a continuing preoccupation. Of course, sub-standard ships had never been entirely eradicated, but it has only been since the 1980s that they have once again been seen as threatening good practice. A press report of a speech made by the head of the Paris MOU in 1993 illustrates the level of concern often expressed by leading figures in the industry (box 7.1).

Estimates of the number of sub-standard ships generally amount to little better than guesswork. The figure of 10 per cent of ships, which seems to be based on PSC detention rates, is quite widely used in Europe. Lord Donaldson, a prominent legal figure in the United Kingdom who chaired an inquiry to consider the prevention of pollution from merchant shipping in the wake of the 1993 *Braer* tanker disaster off the Shetland Islands,[3] was quoted as saying that there was "clear evidence" that 9 to 10 per cent of all ships visiting north-west European ports were sub-standard.[4] In the absence of other publicly available data, this figure is the most defensible, even though it must certainly be an underestimate. The reach of European PSC is stretched in all member countries and it is generally acknowledged that there are not enough

---

Box 7.1   Bid to cut disgrace of sub-standard ships

By Jim Mulrenan

A call for increased cooperation between all parties with a genuine interest in maritime safety "to make the world too small for sub-standard ships" was made by Captain Henk Huibers, the head of the Paris MOU secretariat. It was imperative not only from a safety and environmental standpoint but also for commercial reasons that action against sub-standard shipping should continue. The shipping industry had a right not to be harassed by unfair competition and it was necessary to get back to a situation in which shipowners could afford to have well-trained crews on well-maintained ships, Capt. Huibers told the conference. PSC was, however, not the remedy against all evils and could never be a substitute for adequate standards and effective enforcement by flag states. "All parties with a genuine concern in the safety of shipping and the welfare of seamen, no matter whether they are flag states, shipowners, underwriters, trade unions, maritime lawyers, charterers or port states, should co-operate, with the ultimate aim to stop the operation of sub-standard ships," he said. "Sub-standard shipping is a sheer disgrace to the whole maritime industry and has done the industry more than enough harm, not only in terms of dollars and cents but also in terms of reputation."

Source: *Lloyd's List* (London), 12 June 1993.

inspectors to ensure sufficient coverage, especially of the smaller ports. PSC in some other world regions is either non-existent or patchy in application, and it is often poorly resourced. If the 10 per cent level is accurate for the relatively well-regulated ports of northern Europe, then the level in many parts of Africa, Latin America, and the Middle and Far East must be substantially higher. Although it must be the case that the incidence of sub-standard shipping varies considerably with region, it should also be recognized that it can often vary between sectors. Market and ship-ownership structures in some sectors, such as mainline container ships and chemical and gas tankers, are extremely well regulated. As outlined in Chapter 1, ownership in these two sectors is highly concentrated and the buyers of shipping services require high standards of reliability. However, in the bulker and general cargo sectors, ownership is fragmented and reliability requirements are often far less onerous; unsurprisingly, it is in these sectors that rates of ship detention and abandonment are relatively high.

In the past, as today, sub-standard ships have generally been defined in terms of the decayed nature of their structure and equipment. A look at the Australian inquiry into the loss, with all hands, of the 94,000 ton, Panamanian-flagged bulker, the *Alexandre-P*, provides a good example of what has come to be regarded as sub-standard. In giving evidence, "the ship's provider said that this was the worst rust-bucket he had boarded in his 15 years of boarding vessels. Shift supervisors concerned with the loading operations said that there were holes in transverse bulkheads and fist-sized holes in hatch coamings. [...] The hull of the heavily corroded ship in her departure condition had been considerably sagged."[5]

Although PSC officers typically focus on comparable issues and, for example, vivid descriptions of badly rusted deck furniture, rotten lifeboats and fire hoses often appear in reports, social standards issues also occasionally feature. In 1994, for example, a Dutch PSC described what he had found on inspecting a ship at the request of police officers:

> The crew had gone on shore to have dinner, but could not pay their bill. The police accompanied the men on board to find the ship had no generators, the crew had had no pay for six months and did not even have a supply of drinking water. The ship was detained. After some weeks, we got a call from a man who said he was the owner. He wanted to talk. He came to visit and described himself as a banker who had some friends who had advised him that he could make money on ships. We asked him if he knew he had to pay money out as well. The owner stayed in port and called me from time to time claiming that everything on board was all right. Eventually the ship got a single voyage certificate to carry out repairs. Finally, I got a call from the social welfare people in Rotterdam to report that the crew was actually drinking water from the port.[6]

The public pronouncements made by leading figures in shipping on the subject are generally concerned with the consequences for the industry of harbouring a sub-standard sector and with whom should be held responsible for maintaining good order. Speaking at a conference in the United States in 1994, Gregory Hadjeileftheriadis, a spokesperson for the Greek company Eletson, argued:

> There is sometimes an assumption that an owner who operated quality tonnage with the best crews would automatically gain a reward for his zeal. In a just world this would be the case. But in reality the quality owner was often up against the sub-standard or marginal operator, who was more than capable of making profits from his lower overhead, which eluded his quality competitor.[7]

This complaint by professional owners of being undercut had been so widely and recurrently heard that, in 1996, the OECD produced an assessment of the competitive advantages accruing to owners of sub-standard ships, followed up by an additional report in 2001 seeking to identify and measure the costs incurred by users of sub-standard ships.[8]

The first OECD report estimated that "a significant percentage of total vessel operating costs could be saved by sub-standard operations". In the second, the OECD made the following comment: "There is a strong incentive for charterers and cargo owners to see the continued existence of low-quality ships, as these help to facilitate inexpensive carriage of their cargoes. Conversely, any move towards eliminating such vessels implies an inevitable rise in freight expenses." This last comment echoes frequently heard calls for cargo owners to be held as accountable as other parties. Lars Lindfelt, managing director of the Swedish P&I Club, argued in 1996 that "ways should be found to make it more difficult for cargo owners to recover losses from shipowners when a sub-standard ship was involved".[9]

Two years later, Spyros Polemis of Seacrest Shipping urged charterers to make certain that the vessels they employed were not sub-standard and insisted that charterers should accept the additional costs of employing good ships.[10] Such comments are a reflection of the frustration experienced by industry professionals, and cargo owners/charterers are not the only targets. Classification societies have been held at fault for inadequate rigour in structural surveys, underwriters for insuring poor ships, flag States for deficient regulation and shipowners for uncaring negligence. In this search to find someone to take responsibility for a state of affairs in which owners of sub-standard ships can exploit their crews and subvert professional standards, it could seem, as the Norwegian brokerage house Fearnley's has put it, that "owners, charterers, insurers, port authorities, governments and classification societies have been passing the buck like a hot potato".[11] The problem, though, is not so much that the various parties are failing to accept their proper responsibilities but that the shipping industry's historical regulatory structure – once integrated by the entire ensemble of a flag State's relevant organizations and institutions (see Chapter 2) – has been fragmented as a result of flagging out to sovereignties incapable of duplicating the web of negotiated consent of the older maritime states, which had learned how to control the marginal shipowner.

It seems that the main problem lies in the fact that the interdependent subsets of the industry – the classification societies, shipowners, flag States, trade unions, charterers, insurers and so on – have yet to find an effective means of imposing good professional standards in the commercial, technical and social aspects of ship operation on a global scale. In the absence of such a means, more reliance is being placed on PSC agencies to enforce IMO and ILO Conventions and Codes as a way of raising minimum standards (box 7.2). This dependence on PSC as a regulator acknowledges the fact that the most effective way of correcting dysfunctions in the markets for shipping services is through the administrative capacities of the embedded maritime nations.[12]

Two concerns have dominated the modern debate on sub-standard ships: the competitive disadvantages incurred by owners and administrations who

---

Box 7.2   Europe urged to back port controls

By Marion Welham

A leading insurer has called on European governments to back PSC in a bid to close the loopholes on sub-standard ships. Roger Nixon, Chairman of the Joint Hull Committee at the Institute of London Underwriters, told *Lloyd's List* that Europe must tighten up to match the more effective Norwegian, Australian and Canadian regimes. Hard on the heels of the PSC committee meeting in Bonn, which agreed to target nine flag states, Mr. Nixon said: "Flag states are just a laugh. You tighten up one flag state and another one starts. It is just ludicrous. You will never get a lasso on all these different flag states."

Mr. Nixon said that PSC should be boosted to cover inspection of the steel work as well as getting to grips with whether crews were properly trained. More resources would be needed. "Most of the flag states are not serious players. They are just in it for the money," said Mr. Nixon. "But port states have a serious interest in the quality of the ship coming in. [...] PSC is the best answer because ports have no axes to grind. [...] If the port authority does not like his ship, they should have no problem about making it pretty damn public."

Source: *Lloyd's List*, 5 June 1993.

operate their ships according to good professional standards and the matter of determining responsibility for the continued existence of sub-standard ships. As regards the former concern, there is no reason to doubt that operators of sub-standard ships have lower costs. The calculations produced by the OECD illustrate the cost savings to be made by operating ships below the standards required by IMO Conventions; the report suggests, for example, that an annual saving of $37,000 could be made simply by undermanning a 20-year-old bulker of 30,000 dwt by two people. Additional savings could be made by regulatory avoidance in respect of the SOLAS Convention requirements and the ILO Merchant Shipping (Minimum Standards) Convention, 1976 (No. 147).[13] Surprisingly, the question of allocating responsibility for the continued existence of sub-standard ships has not been the subject of any inquiry or research involving closely reasoned argument. At various times and in addition to owners and flag States, insurers, charterers and classification societies have all been held to be at fault, but there can be little doubt that responsibility for the condition of a ship and its crew rests with its owner, while the State represented in the ship's flag and registry is responsible for ensuring the owner's compliance with international Conventions and for properly exercising a duty of care so that others are not victims of the owner's negligence.[14]

The debate on sub-standard ships has also suffered from a lack of definitional precision and economic analysis of sub-standard shipowners. It was only with the publication of the OECD's 2001 report that a clear specification of criteria became available. The report states that a ship is sub-standard when it:

- is technically unsound;
- fails to comply with mandatory international Conventions;
- is irregularly maintained;
- has insufficiently trained and qualified crew;
- has poor employment conditions for crew;
- has poor shore-based management.

The OECD did not attempt to specify whether all or just some of these criteria are sufficient to determine whether a ship is sub-standard.

As far as the economics of ownership are concerned, the OECD report states that when freight earnings are low "irresponsible owners tend to cut back on vessel maintenance [and] when markets subsequently rise, these owners are too concerned about keeping their ships trading, rather than undertaking any backlog of repairs".[15] These observations are almost certainly accurate but they refer to *specific* patterns of behaviour rather than to the general commercial calculations made by owners of sub-standard ships. A brief discussion of these considerations suggests that, rather than there being a group of owners who consistently operate poor ships, it may be more useful to think in terms of a category of marginal owners who are more or less likely to operate sub-standard ships according to trading conditions.

Whatever the phase of the business cycle, commercial advantages are likely to accrue to those owners operating their ships with poor technical and social standards, since in any given market owners with the lowest costs will enjoy the highest margins. However, it does not follow that such owners invariably operate sub-standard ships. When markets are buoyant, the marginal operator will be anxious to avoid detention or arrest and will, therefore, pay more attention to the condition of ships and crews, satisfying creditors to ensure that the ship can continue to earn high margins. Conversely, when markets subside, the marginal operator will cut costs and hope to escape pursuing creditors and the PSC net. If, however, these marginal owners are fleet owners and operate some ships sufficiently above the margin to escape detention or arrest, they will not easily be squeezed out of the market. And even if they are, it is likely that they will have enough expertise and access to capital to return to marginal operation when freight markets turn upwards again. If this analysis is correct, it would seem that the only way to exclude them permanently from trading would be to put in place a global licensing system for shipowners, similar to the one that exists in civil aviation.

Abandoned seafarers

Large numbers of seafarers are being abandoned on a recurrent basis. The problem is a global one in that it is not confined to any particular world region and it illustrates the conditions typical for those seafarers employed aboard sub-standard ships. Not all owners of sub-standard ships abandon their crews, although operating ships of this sort does involve resorting to commercial and operational practices that are at the margins of economic viability. The possibility of crews being abandoned aboard sub-standard ships, on which all costs are shaved, particularly those related to regulatory compliance, is high. If the conventional assumption that 10 per cent of ships are sub-standard is accepted and that, on average, these ships have crews of 15 people, then at any one moment some 60,000 seafarers are at risk of being abandoned.

Usually, seafarers find themselves abandoned when their ships have been placed under legal arrest by creditors or when the owners are unable to meet the costs of crew wages, bunkers or repairs resulting from collisions, weather damage, class survey requirements or detention by PSC inspectors. In these cases, abandonment almost invariably applies to entire crews. There are also cases in which ships set sail, leaving behind crew members who are owed wages and with no provisions for repatriation. These seafarers have either been physically ejected from the ship (often for complaining about conditions) or discharged owing to injury, illness or dismissal. Abandonment, then, can be defined as a refusal on the part of the owner to acknowledge obligations to crew members as required by either customary duty of care, contracts of employment (both implicit and actual) or by international Conventions and flag State maritime legal codes.

The duration of abandonment and the time it takes to reach a resolution can vary from several weeks to as long as several years; indeed, some cases are never resolved. Living and working conditions commonly deteriorate rapidly after abandonment, although the impact varies according to the country in which abandonment occurs, the physical condition of the ship, the remaining supplies of food and fuel and the extent to which the crew receive support from statutory and voluntary organizations through local and national media exposure.

Since the mid-1990s, the shipping industry has witnessed a number of major company collapses that have led to ships and their crews being abandoned. In the past seven years, Adriatic Tankers (1995–96), UNIMAR (1996), Regency Cruises (1995–97), Baltic Shipping (1995–96), Blasco (1996–97), Dragonix (1997), Navrom, Romline and Petromin (1997–98) and Renaissance (2001) have all collapsed, all of which were well-publicized cases. However, abandonment is not a new phenomenon, although, owing to the lack of systematic study of a suitable period of years, the extent of the problem is difficult to establish. Existing evidence in a collected if raw form can be found in the records of the ITF's Actions Department, the New York-based Center for Seafarers' Rights and the justice and welfare section of the Mission to Seafarers. Other evidence is scattered around the world in the files of local newspapers, shipping agents, trade unions and seafarers' missions. The accessible records at the ITF and the two mission organizations are, therefore, inevitably incomplete. These organizations only have offices and centres in the larger of the world's ports and although these ports may be networked with satellite regional ports, there are significant areas of the world – in Africa and south and south-east Asia – where the three reporting organizations have, at best, a thinly stretched presence. It should also be noted that even in those world regions where the ITF and the International Christian Maritime Association (ICMA)-affiliated organizations have an established presence, the density of their intelligence coverage of ships is not uniformly high. None of these organizations, even in their "heartlands", has sufficient resources to generate adequate knowledge of problem ships. Each of them depends to a very large degree on information passed on by shore workers and officers of agencies routinely coming into contact with ships' crews. Owners' agents, cargo surveyors, port officials, port health officers, dock and river police, customs officers, dockers, ship repair workers, tugmen, lorry, bus and taxi drivers are all receivers and potential transmitters of relevant information about crews.

Taken together, those who have contact with ships and crews are the first link in the chain of the informal information exchange network holding pieces of knowledge about shipboard conditions in any given port. Where they are willing, these network members, without being in any way imperatively organized, can directly or indirectly by word-of-mouth bring problems to the attention of organizations concerned with seafarers' welfare. However, informal systems are at best haphazardly efficient and it is clear that abandoned seafarers are only unfailingly logged and attended to in highly organized States, so that, while it is hard to imagine that abandoned seafarers would pass unnoticed in Rotterdam or Singapore, Australia or Japan, one might be less confident if the regions were Central America or Eastern Europe. In short, the available data about to be examined, understate the extent of abandonment.

In 1999, the ITF and the two ICMA affiliates between them were involved, to a greater or lesser degree, in 97 cases of abandonment. The ITF was notified of 55 cases, but since it was only directly involved in 40 of them, the data presented below in table 7.1 include only those 40 cases. The same criterion for inclusion of data (direct involvement) has been applied to the other two reporting organizations – the Center for Seafarers' Rights and the Mission to Seafarers.

As table 7.1 shows, the data are not uniformly complete; there are 19 cases in which the numbers of people are not recorded and 16 cases in which their nationalities are unrecorded. The data also fail to specify the extent to which whole crews were abandoned, although it would seem reasonable to assume that all crew members were involved in each case except for five ships where the numbers were small. On average, some 18 seafarers per ship were abandoned and, assuming this average applies to those ships short of data, this leaves a total of 2,149 people of 38 different nationalities. With only a very few exceptions, the seafarers were abandoned away from their home countries. Fifty-one of the ships had single nationality and 30 had mixed nationality crews. Nineteen ships had Ukrainian crews, 17 ships Russian, 12 ships Indian, 12 ships Romanian, ten ships Greek, nine ships Filipino, six ships Indonesian and six ships Pakistani nationals aboard, either in mixed or single nationality crews.

The global seafarer

Table 7.1 Abandoned seafarers, 1999

Name of vessel	Flag State	No. of crew	Nationality of abandoned seafarers	Port/Country	Source
Sea Star	ANT	n.a.	Peruvian	Hong Kong	MtS
Campo Duran	ARG	35	Argentinian, Ghanaian, Greek, Filipino	Brooklyn	CSR
Star Glory	BAH	22	Chinese	Indonesia	MtS
Anatolia Sun	BZE	20	Ukrainian	Bremen	CSR
Bagermeyster Grushin	BZE	71	Ukrainian	Taipei	ITF
Hope Okinawa	BZE	12	Myanmar	Pusan	ITF
Lakhta	BZE	22	Russian	Vladivostock	MtS
Mac Pole	BZE	n.a.	Myanmar	Pusan	MtS
Nablus	BZE	13	Ukrainian, Indian	Bizerta	ITF
Sea Johanna	BZE	21	Pakistani, Tanzanian, Indonesian, Burmese, Indian	Mombasa	MtS
Ocean Wrestler	CYM	13	Filipino, Indonesian	Tampa	CSR
Achilles 1	CYP	2	Greek, Yugoslavian	Bejaïa	ITF
Golden Falcon	CYP	n.a.	n.a.	Singapore	MtS
Rio Aroa	CYP	2	Ukrainian	Barcelona	CSR
Sotiras	CYP	n.a.	n.a.	Singapore	MtS
Kherson	GEO	26	Georgian	Avonmouth	ITF
Mana	GRE	23	11 Greek and 12 mixed	San Antonio	MtS
The Theonymphos	GRE	19	Greek, Romanian, Salvadorian, Indonesian, Filipino	Ghent	MtS
Alma 1	HON	10	Ukrainian, Georgian, Russian	Ancona	ITF
Johalison	HON	n.a.	Indian, Iranian, Iraqi, Bangladeshi	Kalba	MtS
Laila H.	HON	8	Egyptian, Syrian, Lebanese	Valetta	ITF
Megamar	HON		Filipino	Rio de Janeiro	CSR
Olga J.	HON	13	Ghanaian	Bourgas	CSR
Reem al Khaleej	HON	45	Indian, Iranian, Iraqi, Bangladeshi	Kalba	MtS
Samuda	HON	15	n.a.	Mumbai	ITF
The Kalba	HON	n.a.	n.a.	Dubai	MtS
Walenburg	HON	6	Ghanaian, Togalise, Cape Verdian, Ukrainian	Cape Verde	ITF
Zaniat al Khaleej	HON	n.a.	Indian, Iranian, Iraqi, Bangladeshi	Kalba	MtS
Bahari Hindi	KEN	33	Romanian, Italian, Kenyan	Somalia	CSR
Free Trader	KWT	1	Indian	Abu Dhabi	CSR
Odincova	LAV	14	Latvian	Reykjavik	MtS

Nicholas	MTA	n.a.	n.a.	Singapore	MtS
Lantic Ruby	MYS	8	Indian	Abidjan	CSR
Kimisis III	MTA	23	n.a.	Vancouver	MtS
Kuzma Gnidash	MTA	n.a.	Russian	Hong Kong	MtS
Nereus	MTA	15	Filipino, Bangladeshi, Greek	Western Africa	CSR
Normar Prestige	MTA	17	Indian	Chittagong	ITF
Pantokrator	MTA	24	Greek, Egyptian, Filipino, Romanian	Rotterdam	MtS
Prams Kunti	MTA	8	Russian, Lithuanian	Chile	CSR
Princess	MTA	26	Ukrainian	Pula	ITF
Provence	MTA	n.a.	n.a.	Durban	MtS
Sun Marsat	MTA	23	Georgian	Zhanjiang	ITF
Terpsichore	MTA	22	Ukrainian	Mongla	CSR, ITF
Vachnadze	MTA	n.a.	n.a.	Durban	MtS
Verona	MTA	8	Mixed	Hamburg	ITF
Zagreb Express	MTA	n.a.	Croatian	Hong Kong	MtS
Nantai Venus	MTA	n.a.	Taiwanese	Hong Kong	MtS
Delta Freedom*	PAK	17	Pakistani	Abidjan	CSR
Delta Peace*	PAK	20	Pakistani	Durban	MtS
Delta Pride*	PAK	23	Pakistani	United States	MtS
Delta Star*	PAK	29	Pakistani	Chittagong	CSR
Ypapadis	PAK	23	n.a.	Vancouver	MtS
Cala	PAN	17	Greek, Tanzanian, Egyptian, Russian	River Humber	MtS
Eli Jeanne	PAN	19	Indian, Romanian, Ukrainian, Sri Lankan	Port-au-Prince	CSR, MtS
Golden Trinity	PAN	23	n.a.	Victoria	MtS
Ideal	PAN	7	Myanmar	Malta	ITF
Kardamyla	PAN	n.a.	n.a.	Singapore	MtS
Litrotis	PAN	n.a.	n.a.	Singapore	MtS
Marine Grand	PAN	15	Indonesian	Kaohsiung	CSR
Matina V.	PAN	23	Filipino, Ukrainian, Moldavian, Greek	Piraeus	ITF
Muzaffar Aziz	PAN	23	Pakistani, Bangladeshi, Indian	Lagos	ITF
Nantai Queen	PAN	n.a.	Taiwanese	Hong Kong	MtS
Normar Pride	PAN	19	Indian	Curaçao	ITF
Ocean Leader	PAN	18	Sri Lankan, Indian	Tunisia	MtS, ITF
Oravita	PAN		Romanian	Dubai	MtS
Queen of Vevey	PAN	26	Russian, Ukrainian, Romanian	Port Stanley	ITF
Star Hope	PAN	17	Korean, Myanmar	Quindao	ITF

/Cont.

The global seafarer

Name of vessel	Flag State	No. of crew	Nationality of abandoned seafarers	Port/Country	Source
/Cont.					
Zoodotis	PAN	23	Greek, Filipino, Indonesian, Romanian	Port Moody	MtS
Focsani	ROM	16	Romanian	Manila	ITF
Mehedinti	ROM	5	Romanian	Mtwara	CSR
Soveja	ROM	20	Romanian	Orinoco River	ITF
Xenia	ROM	9	Romanian	Casablanca	ITF
Ekaterinburg	RUS	10	Russian	Limassol	MtS
Kamchatskiy Beret	RUS	25	Russian	Beihai	ITF
Krhustalnyy Bereg	RUS	n.a.	n.a.	n.a.	MtS
Kutuzova	RUS	9	Russian	Kuwait	ITF
Langeri	RUS	15	Filipino	Durban	MtS
Osha	RUS	27	New Zealander, Russian, Ukrainian	Auckland	
Penzhinskiy Zaliv	RUS	27	Russian	Conakry	ITF
Rostov	RUS	7	Russian	Piraeus	ITF
Tarasovk	RUS	16	Russian	Jebel Ali	ITF
Trunovsk	RUS	9	Russian	Kuwait	ITF
Turkmenistan	RUS	25	Russian	Shanghai	ITF
Ussuriskaya Tayga	RUS	23	Russian	Lagos	ITF
Colinda	SGP	3	Myanmar, Indonesian, Bangladeshi	Cebu	CSR
Equator Grand*	SGP	24	n.a.	Singapore	MtS
Aretti	STP	5	Ukrainian	Mersin	CSR, ITF
Gedaref	SDN	n.a.	n.a.	Rotterdam	MtS
Danny F11	SVC	n.a.	n.a.	Portland	MtS
GTS Krista	SVC	32	Ukrainian	Rijeka	ITF
Petr Pervy*	SVC	26	Ukrainian	Dubai	MtS
Prince Albert	SVC	12	Ukrainian	Liverpool	ITF
Sandrien	SVC	22	Ukrainian	Mobile	ITF
Tirana	SVC	15	Greek, Bulgarian, Ukrainian, Albanian, Romanian,	Brindisi	ITF
Al Ghazi J.	SYR	12	Syrian, Egyptian, Sudanese	Novorossiysk	ITF
Anatoli Gankevich	UKR	50	Ukrainian	Las Palmas	ITF

Note: n.a. = data not available. * Might have been abandoned earlier but only reported in 1999.

Key: MtS = Mission to Seafarers; CSR: Center for Seafarers' Rights. ANT = Antigua and Barbuda; ARG = Argentina; BAH = Bahamas; BZE = Belize; CYM = Cayman Islands; CYP = Cyprus; GEO = Georgia; GRE = Greece; HON = Honduras; KEN = Kenya; KWT = Kuwait; LAV = Latvia; MTA = Malta; MYS = Malaysia; PAK = Pakistan; PAN = Panama; ROM = Romania; RUS = Russian Federation; SGP = Singapore; STP = Sao Tome and Principe; SDN = Sudan; SVC = Saint Vincent and the Grenadines; SYR = Syria; UKR = Ukraine.

Table 7.2 Abandoned seafarers by ship type, 1999

Ship type		Number
General cargo	▲▲▲▲▲▲▲▲▲▲▲▲▲▲▲▲▲▲▲▲▲▲▲▲▲▲▲▲▲▲▲▲▲▲▲▲	36
Bulk	▲▲▲▲▲▲▲▲▲▲▲▲▲▲▲▲▲▲▲▲▲▲	22
Fish cargo	▲▲▲▲▲▲▲▲▲▲▲	11
Tanker	▲▲▲▲▲▲▲▲▲	9
Container	▲▲▲▲	4
Ro-ro	▲▲▲	3
Dredger	▲▲	2
Livestock	▲▲	2
Passenger	▲▲	2
Timber carrier	▲	1
Tug	▲	1
Missing	▲▲▲▲	4

Sources: See table 7.1.

The average age of the abandoned ships was 23. The newest ship was 5 years old and the oldest was built in 1958. Table 7.2 categorizes the abandoned ships according to their types and shows that, in 1999, general cargo ships, together with bulk carriers, accounted for almost 60 per cent of abandoned ships, although they made up only 44 per cent of the world fleet. The over-representation of general cargo ships and bulkers is consistent with the general view that sub-standard ships are concentrated in these sectors.

Table 7.3 shows abandoned ships according to their flag State. Although the ships are registered in 24 different flag States, they are clustered in a smaller number of states. Almost 70 per cent of abandoned ships were attached to just six flags: Panama (16 per cent), Malta (15 per cent), the Russian Federation (13 per cent), Honduras (10 per cent), Belize (7 per cent) and Saint Vincent and the Grenadines (6 per cent).

An examination of the subsequent histories of the abandoned ships using data from the *Lloyd's Ship Register* for 2000 shows that, of the abandoned ships reported here, 14 were broken up and two were a total loss, their shipwrecked crews subsequently being abandoned. Thirty-five of the 97 ships were subsequently reflagged, more than 70 per cent of them to Belize, Cambodia, Malta, Panama, Saint Vincent and the Grenadines and Sao Tome and Principe, that is, to flags with both poor abandonment and PSC detention records. These same flag States also received low ratings in the SIRC *Flag State audit 2003*.[16]

Table 7.3 Number of ships abandoned, by flag, 1999

Flag	Number of ships
Antigua and Barbuda	1
Argentina	1
Bahamas	1
Belize	7
Cayman Islands	1
Cyprus	4
Georgia	1
Greece	2
Honduras	10
Kenya	1
Kuwait	1
Latvia	1
Malaysia	1
Malta	15
Pakistan	5
Panama	16
Romania	4
Russian Federation	13
Saint Vincent and the Grenadines	6
São Tomé and Príncipe	1
Singapore	2
Sudan	1
Syria	1
Ukraine	1

Case notes from Sri Lanka, Tunisia and the United Kingdom

This section attempts to summarize abandonment data in a form that adequately captures the nature of the event itself, the way the event was handled by the relevant agencies, the consequences for seafarers and their families and the eventual resolution. This is done by looking at three cases recorded in the ITF's files and then by examining a much fuller case study based on the records of the Mission to Seafarers and further research conducted by the SIRC. This case study follows the experiences of a single crew between 1997 and 2001 and is looked at in some detail.

Sri Lanka: *Muzaffar Aziz*. Registered in Panama. Crew of 14 Pakistanis, eight Bangladeshi and one Indian. General cargo ship of 8,922 gt, built in 1978.

In October 1998, while their ship was in Colombo, Sri Lanka, the crew members wrote the following "notice" to the Colombo harbour master, the ITF, the Panamanian Registrar General of Shipping, the Embassies of Pakistan and India and the Government of Sri Lanka:

> This is to bring to your kind notice that we, the following crew members of MV *Muzaffar Aziz*, presently at the port of Colombo, have been unpaid for many months. On account of this, we are facing serious domestic problems. Most of our families have no money to provide food for our children and to meet education expenditures. Payment of the children's school fees has been delayed, and most of the children have been expelled. Some of the crew members whose children are getting married in the near future have no money to make the necessary arrangements. These domestic problems have caused all the crew much distress. Under the present circumstances, the following crew members have finally decided not to sail the vessel until and unless our wages are paid up to date.
>
> We, the crew members, request the authorities to help us in this serious matter.

The crew's plight went unnoticed and the ship and crew were abandoned in Lagos, Nigeria, in January 1999 without food, fresh water or gas oil for the ship's generators. After a year in Lagos and severe problems of sickness among the stranded crew, the bank holding the ship's mortgage requested that the ship go back to sea and trade. Following negotiations, about $30,000 were transferred to family members of the crew, although the total sum owed to the crew amounted to $150,000. The ship sailed to Gibraltar, where once again it was abandoned by both the company and the bank. In the last communication received from the ship, the master reported that he intended to sell some of the ship's spare parts to ensure that the crew had something to eat.

Tunisia: *Nablus*. Registered in Belize. Crew of nine Ukrainians and four Indians. A small general cargo ship of 1,530 gt, built in 1966. The owner's name is unknown but has an address in Turkey.

The ship was arrested in Bizerta, Tunisia, in January 1999 by the cargo owners because of irregularities with the cargo. The crew had not been paid since October 1998. The agent's fees were also unpaid, although he continued to supply the crew with enough food to keep them from going hungry.

The crew contacted the ITF in London in March. As soon as the crew had set a legal action in motion to recover their wages, the owner attempted to get them off the ship without paying them and dismissed some of the crew for refusing to join another ship. The local police and port authorities were sympathetic to the plight of the crew and agreed that they should not be sent off the ship without having been paid, thereby preventing the crew from being evicted. The agent eventually withdrew because the expenses he was incurring for supporting the crew were making him bankrupt. The Indian and Ukrainian Consulates declined to handle the case. The owner made no contact with the ship and the Turkish Embassy in Tunis said that they could not trace the owner.

In April 1999, a local lawyer agreed to act on behalf of the crew, and money was advanced by the ITF to provide food. The judge informed the lawyer that a mandate from the crew was not enough and that they should get one from their countries' representatives, but the respective consulates refused to sign the lawyer's mandate. After signing the power of attorney (that is, authorization to the lawyer to act on their behalf), the crew was repatriated with an advance from the ITF. The ship eventually was sold. However, as late as November 1999 the crew was still waiting for their claims to be settled.

United Kingdom: *Kherson*. Registered in Georgia. Crew of 26 Georgians. Tanker of 17,824 gt, built in 1978.

The vessel arrived at Avonmouth in the United Kingdom from Port Sudan, Sudan, in June 1999 with a cargo of molasses. The vessel was detained by PSC on the day of her arrival. About £12,000 of repair work was needed to bring the ship up to minimum standards, but since the ship's owner had accumulated worldwide debts of £80 million, he was unable to provide local contractors with the necessary financial guarantees.

After the ship had been detained, it became apparent that the owners had not sent any money to the ship for several months and that the crew, who had been aboard for 12 months, had not been paid for 11 of those months. Food quickly ran out and the ratings instigated legal proceedings to have the ship placed under arrest. Initially, there was some conflict between the officers and ratings regarding the legal action. All the seafarers were concerned about their families. "We have been working without money for 11 months. We have families at home but we can't send them anything. We are very poor. It's a very big problem," said one of the crew.[17]

Local people, mainly organized by the missions, helped out by delivering emergency supplies and organizing social events. Advances on outstanding wages were paid to crew members by the ITF, while repatriation costs were paid by the Admiralty Marshal, the British Government's legal agency responsible for the arrest of the ship. The cost of crew repatriation was also undertaken by the Admiralty Marshal. The last group of 11 seafarers was repatriated in December 1999. The ship was sold in March 2000, enabling both the ITF and the Admiralty Marshal to recover their costs.

Case study: the *OBO Basak*

In late 1996, Turkish-owned Marti Shipping managed a fleet of nine ships amounting to 1.1 million tonnes and 10 per cent of the entire Turkish-flagged fleet. Six of these ships were owned by Marti and three were chartered by the company.[18] Marti formed many one-ship sub-companies sharing the same addresses and telephone numbers. The company also had offices in the main Turkish ports and repair workshops in Istanbul, in total employing around 500 people. For many years, the firm operated a system whereby, for tax purposes, it officially contracted crews for a very tiny salary, giving most of the money in cash. At various times in 1997 the entire Marti fleet was arrested in different ports around the world.

The 103,325 dwt, 1973-built and Marti-owned OBO carrier, the *OBO Basak*, with a crew of 29 Turkish officers and ratings, was placed under arrest in Dunkirk, France, on 9 July 1997, in a joint action by creditors. The ship's ratings only found out that the ship had been arrested a week after the event – the arrest notice had been posted on the ship's bridge (normally kept locked in port and therefore inaccessible to the crew) in French with no translation – via the Russian captain of another ship in the port who had informed the port chaplain of Dunkirk's Mission to Seafarers, who promptly went aboard the *OBO Basak* to meet the crew. As a result of the chaplain's intervention, a group of crew members was subsequently able to speak to a French ITF inspector, who arranged for them to sign a power of attorney with an ITF-retained French lawyer. The following day, and acting under instructions from the owner, the captain and chief engineer left the ship, without informing the crew. Two days later the remaining crew members were faxed notices of dismissal, except for the mate (who had become the acting master) and three other officers who had not joined the arrest action. With 23 of the crew now represented by a lawyer, the number of parties to the arrest of the ship eventually increased to a total of 23, including a south-east Asian ship-repair company: the owners of the *OBO Basak* had left a trail of debt around the world which had finally caught up with them.

When the ship arrived in Dunkirk, many of the crew had not been paid for nine months. Food was running out, as was oil for the ship's generators. Despite repeated requests to Marti from the acting master, no money arrived for the crew or their families. The seafarers finally successfully appealed on television for assistance from the community, while the Mission to Seafarers made provisional arrangements with the port authority, who agreed to pay for fuel oil, fresh water and so on.

On 12 August, some members of the crew wrote letters of appeal to the French public to explain why they were taking this action. Here are a few examples:

I haven't received any wages for the past six months. My wife and children at home are suffering. They are being looked after by neighbours and relatives. I haven't even got enough money in my pocket to buy a razor to shave. I don't know what to do. Please help us!

(motorman)

My family haven't received any money for the past 10 months. My relatives have been supporting my family but they cannot do it any more. I want to have my money and go home.

(An AB, who did not say in his letter that his wife had had a baby and was being held "hostage" by the hospital because she was unable to pay her bill.)

In the past ten months I have only received $100. I live in a rented house and my wife receives expensive medical treatment; my son is doing his unpaid compulsory military service and I am the only breadwinner. My neighbours cannot support my family any more. We have been here since 7 July. None of the officials from the company has come to see us. We have been completely abandoned. The only news we get from the company, through the second officer, is that "if you take legal action, you will pay for it". They should not have done this to us. We need your help. Please, please, please!

(bosun)

Around the time that these letters were being written but before they had been released, copies of a telex were sent to each rating:

In the application of Article 14 of the Maritime Labour Code, your work contract is ended. In conformity with Article 21 of the Maritime Labour Code, all the necessary steps have been taken for your repatriation: airline ticket and expenses for the journey.

If within one week you have not responded to this proposal, in conformity with Article 25/11 of the Maritime Labour Code, you will lose the provision of repatriation offered and you will return at your own expense.

The crew was advised not to respond on the grounds that judgement had not yet been given in the Dunkirk court in respect of a hearing to establish the legitimacy of their claim to be regarded as a creditor and the value of their claim. They were told that should they return home, they would be disqualified from their action. Some crew members accepted the company's offer of repatriation but in the event the company did not respond to their requests and so the claim for creditor status proceeded. The crew's lawyer argued that, since none of the crew held what could be recognized as a contract and the case was being heard in a French court, French rates of pay were appropriate. The court in Dunkirk then ruled that the crew had a legitimate claim to be regarded as creditors and that the Turkish seafarers should receive 70 per cent of their claims, based on French seafarers' wages.

Soon after the court hearing, the local seafarers' mission, with the support of the ITF, applied to the local immigration office to obtain safe conduct of the crew for repatriation. The immigration office refused on the grounds that seafarers, having arrived in the country by sea, may only leave by sea and they had no official documents to say that they could leave the ship. The harbour master also applied to the immigration office to refuse repatriation on the grounds that the ship would not be secure. Eventually, the harbour master agreed that only eight seafarers need remain aboard, provided he was able to nominate the various ranks required for the safety of the ship. Meanwhile, the Mission to Seafarers persuaded the immigration authorities to allow the crew to be repatriated. In the meantime, the crew sent messages by fax to the Turkish Embassy in Paris asking for help; no replies were received.

The last rating from the original crew of the *OBO Basak* who had arrived with the ship in July finally left Dunkirk on 4 October 1997. Repatriation costs were met by the ITF and each seafarer received £2,850 in cash as an advance in the event of a successful claim for unpaid wages. The cash advance came from the Mission to Seafarers (£200), the ITF (£900) and Dunkirk's Port Authority (£1,750).

A replacement crew of eight stayed on board until the vessel was sold (in March 1998). Meanwhile, another of Marti's ships, the *OBO Selim*, had been placed under arrest in Gibraltar in September 1997 and sold there by the Admiralty Marshal, the British judicial agent acting for creditors in cases of ship arrest. The crew was repatriated to Turkey without their back pay having been settled: the company owed them, on average, five months' wages. Five of the *OBO Selim* crew members were told by the company that the *OBO Basak* was ready to sail after its court case had been resolved. Wages owed to them would be paid as soon as the ship began to earn money again. However, if they went straight home, they would receive nothing for a long period of time. Accordingly, they agreed to go to Dunkirk, unaware of the events unfolding there. Marti had also sent another three seafarers to Dunkirk from Turkey. The last of these was a new master, who arrived in late January 1998. He had been told by the company that the ship was about to sail to Istanbul and had no knowledge of what had been happening in Dunkirk in the previous six months.

Box 7.3   Twenty-one [sic] Turkish seafarers abandoned in Dunkirk
         Their vessel was arrested, the master disappeared, they are
         penniless

There are 28 of them. Twenty-eight Turkish seafarers, unpaid. Abandoned by their captain and their employer. Ignored by their Government. Virtually prisoners aboard their ship in the port of Dunkirk. After six weeks, the shipowner – Marti Shipping – has been silent and invisible. The captain of the bulk carrier *OBO Basak* left the ship along with the contents of the safe. Shortly after its arrival early in July, the *OBO Basak*, whose owners have left a worldwide trail of bad debt, was arrested by the French authorities at the request of its creditors.

Only after the alarm was raised by an officer of another ship in the port was it discovered that aboard the *OBO Basak* there were about 30 penniless seafarers who had received no wages for nine months. The crew had been afraid to reveal their situation for fear of reprisals. Pressure had been exerted on them by the shipowner to keep quiet. Now the Mission to Seafarers and the Franco-British Seamen's Club are caring for the crew by coordinating food and other provisions supplied by local voluntary organizations. The port authority has provided the ship with water and fuel.

Aboard ship the crew works normally so that, if necessary, the *OBO Basak* could sail immediately. Until a few days ago none of the crew dared leave the ship for fear that by doing so they would forfeit their chances of getting the wages owed them. A Dunkirk lawyer, who is giving his services free of charge, has now assured them that they can return home without jeopardizing their chances of being paid. "Return to Turkey? But with what money?" asks a member of the crew. According to the Reverend Tony Rimmer, Chaplain of the port of Dunkirk, the ITF has agreed to pay their fares after an embarrassing silence from the Turkish Embassy. Back in Turkey, the situation for the majority of the families is serious. Without any income, some families have had their electricity supplies cut and others face eviction from their houses and apartments. "What is happening to us is less serious than it is for our families," says the electrician of the *OBO Basak*. "Here, thanks to the solidarity of the different associations, we can live more or less in a normal way, but our families have nothing."

Dunkirk's commercial court has ruled that the shipowner has until December to reach an agreement with his debtors, who are owed some Ffr30 million [US$4.8 million]. Otherwise, the bulk carrier, which has a value of US$4 million, will be auctioned. Even then the crew will have to wait some months before receiving their wages. According to the Reverend Rimmer, abandonment of ships and crews is all too common. Last year, around 50 vessels were arrested in French ports, most of them with unpaid crews and shortages of food and supplies. "We will shortly be meeting the EU Commissioner for Transport to see if we can organize a solidarity fund for the abandoned crews. We have to hope that European pressure on ships' flag states will make them accept their responsibilities," says Tony Rimmer.

Sub-standard ships and abandoned seafarers

> In a separate development, the ITF has asked the French Government not to ratify the Franco-Turkish Commercial Convention drafted by the Alain Juppé Government. This proposed that commercial disputes between Turkish citizens in France would not be heard by French courts. An indignant Tony Rimmer said: "If this Convention is ratified it would mean that the courts would not be able to intervene in cases like that of the *OBO Basak*."
>
> Source: *Libération* (Paris), 17 Aug. 1997.

In January 1998, the *Basak*'s electricity, supplied from ashore by the port authority, was cut off. Since there was no fuel aboard for the ship's generator and therefore no adequate heating and lighting, the health of the remaining crew rapidly deteriorated in the winter months. One crew member became so ill that he had to be repatriated. Another was badly bruised following a fall on deck. Lacking access to health care, the local Turkish community "lent" the papers of a local resident to the injured man so that he could receive professional medical treatment.

The *OBO Basak*'s crew was involved in a series of court cases, the last of which is still ongoing. The first case was heard in a local court and established the right of the crew to be considered a creditor, along with the other parties who had initiated the arrest of the ship and stood to gain from any subsequent sale.

Marti Shipping, however, took the local court's ruling to the Court of Appeal in Douai. The appeal was upheld, with the court ruling that under a treaty agreement between France and Turkey, claims by Turkish citizens against other Turkish citizens had to be heard in Turkish courts. The French lawyer then advised that the Appeal Court ruling could be successfully challenged in the Supreme Court, but that he was not qualified to conduct cases at that level. Therefore, the Mission to Seafarers in Dunkirk asked the ITF to provide the funding for a study to evaluate the prospects of a successful appeal, to which the ITF agreed.

Meanwhile, the sale of the ship had been postponed by about six months because of the appeal by Marti. In March 1998, the ship was finally sold at auction for Ffr 9.2 million upon which the port presented a Ffr 8.5 million bill for port dues. Since in French law state bodies are privileged creditors, virtually the whole of the proceeds of the sale went to the port authority.

The arguments put by the seafarers' legal representatives to the Supreme Court were based mainly on the Brussels Convention of 10 May 1952, according to which, in matters of international law, the jurisdiction before which the claim should be brought is that in which the attachment of the vessel took place – France in this case – and only then if another condition of determining jurisdiction is fulfilled. For the purposes of this case, the other relevant criterion was that the debt was created during the course of the journey during which the seizure took place.

The Supreme Court accepted this argument and decided that:

> looking at Article 7 I c of the Brussels Convention of May 10, 1952, which harmonizes various rules on the "saisie conservatoire" (i.e. protective attachment) of a sailing vessel;

> according to the terms of the text, the national courts of the State in which the seizure of the vessel took place are competent to judge the merits of the case, as long as the debt is created during the course of the journey during which the seizure took place;

> the Court of Appeal decided that the French courts were not the appropriate jurisdiction to hear the claims for unpaid wages of the sailors of the *OBO Basak*, which was the object of the seizure in the port of Dunkirk, notably at the demand of these creditors.

As such, the Court of Appeal misapplied the Article.

This decision on the question of jurisdiction was an important one as it could set a precedent for all future cases involving foreign seafarers in France. However, there needs to be an additional court case to secure this. The Supreme Court's ruling applies only to this particular case unless and until the court rules that this particular judgement is acceptable as a precedent. At the time of writing, the court case was still continuing and the chances were high that the seafarers would win and obtain indemnities in accordance with French law; however, this would only be a technical victory for the *OBO Basak* crew because no financial compensation for lost wages would ensue. However, a successful outcome would establish legal principles capable of improving the rights of foreign seafarers abandoned by their employer in France.

A similar case came to court in France at around the same time. A Romanian vessel, *Oscar Jupiter*, was abandoned and then placed under arrest in Nantes in January 1998. In 1999, the Court of Appeal of Rennes ruled similarly to the Dunkirk Appeal Court in the case of the *OBO Basak*, saying that the crew could have no claim in respect of wages in a French court and that the case should be heard in the Industrial Tribunal of Constanța, Romania.[19] The Romanian crew was repatriated without being paid wages due to them.

The crew of the *OBO Basak* returned home to find their families in difficult circumstances. They had been away for between six and eight months without pay and now faced the possibility of being blacklisted and without work for months. Indeed, in many cases their return home was no less difficult than their detention in Dunkirk. One crew member reported:

When I returned from Dunkirk, the family was relieved and very pleased to see me. All the time they asked questions about what had happened in Dunkirk. "How did you survive?", "How was morale on board?" – things like that. When we were in Dunkirk, when we could not easily communicate with our families, we both played down to each other our real problems so as not to worry each other. But a couple of days after my arrival home, I faced the reality and I felt cheated, humiliated by the company. There was pressure on me to start working immediately as there was no money, nothing to eat, and creditors were visiting the house all the time. Then the arguments started. "Why did I stay there that long?" "Why didn't I leave the company earlier?" I remember smashing the glass door in the living room with frustration after one of these arguments.

This situation was not exceptional. Most of the families had no money. They had borrowed from extended families, friends and neighbours. Since the company had not paid the crew's national insurance contributions for two years, they had no health cover and had to pay all their medical care themselves. Several had had their furniture and personal effects removed by bailiffs. Many had been told by their landlords to leave. Telephones had been disconnected, which, apart from making communicating home extremely difficult while they were in Dunkirk, also meant that, once home, it was difficult for prospective employers to get in touch with them.

Wives had borrowed money from neighbours so that they could travel to the company's offices to try to get some of the money owed to them; one wife travelled for 12 hours and another for eight. At the offices, some were verbally abused by the staff and only occasionally given small sums – sometimes not even enough to pay the ferry home. Others took their sick children along to show how needy they were and to try to shame the company into paying. Some of the women were given post-dated cheques that bounced.

Several families became dependent on the goodwill of neighbours, who gave them second-hand furniture, mattresses and so on. All the wives had run up debts with their local shops and one wife spoke of a trader who had offered to cancel the debt if she would sleep with him. Neighbours no longer called in, suspecting that families would ask for yet more money. This meant that many of the families became steadily more isolated in their own communities.

The circumstances of the *OBO Basak*'s crew are typical of many other cases, except that in this particular instance the crew had been "fortunate enough" to have been abandoned in a port with efficient and experienced seafarers' welfare services. The port chaplain, well-known for his organizing skills, was able to develop a programme of coordinated action with other agencies and generate front-page publicity in the French national press.

As this discussion of cases of abandonment shows, the central issues that need to be dealt with are ensuring that repatriation is quickly arranged and that wages owing are paid. It may well be true that wage claims can often require juridical interpretation, but it is clear that there are no existing instruments that make direct solutions available to crew members. In the circumstances, they may, therefore, have no alternative but to engage in the cumbersome procedures involved in arrest and civil actions, even though stranded crew members will have neither the financial resources nor the local legal and political knowledge to pursue a claim. And when there are no provisions in local legislation for the nomination of parties responsible for the welfare of the crew during the period of abandonment or voluntary organizations are poorly organized or non-existent, seafarers are usually left to look after themselves.

Towards global protection

The immediate issues faced by abandoned seafarers are few in number and uncomplicated: all that abandoned seafarers need is to be provided with food and accommodation and competent socio-legal advice, while arrangements are made for them to be repatriated and any wages owing paid. But if their needs and the necessary arrangements to meet them are themselves straightforward, the difficulties quickly become apparent once the multiplicity of institutional practices and legal systems and precedents that are to be found in the ports and States of the world and the absence of globally uniform procedures for dealing with abandonment are taken into account.

Below is a list of ILO and IMO Conventions and other international treaties that contain provisions relevant to the abandonment of seafarers:

ILO Conventions
- Repatriation of Seamen Convention, 1926 (No. 23)
- Repatriation of Seafarers Convention (Revised), 1987 (No. 166)
- Seafarers' Identity Documents Convention, 1958 (No. 108)
- Seafarers' Identity Documents Convention (Revised), 2003 (No. 185)
- Recruitment and Placement of Seafarers Convention, 1966 (No. 179)
- Seafarers' Welfare Convention, 1987 (No. 163)
- Protection of Wages Convention, 1949 (No. 95)
- Protection of Workers' Claims (Employer's Insolvency) Convention, 1992 (No. 173)
- Seafarers' Wages, Hours of Work and the Manning of Ships Recommendation, 1996 (No. 187)

- Shipowners' Liability (Sick and Injured Seamen) Convention, 1936 (No. 55)
- Merchant Shipping (Minimum Standards) Convention, 1976 [and Protocol, 1996] (No. 147)
- Seafarers' Welfare Recommendation, 1987 (No. 173)

IMO Convention

- Convention on Limitation of Liability for Maritime Claims, 1976

International treaties

- International Convention relating to the Arrest of Sea-Going Ships, 1952
- International Convention on the Arrest of Ships, 1999
- International Convention on Maritime Liens and Mortgages, 1993
- UNCLOS, 1982

The ILO Repatriation of Seamen Convention, 1926 (No. 23), ratified by 45 States since 1926, was put in place to try to ensure the repatriation of seamen landed in foreign ports due to desertion, sickness or imprisonment rather than abandonment. Although establishing a seafarer's right to repatriation, it failed to specify who was to pay. However, the Repatriation of Seafarers Convention (Revised), 1987 (No. 166), expressly places the responsibility onto the shipowner. The problem, however, is that, in cases of abandonment, the shipowner tends to disappear, making the recovery of expenses advanced by the port State or the country highly unlikely. According to this Convention, it is only when shipowners fail to meet their obligations to repatriate that the State in which the ship is registered becomes responsible. If the flag State then fails in its obligations, the seafarers' country of origin or the country in which they are stranded may repatriate and, in doing so, is entitled to recover the cost from the ship's flag State. A survey of national repatriation laws, conducted by the Center for Seafarers' Rights, shows that, although most countries have placed the responsibility for repatriation on the shipowner, there seems to be no clear mechanism for determining when shipowners may be deemed to have failed in their duty to repatriate.

The Recruitment and Placement of Seafarers Convention, 1996 (No. 179), is another relevant Convention but it does not require the placement (crewing or manning) agencies to repatriate. The subject matter of the Shipowners' Liability (Sick and Injured Seamen) Convention, 1936 (No. 55), is only partially relevant. With regard to the Protection of Wages Convention,

1949 (No. 95), and the Protection of Workers' Claims (Employer's Insolvency) Convention, 1992 (No. 173), which cover all workers, employees are ranked as privileged creditors, but the Conventions do not specify that crew members should receive all wages due. It is also worth noting that the International Convention on Maritime Liens and Mortgages, 1993, gives liens for crew wages lower priority than other claims. Where wage questions are concerned, the ILO Protection of Wages Convention, 1949 (No. 95), and the Protection of Workers' Claims (Employer's Insolvency) Convention, 1992 (No. 173), are not suited to the question of wage payment defaults by employers. It would be administratively and politically difficult for flag States to meet wage defaults from public funds and even more difficult in the case of port States. Public accountability would certainly require the retrieval of defaulters' funds from the original defaulter, that is, the shipowner, and it is not clear how these claims could be effectively and economically pursued. It would be difficult for States to undertake responsibility to pay seafarers' wages from public funds. In short, and taking together the various instruments noted in this paragraph, none is appropriate to cases of abandonment.

It is often pointed out that, whereas IMO instruments, which have an essentially technical content, have been ratified by more than 100 States, less than half that rate of ratification has been achieved by ILO instruments, the contents of which are primarily socio-economic. This disparity can be explained by the fact that, without the certification signifying compliance with IMO Conventions, ships as structures would be unable to engage in worldwide trades. States are, therefore, effectively obliged to ratify these instruments, particularly now that PSC regimes can enforce compliance. Uniquely among ILO maritime instruments, the wide acceptance of the Merchant Shipping (Minimum Standards) Convention, 1976 (No. 147), stems from the fact that it was made mandatory and enforced by the member States of the Paris MOU on PSC.

A few of the ILO maritime Conventions are more than 40 years old and do not entirely address current global shipping conditions. On the other hand, some of the more recent international instruments that do have potential relevance for abandonment issues, such as the 1993 International Convention on Maritime Liens and Mortgages and the 1999 International Convention on the Arrest of Ships, have yet to receive ratification to bring them into force.

In addition to the ILO and IMO Conventions and other international treaties, some flag States have insurance schemes and special funds to deal with cases of abandonment. Globally, however, there are no effective insurance schemes that provide support during abandonment and cover the payment of wages owing and repatriation. For example, Liberia requires its vessels to carry P&I insurance or to prove financial responsibility to cover repatriation problems. However, the Liberian administration's experience has shown that this system can still fail: although Liberia requires annual proof of financial responsibility, unscrupulous shipowners can allow their insurance to lapse, which would probably only be discovered by the authorities after a problem had arisen.[20]

Under Norwegian legislation, shipowners are responsible for repatriation costs and the payment of the crew's wages in the event of the owner's bankruptcy. Every shipowner belonging to the NIS has to provide a guarantee that the seafarers will be repatriated and that eight weeks of their wages will be paid; any ship that fails to meet these requirements will be removed from the register. Singapore has a specific fund to assist seafarers stranded on ships abroad (the Singapore Stranded Seafarers' Fund). These provisions are valuable but the global nature of the shipping industry means that seafarers need globally recognized protection against abandonment. Positive moves in this direction are currently being made by the ILO and IMO.

Three sessions of a Joint IMO/ILO Ad Hoc Expert Working Group on Liability and Compensation Regarding Claims for Death, Personal Injury and Abandonment of Seafarers were held between 1998 and 2001. At the end of the third session a draft resolution and associated guidelines were finalized. The draft resolution on providing financial security in case of abandonment states that "abandonment of seafarers is a serious problem involving a human and social dimension and recognizes that, given the global nature of the shipping industry, seafarers need special protection".

The issue is straightforward: if shipowners are not properly financially secured, seafarers may not receive remuneration due or be promptly repatriated. The resolution acknowledges the core of the problem by affirming that provision for repatriation, maintenance while abandoned and payment of wages due should form part of the seafarer's contractual and/or statutory rights and should not be affected by the failure or inability of shipowners to meet their obligations. The resolution also recognizes that, in cases where shipowners fail to meet their obligations, flag States and, in some cases, the State of which the seafarer is a citizen or the port State, can be expected to intervene.

The resolution's guidelines propose that shipowners should have in place an adequate financial security system to provide for repatriation expenses without any cost to the seafarer and for the maintenance of the seafarer from the time of abandonment to the time of arrival at the place of repatriation. It might take the form of a social security scheme, an insurance scheme, or a national fund. The seafarer should have a right of direct access to the financial security system, which should apply to all seafarers irrespective of nationality. The payment of all outstanding remuneration and contractual entitlements should be covered, as well as the payment of other expenses incurred by the seafarer during the period of abandonment and arising from it, including repatriation.

The guidelines also state that shipowners should ensure that ships engaged on international voyages should hold a certificate attesting to the existence of a financial security system in the event of abandonment of seafarers and that it should be posted in a prominent position. Shipowners should also display the contact details of the people or entity responsible for handling claims covered by the guidelines.

The final resolution and guidelines were adopted by the IMO at its 22nd Assembly in November 2001 to take effect from 1 January 2002.[21] However, IMO resolutions and guidelines are not mandatory and have no legal effect until promulgated in States' law. States normally consult interested parties before implementing resolutions and guidelines and, at the time of writing, the outlook was not good. Many P&I Clubs publicly announced that they would find it impossible to comply with all the terms of the guidelines.[22] In a submission to the ILO's Legal Committee, representatives of the International Group of P&I Clubs declared that clubs could not attest to certificates that stated that the insurance would:

- notify seafarers of the cancellation or non-renewal of insurance. (It was pointed out that it would not be practicable for clubs to notify individual seafarers as they do not have crew lists or details of individuals employed by their members, which, in any event, change on a day-to-day basis. It was suggested that it would effectively be impossible for any insurer to comply with such an obligation.)

- pay all the claims arising during the period for which the certificate is valid. (It was pointed out that since the payment of claims is always subject to club rules and members' terms of entry, P&I Clubs could not comply with this requirement. As far as the insurance system is concerned, the International Group of P&I Clubs also stated that the clubs covered most but not all of the shipowner's legal liabilities and that as a matter of long-standing principle bankruptcy was not covered.)[23]

It was made clear that if these conditions were retained, Group Clubs would not be in a position to issue appropriate certificates.

Compared with other human rights infringements inflicted on migrant workers, the scale of abandonment of seafarers is not huge. But in its very extremity it does illustrate the essential nature of the problem of employment abuse. Crews are not abandoned or subjected to lesser abuses because of the moral inadequacies of the abusing parties. Shipowners and their agents do, of course, have a duty of care for seafarers in their employ and to that extent are culpable when they abandon their crews. However, these owners are also embedded in the economic and political logic of their industry and if they operate at the margins of economic and regulatory structures it is inevitable that sometimes some owners will be unable to honour their commitments. Abandonment is unquestionably a callous act. But it is also an act of desperation borne out of desperate circumstances. In general, these "circumstances" are the (changeable) economic and regulatory structures of world shipping. It is clear that abandonment is a structural problem that can only be resolved by the industry. And the Resolution and Guidelines on Provision of Financial Security in Case of Abandonment of Seafarers adopted by the IMO goes some way to addressing the problem.

Notes

[1] Quoted in OECD: *The cost to users of sub-standard shipping* (Paris, Directorate for Science Technology and Industry, 2001).

[2] For a fuller account of the collapse of Adriatic Tankers, see Alastair Couper et al.: *Voyages of abuse* (London, Pluto Press, 1998).

[3] Lord Donaldson inquiry into the prevention of pollution from merchant ships: *Safer ships, Cleaner Seas* (London, HMSO, 1994).

[4] *Lloyd's List*, 11 Dec. 2001.

[5] *Lloyd's List*, 10 Jan. 1991.

[6] *Lloyd's List*, 8 Feb. 1996.

[7] *Lloyd's List*, 18 Mar. 1994.

[8] OECD: *Competitive advantages obtained by some shipowners as a result of non-observance of applicable international rules and standards* (Paris, 1996); op. cit., 2001.

[9] *Lloyd's List*, 3 Oct. 1996.

[10] *Lloyd's List*, 15 Oct. 1998.

[11] *Lloyd's List*, 5 Aug. 1992.

[12] For a detailed discussion of the nineteenth-century development of the United Kingdom's maritime administration as a direct response to market dysfunctions, which has many contemporary resonances, see P. G. Parkhurst: *Ships of peace*, Vol. 1 (New Malden, Surrey, privately published, 1963).

[13] OECD, op. cit., 1996.

[14] "Duty of care" is a legal principle requiring persons to exercise due care in their actions so that other persons may not suffer due to negligence.

[15] OECD, op. cit., 2001.

[16] SIRC: *Flag state audit 2003* (Cardiff, 2003).

[17] *Bristol Evening Post* (Bristol), 9 Aug. 1999.

[18] *Lloyd's List Turkey Supplement* (London), Oct. 1996.

[19] Quoted in Chaumette: *Marins abandonnés* (Nantes, Faculty of Law and Political Sciences, University of Nantes, 2000).

[20] Center for Seafarers' Rights: *There is no place like home: Repatriating the industry's seafarers* (New York, 1998).

[21] IMO Assembly Resolution A.930(22), adopted on 29 November 2001.

[22] The Japan Ship Owners' Mutual Protection & Indemnity Association: *Special Circular*, 2001/12/21 (Tokyo, 2001).

[23] See IMO/ILO: *Final Report of the Joint Maritime Commission's Ad Hoc Expert Working Group on Liability and Compensation Regarding Claims for Death, Personal Injury and Abandonment of Seafarers* (Geneva, 2001).

CONCLUSION

Lashing containers, homeward bound

There have always been serious and well-informed people in the various branches of the shipping industry who have understood the critical importance of recruiting and then sustaining a resourceful and highly motivated seafaring workforce. There have also been periods in the modern epoch when the ambition of professionals operating ships with all-round excellent crews, from shipmasters and chief engineers to motormen and messmen, has been as close to attainment as could reasonably be expected. Few with long enough memories would disagree that a high point in these respects was achieved in the 1950s and 1960s, a period of relative stability and historically high rates of growth in world trade during which companies widely known internationally for operating good ships and based in nations with respected maritime administrations effectively set standards of best practice. Not all companies and their ships either aspired to or attained those standards and there were often substantial differences between the best and the worst. However, there was a floor and it was not so low that prominent industry figures felt the need to speak publicly about sub-standard ships and the need to drive them out. During that "high point of standards" period, shipping companies, seafarers and the entire support infrastructure of insurers, classification societies and maritime administrators together formed national shipping communities with powerful legal and normative means to ensure that the floor was high enough to keep out sub-standard shipowners.

The socio-legal mechanisms that encouraged high operational standards and set limits designed to mitigate the damaging effects to seafarers and professional shipowners of execrably unprofessional competitors collapsed under the weight of the recession of the 1980s and the ensuing rush to deregulate. Flagging out, usually to regimes devoid of maritime administrations as well as commercial, social and political infrastructures, freed owners from legal and normative restraints and left them to determine for themselves their own levels of professional standards. This led to what was later described by the investment bank Warburg Dillon Read as a period of "valiant but mutually destructive competition", during which serious professionals knew perfectly well that best-practice standards were on the slide. That period now belongs to history, but like all significant events of the recent past, it has left its mark. The desperation of that time is still vividly felt by those who lived through it, while the organizational transformations that it produced – arguably the most significant since the transition from sail to steam 120 years ago – can be seen as the industry moves steadily towards global regulatory regimes.

In the rapidly developing global epoch, the shipping industry no longer trades internationally from highly organized national bases where all shipping activities are interrelated. Shipowners and seafarers still have national identities: as corporate entities or individuals, they are attached to particular States. But this sense of attachment to a State is often nominal. For shipowners, the location of their command activities in a particular State is principally determined by convenience or contingency and is mostly irrelevant to the way business is conducted and the ships managed. The situation for seafarers is similar, since most of the ships they sail in are registered to States which for them are irrelevant. On the other hand, living at sea is merely an alternative to living somewhere else, typically the seafarer's State of origin. Seafarers are attached to their origins because where they come from is where they are rooted. *Their* attachment to their home State is not a matter of convenience or contingency; it is compulsively personal. Of course, these same personal attachments also apply to shipping company executives as private individuals, but not in the case of the corporate entity that they are charged with managing. Companies as companies in the global epoch cannot afford to have unequivocal national attachments. Seafarers as seafarers cannot afford *not* to have them. A recent French book on the lives of merchant seamen has the title *Ni morts, ni vivants: marins!*, which translates as Neither dead nor alive: sailors![1] Once aboard ship, there is indeed a sense in which seafarers are neither dead nor alive because they mortgage the present against the future expectation of living fuller lives during their periods of return. Seafarers also incur other opportunity costs. A recent analysis of risk exposure incurred by shipping industry stakeholders shows that the risks for seafarers are substantially higher than for any other interested party.[2]

The lack of equivalence between the shipowner as a corporate entity and the seafarer as a private individual may today be inescapable, but it does not follow that it is in the interest of shipowners to ignore the fact that seafarers also have a collective existence, which consists in the pool of skills and experiences they hold and on which shipowners depend completely. Without crews, ships are, after all, merely inert and useless artifacts. Accordingly, shipowners have a powerful interest to ensure that they can recruit and then retain crews with the necessary range of talents.

This interest in the condition of the labour force becomes more or less apparent according to the extent to which shipowners are faced with financial crises and, in those moments, are able to employ significantly cheaper crews. One of the more important facts of globalization as it has occurred in shipping is that it would not have happened at all if shipowners had been unable to change their sources of seafaring labour. Now that the industry has become global, it can no longer switch *rapidly* to new sources of supply. This is partly because, in the short term, sufficiently large new sources of suitable labour are not available.[3] It is also because the process of globalization itself, coupled with significant developments in domestic politics in many parts of the world, has led to the emergence of what, for want of better words, might be described as a global regulatory system increasingly focused on labour issues.

To reiterate, globalization was first the result of the crisis in shipping of the 1980s. Entirely coincidentally, this crisis overlapped at each end of that decade with the arrival of the environment as a political issue and a sequence of large pollution incidents involving tankers in Europe, North America and Japan.[4] Two of these incidents were especially important. The stranding of the *Amoco Cadiz* off the coast of northern Brittany in 1978 led directly to the creation of Europe's PSC regime (the Paris MOU) and subsequent emulation by alliances of countries in other world regions, notably in the Pacific (the Tokyo MOU). The stranding of the *Exxon Valdez* in Alaska in 1989 speeded up the growth, reach and deterrent policies of the new PSC organizations specifically aimed at ridding the markets of sub-standard ships of all types. It spurred the oil majors to regulate, decisively and effectively, quality standards in the tanker market through its SIRE system and provoked the Government of the United States into creating legislation to ensure that double-hulled tankers are adopted worldwide. These developments all came on stream in the 1990s as the industry emerged from the wasteland of the 1980s and, in the manner of all survivors, began to take a critical look at itself. The main issue was obvious: the importance of having skilled seafarers.

The BIMCO/ISF-sponsored studies on supply and demand, published serially throughout the 1990s, unerringly focused on the training deficit and the growing probability of shortages of well-trained officers of the 1980s. Industry professionals, many of them trained in the "high point of standards" era, found that many of the new recruits had been inadequately trained and even held corrupt certification. These experiences led to the 1995 revision of the IMO's STCW Convention of 1978 (fully implemented in 2002) and an IMO-sponsored study of fraudulent certification, reported in 2001. Behind the scenes in all these and other activities at the IMO and ILO, ad hoc alliances between national delegations, shipowner organizations, insurers, classification societies and trade unions met. As the levels of contact and deals done between them rose, so did it begin to look as if the key aspects of the regulatory regimes of the older and more embedded maritime nations were beginning to reappear, this time on a global stage. This perspective was reinforced in 2000 with a collective bargaining agreement between IMEC and the ITF. It was further consolidated by the agreement reached between employers and trade unions at the ILO's 2001 meeting of the Joint Maritime Commission with the aim of reviewing all ILO Conventions concerned with the living and working conditions of seafarers. In the meantime, the IMO implemented new measures to improve safety at sea with its 2002 International Safety Management Code, conducted under its aegis an extensive set of risk assessment studies of bulk carriers and launched discussions on the proper responsibilities of flag States.

The consolidation of companies to form larger units and tactical commercial alliances in pools have all helped the tendency towards greater global regulation. Pools do not entail any kind of merging of management practices but they do bring companies into closer relations with each other and help to establish common understandings of good practice. Where crewing is concerned, mergers obviously help to establish a wider reach of good practice when they are between close equals that are each positioned towards the top end of their markets. There have been a number of extremely significant mergers among container, tanker, car carrier, chemical tanker and reefer companies and there can be little doubt that the net effect has been to stabilize the labour market. These larger companies all expect consolidations to help them to establish greater market share and to compete as much on quality grounds as on price. This has eventual benefits for seafarers, because big companies competing with each other for quality delivery understand the critical importance of reliable crews and, therefore, begin to think strategically about their seafarers. As do the larger ship-management companies – and for exactly the same reasons.

This rediscovery of strategic thinking – it was, after all, strategic thinking on labour issues that was a characteristic of the best-practice companies of the

1960s and 1970s – must, however, be conducted on a global scale. This book has put great emphasis on the global labour market for seafarers for the good and simple reason that it is there and is likely to prove permanent. The structure and multinational composition of that market is now too established to change rapidly and it follows that the ability of crew managers to choose single nationality crews will be increasingly restricted. Crew managers will, therefore, accumulate more and more experience of mixed nationality crews and the more experience they have, the more likely they are to favour them. The corollary of this for seafarers' trade unions is that, although they will continue to be nationally based, they will be increasingly obliged to act like transnational organizations. This is another development that should contribute to integrating the network of organizations and associations that bring stability and order to the industry to the benefit of everyone in world shipping.

Notes

[1] Maurice Duval: *Ni morts, ni vivants: marins!* (Paris, Presse Universitaire de France, 4th edition, 2002).

[2] SIRC: *Bulk carrier vessels: Stakeholder analysis* (Cardiff, 2001).

[3] This shortage of new labour is not a real shortage in the sense that it would be hard to find people willing to work in the industry. Potentially, there are millions of people in Africa, Asia and Latin America who would need little inducement, provided there were IMO-approved training schemes in their countries or regions.

[4] The incidents involving bulkers, which caused far greater loss of life, only attracted significant attention within the shipping industry because of the persistence of the Derbyshire Families' Association, the British seafarers' trade unions, the ITF and *Lloyd's List* journalist, Michael Grey.

INDEX

Note: Page numbers in *italic* refer to figures; **bold** refers to tables and boxes; superscript refers to footnotes.

abandoned crews 159, 165–7
   case studies 172–82
   international conventions and treaties 182–7
   by ship type **171**
   statistics (1999) **168–70**
accidents and emergencies 132–4, 155–6
   compensation for 155–6
   families and 155
accommodation 124–7
   deficiencies 127–8, **128**, **129**, 130–1
Acomarit 22, 89
Adriatic Tankers 14, 159, 166
agency fees 79–80
Albania **36**
alcohol
   and accidents 134
   and disease 136
   social consumption 101
Alexandre-P, loss of 161
Algeria **36**, **128**
Amoco Cadiz, France (1978) 26[17], 191
Anglo-Eastern Group 68, *69*
Anguilla (second register) 33, **33**
Antigua and Barbuda (FOC) **31**
   crew complaints 92
   ITF TCC Agreements **115**
   loss rate 37
   PSC-verified deficiencies **128**
A.P. Moller 11

Apostleship of the Sea, 106, 156
Argentina **37**
Aruba (FOC) **31**
Asian Maritime Conference (1965) 60
Atlantic Sea, detained 127
Australia **32**, 85
   inquiry into loss of *Alexandre-P* 161
Australian seafarers
   family relations 147, 148–9, 150
   health and lifestyle 138
   occupational fatalities 134
   stress 138–9
   trade unions 89
   women 80
Austria **37**
Azerbaijan **36**

Bahamas (open register) 29, **31**, **32**
   crew complaints 92
   ITF TCC Agreements **115**
   loss rate 37
   PSC-verified deficiencies **128**
   ratification of conventions 39, 40
Baltic Shipping, collapse 166
Baltic States 12–13
   crews from **67**, **77**, 86
Bangladesh **36**
   wage rates 109–10, *110*

banks
    capital funding by 13–15, **16**, 17, *17*
    relational banking 14, 15
Barbados (FOC) 31
    ITF TCC Agreements 115
    PSC-verified deficiencies **128**
    ratification of conventions 40
Barber International 21, 68, 89
    manning **77–8**
Belgium 3, **32**, 80
Belize (FOC) 29, **31**
    crew complaints **92**, 171
    detention rate **36**
    ITF TCC Agreements 115
    loss rate **37**
    PSC-verified deficiencies **128**
Bermuda (FOC) **31**, **33**, 34, 89
    ITF TCC Agreements 115
BIMCO (Baltic and International Maritime Council) 7
BIMCO/International Shipping Federation (ISF)
    2000 Manpower Update 47, 61, 93[4]
    on officer training 81, 87, 192
Blasco, collapse 166
Blue Funnel *see* Ocean Transport
Bolivia (FOC) **36**, 39
bond money 79–80
BP Tankers 89
BP-AMOCO, shipping management 20
Braer, Shetland Is. (1993) 26[17], 160
Brazil **33**, 69, 81
bridge systems, integrated 23
British Virgin Is., second register **33**, *33*
Bulgaria **36**, **128**
Bulgarian seafarers **67**, 86, *110*
bulk cargo trade 6, 12
bulk carriers
    crews *62*, **62**, *76*, 112
    losses 193[4]
    standard of ships 161
    turnaround times **105**

Cambodia (FOC) 29, **31**
    crew complaints **92**, 171
    detention rate **36**

ITF TCC Agreements 115
loss rate **37**
PSC-verified deficiencies 44, **128**
regulatory regime 42, 44, 45, 50
Canary Islands (FOC) 29, **31**, 33, **33**, 34
Cape Verde **36**
capital funding *see* banks
car-carrier trade 11–12
    turnaround times **105**
cargo handling, and containerization 24–5
Carnival (Airtours) 18, 19, *19*
Cayman Islands (FOC) **33**, 34, **115**
Center for Seafarers' Rights (New York) 166, 167
certification
    and compulsory training 153
    fraudulent 83–5, **84**, 87, 192
    see also STCW; training
Channel Is., second register 33, *33*
Chao, T.Y. **16**
charterers, and shipping standards 162
Chase Manhattan Bank **16**
chemical tankers 11, 76
chemicals, exposure to 136–7
Chile **37**
China 4[1], 9, 39
    loss rate **37**
    national crews 69–70, 75
    officer supply 68, 73, *74*
    ownership of open registry fleets **32**
    second registers 33
Chinese seafarers 63, *65*, **67**
    family relations 153, 154–5
    Seafarers' Wives Committee 156
    training provision 86
    wage rates 112
classification societies 162, 163
coastal shipping 132
    labour market 68–9
collective bargaining 88–9, 90, 91–3
collisions 132
communication
    hazards from problems of 102, 103
    in mixed nationality crews 102–3
    ship–shore (families) 151–3

Index

compensation 155–6
complaints procedure
    ITF and 91–2, **92**
    see also abandoned crews
computers 152, 153
Concordia, crewing levels 61, 87
conditions on board ship
    accommodation 124–7, **128**, **129**
    leisure facilities 124, 125, 126, 140
    medical care 140
conditions of work 18, 107, **108**, 118
    historical 96
    on *Mallard* 95–6
    see also occupational safety
Congo 37
container trades 10, 11, 17–18
    crewing levels 62, **62**, 76
    standard of ships 161
containerization 1, 24–5
    effect on employment 58
    new ports **107**, 108
    and turnaround times 104
Contoro, crew **71**
Cook Islands (FOC) **31**, 33, **33**
crew costs 2, 17
    and new labour sources 60–1
    reduced by flagging out 59–60, *60*
crewing agents 75, 78, 79–80, **79**, 116–17
crewing levels 61–2, **62**
    and shore leave 106–7, **106**
    and social life 124–5
    and training 87
crews 18, 60
    age of ratings *64*, *65*
    demand for 47, 75, 78
    division of labour 62–3
    English-language ability 72
    national 57–8, 69–71
    nationality choice 72–3
    officer/rating interaction 98–9
    ship-management companies 21–2
    single nationality 68, 69, 72, 75
    sources 66, **67**, 68
    on sub-standard ships 161

    see also abandoned crews; labour market; mixed nationality crews; officers; seafarers; training
critical incident stress debriefing (CISD) 140
Croatia
    detention rate **36**
    officer supply 73, *74*
Croatian seafarers **67**, 112
    junior officers 73
cruise ships 18–19, **18**, **19**
    agency fees 79–80
    employment levels 2, 61, 63
    hotel crew 63, 66, 80, 112
    passenger/crew ratios 66, **67**
    tip earnings 112, 113
    wage rates 112–13
Cyprus (FOC) 21, 29, **31**, 32
    crew complaints 46, **92**
    detention rate **36**
    employment contracts **115**, 117
    loss rate **37**
    PSC-verified deficiencies **128**
    regulatory regime 40, 44

Danish seafarers 59, 88
    health and lifestyle 136, 138
    occupational accidents and fatalities 131, 132–3, 134
    training schemes 88
    women 80
Denholm's 20, 22
Denmark 25, **32**
    see also DIS
detention rates 35, **36**, 55[15]
    and abandoned crews 166, 171
    sub-standard accommodation and food 127
DIS (Danish International Ship Register) 3, 32, **33**
    crew complaints **92**
    mixed nationality crews 71
    and trade unions 88
discrimination
    against women 99–100
    on race/nationality grounds 99

disease
 and alcohol 136
 cancers 136–7
 cardiovascular 135, 136
 hepatitis 135, 136
 HIV/AIDS 137
 STDs 137, 138
 see also health
dispute procedures 89–90
distress and safety systems, integrated 23
Donaldson Inquiry (1994) (UK) 132, 160
Dorchester Marine 89
Dragonix, collapse 166
dry commodities 6, **105**
 see also bulk carriers
Dunkirk (France), *OBO Basak* abandoned at 175–80

East Germany 12
Eastern Europe
 privatization 12–13
 seafarers 58, 78, 116
 shipbuilding 9
 training provision 86
Egypt **36**, **128**
Eletson company 162
email 152
embedded maritime nations 4[1], 25, 58
 regulatory regimes 39, 51–2, 163
 training establishments 85–6
 see also flag States; flags of convenience
employment
 insecurity of 18, 97, 100–1
 levels 58, 61, 63
 by ship-management companies 20–2
employment contracts 91, 92, 116–17
 and access to benefits 117
English language
 as common working language 102
 factor in crew selection 72, *77*, 78
environmental issues 191
 oil tankers 25, 26[17]
 tonnage tax (Norway) 43
Equatorial Guinea (FOC) **31**, 39

 detention rate **36**
 loss rate **37**
 regulatory regime 45, 50
Estonia 12–13, **128**
Europe 9, 13
European Commission, on training and recruitment 94[18]
European Union, Brussels Convention (1952) 179–80
Evergreen, Taiwanese liner company 70
Exxon Valdez, Alaska (1989) 26[17], 191

Faeroe Is., second register 33
Falkland Is., second register 33, **33**
family relations 145–6
 and abandoned seafarers 176, 181
 company policies and 153–6
 debt 153–4
 and health and safety 148–50
 sailing opportunities for partners 154–5
 sexual fidelity 146, 147
 ship–shore communication 151
 social isolation 150–1
 and stress 138–9, **139**, 146–7
 support organizations 156
fatalities
 human error 132
 off-duty 134
 ship failure 132
Fearnley's, Norwegian brokerage house 162
feeder ships, crew conditions 18
ferry trade *see* ro-ro
Filipino seafarers 47–8, 58, 60, 63, *65*, **70**, 73
 employment contracts 116, 117
 labour standards 88, 89
 officer supply 73, *74*, 110
 recruitment 78, 79
 Seafarers' Wives Associations 156
 training provision 47, 82, **82**, 86
 wages *110*, 111
 women 81
 see also Philippines
Finland, second register 33
Finnish seafarers 80, 135, 138

Index

flag States and regulations 27–8, 53–4, 190
　abandonment rates 171, **172**
　deficiencies reported **128**
　enforcement 41–2
　good practice 44–8
　and ownership of fleets 53–4
　regulatory regimes 38–44, 50
　regulatory standards 51–3
　and sub-standard ships 162–3
　unregulated 50
flags of convenience (FOCs) 1, 3, 28–9, **31**
　crew complaints against **92**
　detentions 35, **36**
　and ITF TCC Agreements 114, **115**
　loss rates 35, **37**
　ownership of fleets 29, **32**
　registration requirements 42
　ship-management companies' use of 22
　tonnage registered under *30*, **31**
　wage rates 111
　see also open registers; second registers
food
　and catering standards 121–2, **122**
　and diet 123–4
　and social life 124
France 3, **33**, 40
　abandonment of *OBO Basak* 175–80
　labour force 58, **59**
　ownership of open registry fleets **32**
French International Ship Register (FIR) 3, **33**, 34
friendships 150–1
Frontline 11

GATT (General Agreement on Tariffs and Trade) 9
general cargo 12, 161
　abandoned 171, **171**
　crewing levels *62*, **62**, *76*, 112
　turnaround time **105**, 119[29]
Georgia 12, **36**, 174
German, seafarers **70**
Germany
　labour force 59, **59**
　ownership of open registry fleets **32**
　ship management companies 20

supply of officers 73, *74*
wage rates 109
women seafarers 80
see also GIS
Gibraltar (FOC) 29, **31**, **33**
　ITF TCC Agreements **115**
GIS (German International Ship Register) (FOC) 3, **31**, 33, **33**, 34
　crews 71, **92**
　ITF TCC Agreements **115**
Glasgow 21
GMDSS (global maritime distress and safety system) 23
Greece 4[1], 40
　crew complaints **92**
　crew nationalities **70**
　ownership of open registry fleets **32**
　supply of officers 73, *74*
Greek seafarers 58, **59**, 111
　seamen's union 117
Green Lily, loss of 100
Grimaldi 11–12
groundings 132
Guinea **36**

Hadjeilleftheriadis, Gregory 162
Hamburg 21
health
　access to medical care 140
　alcohol consumption 136
　diet 123–4
　gastrointestinal disorders 123–4
　mortality rates 136–7
　occupational 134–40
　smoking 138
　see also disease; mental health; stress
health screening
　Panama 45
　regulatory (Norway) 45
Heng Ya, detained 127
hierarchies
　on board ships 95–6
　occupational 98, 100
high-speed ships 24

Hoegh Lines 95
Hoegh Mallard, conditions on 95–6
Honduras (FOC) 28, **31**, 45
  crews **92**, 171
  detention rate **36**
  ITF TCC Agreements **115**
  loss rate **37**
  PSC-verified deficiencies **128**
Hong Kong, China (open register) 21, **33**
  ITF TCC Agreements **115**
  ownership of fleets **32**
Hong Kong seafarers 83, 131
  training standards 82, 83
  wage rates 109
Huibers, Captain Henk **160**
Hyundai Heavy **10**, 12

IACS (International Association of Classification Societies) 43
ICMA (International Christian Maritime Association) 166, 167
ICS (International Chamber of Commerce) 7, 134
ILO (International Labour Organization) 25
  Accommodation of Crews Convention (Revised), 1949 (No. 92) 125, 126
  Accommodation of Crews (Supplementary Provisions) Convention, 1970 (No. 133) 125, 126
  Asian Maritime Conference (1965) 60
  Characteristics of international labour standards 40–1
  Continuity of Employment (Seafarers) Convention, 1976 (No. 145) 93
  Conventions 39–41
  and enforcement 163
  Food and Catering (Ship's Crews) Convention, 1946 (No. 68) 121, 125, 126
  global standards 48–50, 52
  IMO/ILO Joint Committee on Training 83
  Joint Maritime Commission (2001) 192
  Merchant Shipping (Minimum Standards) Convention, 1976 (No. 147) 39, 40, 93, 126, 127, 164, 183, 184
    Protocol, 1996 93, 126, 183
  Protection of Wages Convention, 1949 (No. 95) 182, 183–4
  Protection of Workers' Claims (Employer's Insolvency) Convention, 1992 (No. 173) 182, 184
  ratification levels 39–40, 50, 184
  Recruitment and Placement of Seafarers Convention, 1966 (No. 179) 182, 183
  Repatriation of Seamen Convention, 1926 (No. 23), and Revision, 1987 (No. 166) 182, 183
  Seafarers' Identity Documents Convention, 1958 (No. 108), and Revision, 2003 (No. 185) 182
  Seafarers' Wages, Hours of Work and the Manning of Ships Recommendation, 1996 (No. 187) 113–14, 118, 182
  Seafarers' Welfare Convention, 1987 (No. 163) 182
  Seafarers' Welfare Recommendation, 1987 (No. 173) 183
  Shipowners' Liability (Sick and Injured Seamen) Convention, 1936 (No. 55) 183
ILO/WHO Committee on the Health of Seafarers (1993) 137
IMEC (International Maritime Employers' Committee), and wage rates 114, 116, 192
IMO (International Maritime Organization) 23, 52–3
  Conventions 25, 26[18], 39, 40, **40**
    on Limitation of Liability for Maritime Claims (1976) 183
  IMO/ILO Joint Committee on Training 83
  International Safety Management Code (2002) 192
  International Ship Information Database 131
  Joint IMO/ILO Ad Hoc Expert Working Group on Liability and Compensation Regarding Claims for Death, Personal Injury and Abandonment of Seafarers (2001) 158[74], 185–6
  ratification levels 39, 50, 184
  Resolution and Guidelines on Provision of Financial Security in Case of Abandonment of Seafarers (2001) 186, 187
  study on fraudulent certification 83–5, **84**, 192
India 4[1]
  officer supply 73, *74*, 110
Indian seafarers 60, *70*, 86
  employment conditions *110*, 116
  trade unions 89

Index

women 80
Indonesia 36
Indonesian seafarers 60, **67**
   training provision 82, 86
   women 80
industrial production, and seaborne trade 7
INMARSAT (International Mobile Satellite Organization) 23, 152
Institute of Employment Research (IER) (UK) 81
insurance
   for abandonment and repatriation 184–5, 186
   rates 52, 55[33]
Inter-Industry Round Table Group 7
Intercargo 7
International Convention on the Arrest of Ships (1999) 183, 184
International Convention on Maritime Liens and Mortgages (1993) 183, 184
International Convention relating to the Arrest of Sea-Going Ships (1952) 183
International Group of P&I Clubs 186
international law 39–41, 50
   on abandoned seafarers 182–7
   Brussels Convention (1952) 179–80
International Ship Information Database 131
International Union of Marine Insurance Conference (1999) 159
Intertanker 7
Intertanko 82
Iran, Islamic Republic of **36**
Ireland 85
ISF (International Shipping Federation)
   and STCW certification 83
   wages survey (1995) 109–10
   see also BIMCO
Isle of Man (second register) 21, **33**, 34, 89
   ITF TCC Agreements **115**
   loss rate 37
ISMA (International Ship Managers' Association) 22
   Code of Shipmanagement Standards 89
Italian seafarers **59**, 80
Italy
   officers from 73
   ownership of open registry fleets **32**

second register **33**
ITF (International Transport Workers' Federation) 47, 90–3, 192
   and abandoned seafarers 167
   Actions Department 91, **92**, 166
   Agreements Department 91
   case notes 172–4
   and case of *OBO Basak* 179
   FOC campaign 90
   Seafarers' Charter 92
   Special Seafarers' Department (SSD) 90
   Standard Collective Agreement (1998) 114
   and STCW Convention 83
   Uniform TCC Collective Agreement 114, 117
   wages survey (1996) (with MORI) 111, 116, 117

Japan 4[1], 9
   crew nationalities **70**
   labour force 58, 59, 89, 109
   ownership of open registry fleets **32**
Japan Maritime Research Institute (JAMRI) 132
jokes 101–2

Kerguelen Islands (French) (second register) 32, 33, 34, **115**
Kherson, crew abandoned 174
Korea, Democratic People's Republic of **36**, 37
Korea, Republic of
   officer supply 74
   ownership of open registry fleets **32**
   seafarers of 60–1, 68, **70**, 72
   seafarers' union 89
   shipbuilding 9, **10**
   training standards 83
Kotuku, near grounding of 133
Kuala Lumpur 21

labour market, global 1, 48, 57–81, 191, 193
   age requirements 78–9
   choice of crews 71–3
   for coastal shipping 68–9
   crew sources 66, **67**, 68
   effect on wages 109

The global seafarer

entry (gatekeeper) payments 78, 79–80
informal networks 2, 68–9
local brokers 68
and mixed nationality crews 66, 193
organization of supply 75, 78, 191
shipping management company tours 66, 67
size 61, *61*, *62*, **62**
use of English tests 78
see also crews
labour markets, national 57–60, **59**, 69
and flagging out 58–60, *60*
labour organizations 49
see also trade unions
Lagos, crew abandoned in 172–3
language
and communication 102–3
see also English
Larsen, Petter **77–8**
Latin America, crews from **67**, 75
Latvia 12–13
crews from **67**, 80
Leader, detained 127
Lebanon (FOC) **31**, **36**, **115**, **128**
letters, family 151–2
Liberia (FOC) 3, 28, 29, **31**, 58
crew complaints **92**
insurance 184–5
ITF TCC Agreements **115**
ownership of FOC fleets **32**
PSC-verified deficiencies **128**
regulatory regime 39, 40, 50
Libyan Arab Jamahiriya **36**, **128**
lifeboats, equipment failure 134
Lindfelt, Lars 162
liner companies 10–11
liquid bulk, turnaround time **105**
Lithuania 12–13
Lloyd's Register of Shipping
abandoned ships 171
World Casualty Statistics 132
loss rates 35, 37–8, *37*
Luxembourg (FOC) 29, **31**, **115**

Macao, China, open register **33**

Madeira, Portuguese second register 33, **33**, 34, **115**
Mailicia, detained 127
Malaysia 4[1], **36**, **92**, **115**
Malta (FOC) 29, **31**, **32**
crew complaints **92**, 171
detention rate **36**
ITF TCC Agreements **115**
PSC-verified deficiencies **128**
regulatory regime 39, 41, 50
Manila, Rizal Park 78, **79**
Maritime and Coastguard Agency (MCA) (UK) 43
maritime education and training (MET), world regime 81–5
Marmara, detained 127
Marshall Islands (FOC) **31**, 47
ITF TCC Agreements **115**
PSC-verified deficiencies **128**
ratification of international conventions 39, 40
Marti Shipping, abandonment of *OBO Basak* 175, 177, 179
Mauritius (FOC) **31**, **36**, **115**, **128**
medical care, shipboard 140
mental health **108**, 138–40
family problems 149–50
isolation 139–40
lack of shore leave 107
solitary drinking 101
suicide rates 136, 138
MET (maritime education and training) regime 81–5
Mission to Seafarers (Dunkirk), and *OBO Basak* 175, 177
Mission to Seafarers (UK) **145**, 156
complaints of conditions 128, **130**
Missions to Seafarers 166, 167
Mitsui-OSK 11
mixed nationality crews 1, 2, 29, **70**, **71**, *74*
communication difficulties 102–3
and global labour market 66, 71–3
seafarers' preference for 97
by ship type 76
MOL 11, 12
Monaco 20, **32**
Morocco **36**

mortgaging
    and debt-to-equity conversions 14–15, **16**, **17**
    of privatized E. European ships 13
Mulrenan, Jim **160**
Muzaffar Aziz, abandoned crew 172–3
Myanmar (FOC) **31**, **67**, **115**, **128**
Mystras II, detained 127

Nablus, abandoned crew 173–4
navigation 23
Navrom, collapse 166
Netherlands 20, 25
    labour force 59, **59**, 70
    second register 3, **33**
    training provision 86
Netherlands Antilles (second register) 3, **31**, **33**, **115**
New York 21
New Zealand **33**, 80
Nigeria **36**
NIS (Norwegian International Ship Register) 21, **32**, **115**
    crews 71, **71**, 88, **92**
Nixon, Roger **163**
noise and vibration 107, **108**, 125, 133, 134, 137
Norway 25, 43, 185
    cruise shipping 18, **19**
    ownership of open registry fleets **32**
    regulations 40, 44–5, 50
    Seamen's Act (1975) 44–5
    see also NIS
Norwegian Cancer Research Institute 136
Norwegian Cruise Line (NCL) **19**
Norwegian seafarers 58, 59, **59**, 68
    Government Seamen's Service 45
    trade unions 88, 89
    training provision 86
    welfare regulations 45–6
    women 80
NUMAST (National Union of Marine Aviation and Shipping Transport Officers) (UK) 89
NYK 12

OBO Basak, abandoned (case study) 159, *159*, 175–82, **178–9**
OBO Selim, arrested (Gibraltar) 177

occupational health 134–40
    access to medical care 140
    audiometric tests 135, 137
    medical examinations 135–6
    morbidity rates 135–6
    physical hazards 137
    see also disease; health; mental health
occupational safety 131–4
    equipment failure 134
    fatalities 131–3, 134
    fatigue 132, 133, 137
    and stress 149–50
    see also noise and vibration
Ocean Transport 19
OCIMF (Oil Companies International Maritime Forum) 55[34], 134
Odfjell 11
OECD
    industrial production and seaborne trade 7
    report on sub-standard ships (2001) 162, 164–5
officer training 63, 81, 85–6
    cadetships 88
    by ship-management companies 21
officer/rating ratios 63, 66
officers
    age of *64*, *65*
    interaction with ratings 98–9
    nationalities of 72–3, *74*
    supply of 73, *74*
    wage rates 110–11
    work in port 106
offshore company incorporation 42, 55[34]
oil tankers 6, 11, 24, 87
    crewing levels 62, **62**, 76
    and exposure to chemicals 136–7
    incidents 25, 26[17], 191
    standard of ships 55[34], 161
    turnaround time **105**
    see also SIRE
open registers 28–9, 52
    and labour markets 58
    and ratification of international conventions 39–40, 50
    regulatory regimes 50, 52–4
    see also flags of convenience (FOCs); second registers

203

The global seafarer

organizational alliances 10–11, 192
Oscar Jupiter, abandoned (Nantes) 180
Osman, detained 127
ownership
    container companies 10
    and FOC fleets 29, **32**
    organizational alliances 10–11, 192
    PLCs 10, 14
    private 10
    single-ship companies 42
    structure 10–17
    and training provision 48
    see also shipowners

P&I Clubs 88, 155–6, 186
    accident claims analysis 132
    insurance 184
    see also Standard Steamship Owners' Protection and Indemnity Association
P&O Cruises 18, **19**
P&O Group 11, 20
Pakistan **36**
Panama (FOC) 3, 28, 29, **31**, 58
    crew complaints **92**, 130, 171
    demand for crew 47
    ITF TCC Agreements **115**
    ownership of FOC fleets **32**
    PSC-verified deficiencies **128**
    regulatory regime 39, 41, 42, 50
    welfare provisions 45, 46
Panamax 24
Paris Memorandum of Understanding (MOU) (1982) 25, 35
    and ILO Merchant Shipping (Minimum Standards) Convention, 1976 (No. 147) 184
    members 55[15]
    and sub-standard ships **129**, 160
    see also port state control (PSC) agencies
passenger ships 24, 132
Perez-Mallaina, Paulo 96
Petromin, collapse 166
Philippines 4[1], **37**, 39, **115**
    see also Filipino seafarers
pilots, Finland 135

Piraeus 21, 68
Poland 12
    Solidarity union **77**, 89
Polemis, Spyros 162
Polish Manning Services **77–8**
Polish seafarers 68, **70**, 77–8
    officers *74*, **78**, 110
    training provision 86
port authorities **163**
ports
    modern 107
    turnaround times 103–7, *104*, *105*, **105**
Portugal **33**, 68
PSC (port state control) agencies 12, 35, 86, 163
    certification checks 82, 83, **84**
    European 160–1, **163**
    and regulatory standards 52–3, 191
    and standards of accommodation and food 126–7, 131
    and trade unions 88
    see also Paris Memorandum of Understanding (MOU) (1982)

Red Ensign Group 34, 88
Regency Cruises, collapse 166
registration, requirements 41–2, 53
registry, offshore 3
regulatory systems 1, 3, 38–44, 191–2
    and economic viability 38, 53, 164
    global 48–9, 191–2
    and international law 39–41
    and labour issues 48–54
    stringency of 50–1, 52
    see also flag States
Renaissance, collapse 166
repatriation 155, 183
    of abandoned crews 176–7, 181–2
Rimmer, Rev. Tony, port of Dunkirk chaplain **178–9**, 181
ro-ro (roll-on roll-off) passenger ships 17
    accidents and fatalities 132
    mixed nationality crews 76
Roger, S. 95–6

Index

Romania 12
  crew complaints **92**
  crews from **67**
  detention rate **36**
  officer supply 73, *74*
  PSC-verified deficiencies **128**
  training provision 86, 88
  wage rates 111
Romline, collapse 166
Rotterdam 68, 149
Royal Caribbean Cruises 18, **19**
Russian Federation 12–13, **32**, 75
  crew complaints **92**, 171
  detention rate **36**
  officer supply 13, 73, *74*
Russian Federation seafarers 72, 78, 86
  wages *110*, 111

Saint Vincent and the Grenadines (FOC) **31**, **115**
  crew complaints **92**, 171
  detention rate **36**
  loss rate **37**
  PSC-verified deficiencies **128**
Salvage Association 81
Samoa **36**
São Tomé and Príncipe (FOC) **31**, 171
satellite communications 22–4
  for line management 23–4
  for navigation 23
Saudi Arabia **32**
Schulte 89
Sea Empress, Milford Haven (1996) 26[17]
Seacrest Shipping 162
seafarers 73, *74*, 145, 190
  age structure 63, *64–5*
  flags of employment **70**
  and labour standards 52–3
  numbers *61*
  shipowners' financial responsibility for 183–7
  shore leave 105–6, **106**, **107**, 145
  social isolation of 96, 102, 103, 124, 139–40, 148, 150–1
  women 78–81
  see also abandoned crews; crew; officers; wages

seafarers' hostels 75
Seafarers' Wives Associations 156
second registers 1, 3, 29, 32–4, **33**
  government controls over 34, 35
  non-active 33
  and ship-management companies 22
shiftworking
  and diet 123–4
  and fatigue 133
ship-management companies 1, 19–22
  as employers 20–2
  and labour market tours 66, **67**
  management buy-outs 20
  officer training 21
  and trade unions 89
  see also Barber International
shipboard society 95–103
shipbuilding industry 7–10
  demolition–newbuild ratio 7–8, **8**
  specialist ships 13
shipowners
  financial responsibility for crews 183–7
  insurance 184–5
  responsibility for shipboard conditions 124–6
  sub-standard and marginal 159, 162, 163–5
  see also ownership
shipping
  increase in size 24
  tonnage (by type) 8, **8**
  see also ships, sub-standard
shipping industry 96, 166, 191
  company policies towards families 153–6
  financial responsibility for seafarers 184–5
  global nature of 25–6
  high point of standards (1950s-1960s) 189–90
  and labour markets 48–9, 61–2
  political economy of 5–6, 25–6
  structural adjustments (1980s) 2, 7–8, 15, 19, 190
  and world trade 6–10, *6*, *7*
  see also flag States; flags of convenience; shipowners
ships, sub-standard 159, **160**, **163**, 191
  and abandoned crews 165

cost savings by operators 162–3, 164–5
defining and identifying 160–5
sector variations 161
shore leave 105–6, **106**, **107**, 145
and crewing levels 106–7, **106**
and family relations 147–8
Sierra Leone, crews from 73, 116
Singapore 21, **32**, 39, **92**
crews from 83, 131
ITF TCC Agreements **115**
Singapore Mercantile Marine Office 140
Singapore Stranded Seafarers' Fund 185
SIRC (Seafarers International Research Centre)
Flag State audit 2003 171
global labour survey 61, 63, 72, 73
study on training and certification 86, 87
on women seafarers 102
SIRE (Ship Inspection and Report Exchange) 55[34], 191
Slater, P. 15, 17
social life 96–103
alcohol consumption 101
jokes 101–2
meal times 124
and occupational hierarchies 98
recreation 95, 101–2, 124, 125, 126, 140
story-telling 97–8
team-building routines 101
for women 102
Sohmen, H. 14, 19
SOLAS (Safety of Life at Sea) Convention 164
South Africa **37**
Soviet Union (former) 12–13
Spain **32**, **33**, 59
Sri Lanka (FOC) **31**, **36**
abandoned crew (case) 172–3
employment conditions 109, 117
ITF TCC Agreements **115**, 117
Merchant Shipping Act No. 52 (1971) 117
Standard Steamship Owners' Protection and Indemnity Association (the Standard P&I Club) 81
Star Cruise **19**
STCW (Standards of Training, Certification and Watchkeeping)

Convention (1978) and Revision (1995) (STCW-95) 82–3, 85, 153, 192
human relationships model 99
private short courses 85
Stolt-Nielson 11
story-telling 97–8
stress 138–9, **139**
of separation from families 145, 146–7
Sudan **36**
suicide rates 136, 138
surveys and inspections 43–4, 50, 52
oil fleets 34[34]
Swan, detained 127
Sweden **32**
labour force 58, **59**, *60*, 80
P&I Club 162
Switzerland 20, **32**
Syria **36**, **37**, **128**

Taiwan, China **32**
Taiwanese seafarers 70, 83, 109
Tanker, crew **71**
tanker companies 11, 61
see also bulk carriers; chemical tankers; oil tankers
technological developments 22–5
effect on shipboard conditions 95, 97
engine-room controls 23
and fatigue 133
ship–shore communications 152–3
telephones 151
mobile 152
Thailand **36**
tip earnings, cruise ships 112, 113
Tokyo Memorandum of Understanding (MOU) 191
Tonga **36**, 44, 50
trade unions 88–93
collective bargaining 88–9, 90, 91–3
in new labour supply countries 89, 90
officers' 93
ratings' 93
see also ITF

training 78, 81–8, 192
   and crewing levels 87
   fraudulent certification 83–5, **84**, 87, 192
   on-board 87–8
   paramedic 140
   provisions for 46–8, 85–6
   of ratings 86–8
   required courses 153
   by ship-management companies 21
   standards of 81–3, **82**
   STCW-95 compliance 82–3, 85
   world MET regime 81–5
   see also officer training; STCW
Tunisia, abandoned crew (case) 173–4
Turkey **33**, 36, 37, 92, 128
   see also OBO Basak
Turkmenistan 36
Turks and Caicos Is., second register 33, **33**
Tuvalu (FOC) **31**, **115**

Ugland, Andreas 82
Ukraine 12–13, 75
   detention rate **36**
   officer supply 73, *74*
Ukrainian seafarers 63, *65*, **92**
   entry payments 78
   training provision 86, 88
   wage rates 112
ULCC (ultra large crude carriers) 24, 87
UNCLOS (United Nations Convention on the Law of the Sea) (1982) 27–8, 183
UNIMAR, collapse 166
United Kingdom 25, 93[1]
   catering standards 121–2, **122**
   Chamber of Shipping 86
   crew abandoned in (case) 174
   crew nationalities **70**
   Marine Accident Investigation Branch (MAIB) 100
   Maritime and Coastguard Agency (MCA) 43
   Maritime Training Trust 48
   Merchant Navy Welfare Board 46
   Merchant Shipping Acts 34
   National Maritime Board 89

Occupational Health Decennial Supplement 136
officer training 85–6
officers' pay rates 110
ownership of open registry fleets **32**
P&I Club analysis of health and safety claims 131–2, 135
regulatory regime 41, 50
second registers 3, **33**
ship-management companies 20
United Kingdom seafarers 46, 58, 59, **59**
   age of *64*, *65*
   medical examinations 135–6, 139
   occupational fatalities 131, 134
   trade unions 88–9
   wage rates 109, *110*
   women 80
United States 13, 20, 69, 191
   2000 Port State Control (PSC) Report 35
   crew nationalities **70**
   ownership of open registry fleets **32**
   port security restrictions 106
   trade unions 89
   wages *110*
Univan ship-management company 21

V-Ships, ship-management company 21, 22
Vanuatu (FOC) **31**, 40, **115**
Viet Nam, crews from **67**
VLCC (very large crude carriers) 11, 87
Voyager of the Seas (cruise ship) 18

wages 109–14, *110*, **111**
   and debt 153–4
   effect of rank on **112**
   ILO Conventions on 183–4
   minimum 113–14
   security bonds ("leave pay") 113
   unpaid 166
Wah Kwong Shipping and Investment 15, **16**, **17**
Wallems 89
Wallenius Wilhelmsen 12
Wallis and Futuna Is., second register 33, **33**

welfare organizations 166
    and abandoned crews 175, 177, 182
    see also Missions to Seafarers
welfare services 45–6
West Africa, crews from **67**
WMU (World Maritime University) 86
women, as seafarers' wives 147–8, 154, 155
women seafarers
    as crew 78–81, 94[13], 102
    on cruise ships 18, 80, 113

discrimination against 99–100
sexual harassment 100, 140
sexual health 138
social isolation 150
working hours 117–18
Worldwide 11
WTO (World Trade Organization) 9

Yannopoulos, G.N. 81
Yugoslavia 12